HOW WR

'What Roslyn Petelin doesn't k   ..., precise writing isn't worth knowing.'

Leigh Sales, host, ABC TV's 7.30

'It's time for a new President for the Republic of Writing: Petelin's book will win her subjects from students to experienced professionals electing to learn why writing is so vital and to follow her lively learning pathways on how to do it elegantly, vividly, and with precision.'

Professor David McKie, Waikato Management School

'*How Writing Works* will be invaluable for all students from undergraduate to doctoral level, especially as a guide to the construction of robust and coherent argument.'

Margo Blythman, Former Director of Teaching and Learning, University of the Arts, London

'*How Writing Works* will be an enormous support for undergraduates and postgraduates who want to be the best writers possible. It will also help to prepare them for success in the communication industries, whether as author, editor, publicist or publisher.'

Jeri Kroll, Professor of English and Creative Writing, Flinders University

'Roslyn Petelin is the best of the best in teaching clear, readable writing. This book will improve the writing of everyone who reads it.'

Lelia Green, Professor of Communications, Edith Cowan University

HOW WRITING WORKS

A field guide to effective writing

ROSLYN PETELIN

SYDNEY · MELBOURNE · AUCKLAND · LONDON

First published in 2016

Copyright © Roslyn Petelin 2016

All rights reserved. No part of this book may be reproduced or transmitted in any form or by any means, electronic or mechanical, including photocopying, recording or by any information storage and retrieval system, without prior permission in writing from the publisher. The Australian *Copyright Act 1968* (the Act) allows a maximum of one chapter or 10 per cent of this book, whichever is the greater, to be photocopied by any educational institution for its educational purposes provided that the educational institution (or body that administers it) has given a remuneration notice to the Copyright Agency (Australia) under the Act.

Every effort has been made to trace the holders of copyright material. If you have any information concerning copyright material in this book please contact the publishers at the address below.

Allen & Unwin
83 Alexander Street
Crows Nest NSW 2065
Australia
Phone: (61 2) 8425 0100
Email: info@allenandunwin.com
Web: www.allenandunwin.com

Cataloguing-in-Publication details are available
from the National Library of Australia
www.trove.nla.gov.au

ISBN 978 1 92526 691 7

Set in 12/15 pt Bulmer MT by Bookhouse, Sydney
Printed in Australia by SOS Print + Media Group

10 9 8 7 6 5

The paper in this book is FSC® certified.
FSC® promotes environmentally responsible,
socially beneficial and economically viable
management of the world's forests.

This book is dedicated to my dear friend Professor Linda K. Fuller, of Worcester State University, Massachusetts, whom I can always rely on to produce perfect prose.

Contents

Preface ... ix

1 How writing works ... 1
    Writing in our contemporary information society ... 1
    What is writing? ... 2
    Vocation or avocation? ... 3
    Writing in the workplace ... 4
    The writing–thinking–learning connection ... 5
    Keeping a journal ... 6
    Inspiration for journalling ... 9
    Writing as a problem-solving process ... 11
    Getting started ... 13
    Producing writing worth reading ... 13
    What characterises good writers? ... 14
    The last word ... 15
    Activities ... 15

2 How reading works ... 18
    Why read? ... 18
    How does reading help writing? ... 19
    Writing for your readers ... 21
    Reading in the workplace ... 25
    Structuring writing for reading ... 29
    Reading critically ... 30
    The last word ... 33
    Activities ... 34

3 How words work ... 37
    Using words well ... 37
    Taking words seriously: style, voice, and tone ... 41
    Choosing words wisely ... 45
    Spoken communication ... 67
    The last word ... 67
    Activities ... 68

4	How sentences and form-class words work	70
	Why study grammar and syntax?	71
	Descriptivism and prescriptivism	74
	Traditional grammar	74
	Syntax	78
	Form-class words	84
	The last word	100
	Activities	101
5	How structure-class words and paragraphs work	107
	Structure-class words, interjections, and paragraphs	107
	Structure-class words	108
	Interjections/exclamations	120
	Analysing sentences	120
	Paragraphs	122
	The last word	124
	Activities	125
6	How punctuation works	130
	Why punctuate?	130
	Categories of punctuation marks	132
	Punctuation patterns	145
	The last word	146
	Activities	146
7	How structure and design work	150
	Shaping the verbal and the visual	150
	Structuring	150
	What is structure?	151
	Design considerations	166
	The last word	174
	Activities	174
8	How genres and workplace documents work	176
	Understanding genre expectations	176
	Writing in a professional context: workplace genres	177
	The last word	202
	Activities	202

9	**How genres and academic writing work**	206
	Research-based writing: How academic writing works	206
	Academic research	208
	What is academic writing?	210
	Critical reasoning	212
	Getting started on research	214
	The last word	234
	Activities	236
10	**How digital writing works**	238
	The inexorable rise of digital media	238
	The early years	240
	Email: insistent and indelible	241
	Writing for social media in the workplace	246
	Organisational websites	246
	Blogs	251
	Twitter	256
	Texting	259
	The last word	261
	Activities	262
11	**How revising, editing, and proofreading work**	264
	Writing with the intention of revising	264
	Revising	265
	Editing	269
	Proofreading	273
	Using computers for writing and editing	277
	What happens in publishing?	278
	Five levels of edit: checklist	278
	Typographical errors	285
	The last word	286
	Activities	287

Acknowledgements	291
Answers to the activities	293
Further reading	301
References	305
Index	315

Preface

Renowned American writing educator Peter Elbow dedicated his book *Writing Without Teachers* (1973) to 'those people who actually use it—not just read it'. I can't endorse his sentiment strongly enough. I'd love everyone who reads this book to use it by putting into practice its heuristics (from the Greek word 'to discover') and strategies in their own writing. Whether your writing is already reasonably good or less than good, following the book's advice and implementing its strategies will exponentially enhance your writing self-efficacy (your confidence and competence). At the end of each chapter there are practical activities, which one of the student readers of an earlier draft of this book said were their favourite parts of the book.

Whether you are a student or a workplace writer, or a creative writer, whether writing is your vocation, your avocation, or both, this book aims to provide you with a substantial and engaging introduction to contemporary writing in plain language with its accelerating demands for succinct and coherent writing. Following this book's advice will enable you to gain control over your words so that you can write the concise, lucid, nuanced, and compelling prose that is so valued in universities and in the professions.

The book will develop your understanding and use of generic structures in academic and workplace contexts and help you to survive and thrive in the writing-reliant arenas of the 21st century. It will help you to use the right words in the right order in the right places at the right time for the right reasons.

The book introduces the core concepts of writing and reading, then follows with a discussion of writing at the word, sentence (including punctuation), and paragraph level. It then covers the structure and design of documents in the most common academic and workplace genres, followed by a chapter on digital writing and a concluding chapter on revising, editing, and proofreading. The book also contains a wide range of resources, with references to useful print and online sites for further reading and learning. One of the student readers of an earlier draft of the book told me to remove the instances of 'Google it!' that I had inserted here and there, because she said that 'millennials wouldn't need that advice'. I have therefore removed the instruction to google, and I know that many non-millennials won't need 'Google it' suggestions but will also spontaneously turn to the glorious resources of the internet to explore rich pickings alluded to in the book.

Although I have written this book primarily for university and workplace writers, I firmly believe that much of the material and advice will be valuable for creative writers, who also need to be their own best editors.

Some of the content in this book is based on material that I wrote for *Professional Communication: Principles and applications* by Peter Putnis and Roslyn Petelin (Prentice Hall, 2nd edition, 1999). I have also adapted a small amount of the material that I wrote and which was published in *The Professional Writing Guide: Writing well and knowing why* by Roslyn Petelin and Marsha Durham (Longman Professional, 1992). Many of the examples have been drawn from my work in consulting about writing and editing to the corporate sphere.

I have made every effort to locate sources and copyright holders of other original material reproduced in the book, but if there are any errors or omissions, I will be pleased to insert the appropriate credit in any subsequent edition.

Roslyn Petelin

1

How writing works

> You have to let words talk to words.
> KEN MACRORIE

Writing in our contemporary information society

Before writing was invented, speaking was the main mode of communication. And while orality—a term derived from the Latin word for the mouth—was central to culture before the invention of writing, writing has become absolutely central to contemporary culture. These days, everyone's a writer—in social, educational, and professional spaces (Pullum, 2014; Yagoda, 2013). Writing is a mass daily experience (Brandt, 2015); journalist Clive Thompson (quoted in Brandt) claims that, worldwide, people produce 3.6 trillion words on the Web every day.

In a 2012 presentation on YouTube, workplace-writing researcher Professor Deborah Brandt describes how, over the last 50 or 60 years, the world economy has shifted from a base in manufacturing goods to a base in manufacturing services, that is, knowledge, ideas, data, and information. She says 'as a consequence of this shift, writing has become the work of our time'. Living in the twenty-first century entails living in a service-oriented information society—known as 'the knowledge economy'. Writing is at the heart of this knowledge economy: it is ubiquitous, demanding ever greater levels of verbal sophistication.

The rise and rise of the internet in our digital era has dramatically upped the ante. Employers want graduates who are problem solvers—variously called 'gold-collar workers', 'knowledge workers', and 'information architects'—that is, graduates who can research, analyse, write, and edit, and who are critical and creative thinkers with technological competence and design sensibility.

Contemporary government, business, education, and industry rely on writing. I can think of no disciplines or professions that aren't critically reliant on the researching, writing, and editing nexus. A recent research project by the Society for Human Resource Management reported that 'two crucial skills lacking in US college graduates both involve . . . writing' (Nguyen, 2015).

Writing is at the centre of all disciplines and professions. We are often judged on the quality of our writing, so it's essential to strive for professionalism. You'll need to write well to succeed in your studies and to have a great career path in whatever profession you enter. The workplace requires a strong grasp of words, grammar, and sentence structure—what is widely regarded as Standard English. Standard English is rather an elastic term, but English holds its place as the language of power and prestige in much of the world.

What is writing?

Writing is a process in which thinking and learning take place. This process is known as the writing–thinking–learning connection. It's a process that results in a communicative product that conforms to grammatical, syntactical, mechanical, and genre conventions. Importantly, writing also performs recognisable social functions that have increased in importance with the rise of social media. We live in what has been called a 'participatory society', where social media consistently provides us with opportunities to interact in global conversations.

People often think that they can't begin to write until they've decided what they want to say, but writing well is a complex skill that develops slowly over time and not necessarily in a linear fashion. Experienced writers know that writing is a difficult, complex, time-consuming, recursive process. They draft so that they can revise ('re-see' what they have written). Put another way, they write with the intention of revising. They write knowing that it's easier to correct than to create, confident that once words are on the page or on the computer screen, those words will 'talk to' other words.

The influential writing teacher Joseph Williams, who wrote the best book on writing at the sentence level that I have ever read, *Style: Toward clarity and grace*, uses a cookbook analogy to explain that 'knowing the ingredients and knowing how to use them is the difference between reading cookbooks and Cooking'. Williams says that 'describing a few of the devices that some graceful writers use . . . is about as useful as listing the ingredients of the bouillabaisse of a great cook and then expecting anyone to make it' (1995, p. 153). He points out that writing success is highly dependent on learning and adapting to the often implicit rules and genre conventions of a discourse community—that is, of the context in which writing takes place.

To understand the conventions, writers need excellent briefing and excellent exemplars to imitate, or, better still, to emulate. They need to be able to identify errors that characterise non-standard English (see Chapter 4). They need to be able to identify rectifiable weaknesses. They need to know how to read for substance and subtext. They need to be able to discern perspectives, inaccuracies, biases, gaps, and blind spots. They need to be able to identify and analyse the rhetorical and stylistic devices that accomplished writers use. They need to be able to analyse, evaluate, and select information, and structure and synthesise it into logical, meaningful, economical, persuasive prose of their own. Much of this competence will come from writing instruction by knowledgeable teachers, but it also comes from the processes of reading and writing.

Vocation or avocation?

Do you aspire to be a writer? Are you a writer already? Do you regard writing as a vocation or an avocation, or, perhaps, both? A vocation—from the Latin verb *vocare*, 'to call'—is an occupation, a calling. It's roughly synonymous with 'career' or 'profession'. An avocation is an activity that one engages in for pleasure outside one's main occupation.

So we have the writer Anton Chekhov, who was a physician by vocation; the composer Alexander Borodin, who was a chemist; the poet William Carlos Williams, who was a paediatrician; the poet and jazz critic Philip Larkin, who was a librarian; the novelist Salley Vickers, who is a psychoanalyst; the novelist Beryl Bainbridge, who was a painter; the novelist Joseph Conrad, who was a sea captain; and the poet Wallace

Stevens, who was an insurance executive. Nick Earls, a very successful Australian writer of fiction, trained and practised as a medical doctor, as did the writer Sir Arthur Conan Doyle. As Robert McCrum (2012) notes in his article 'Against type: Writers with other careers', 'There is a lot to be said for writers who don't just write'.

The American poet Robert Frost moved from a vocation, university teaching, to his avocation, poetry, but declared their intertwining in the final stanza of his poem 'Two Tramps in Mud Time':

> But yield who will to their separation,
> My object in living is to unite
> My avocation and my vocation
> As my two eyes make one in sight.

Whether writing is your vocation or avocation, a great deal of your success in life will hinge on whether you can communicate effectively, and, if you can embrace and even become excited about the range of possibilities writing well opens up, it will add pleasure to and enrich your working life.

Writing in the workplace

Some years ago, I used the terms 'working writer' and 'writing worker' to distinguish between professionally trained writers (career writers) and those who are not necessarily trained as professional writers but whose jobs require them to write (Petelin, 2002).

The **working writers** are journalists, reviewers, copywriters, novelists, scriptwriters, playwrights, poets, bloggers, digital content creators, technical writers, etc. The **writing workers** are lawyers, accountants, marketers, economists, managers, engineers, architects, nurses, technologists, scientists, public affairs and information officers, researchers, software developers, etc.

Although writing is a mainstream activity in most professions and an employee's writing ability is likely to be critical to their career path, many of those who write in the workplace regard writing as marginal; they do not see it as essential to their working lives. They are not reflective about its importance because writing is often a rather invisible activity in organisations. Untrained writers think that because they can talk they can write. That's not necessarily so. In most Australian universities, writing is under-taught, undervalued, and under-researched. Its importance in organisations often goes unnoticed until there's a document-related crisis. Writing is feared by many workers who are not hired as writers but find that a substantial part of their day, and sometimes their night, is spent writing. Such a worker may not consider themselves to be a writer by profession, but they find that they are one by default. As I mentioned earlier, Brandt's North American research on literacy in the workplace (2015, p. 7) revealed an intensifying use of writing for work. These writing workers need to know about the writing–thinking–learning connection.

The writing–thinking–learning connection

Language scholars have long argued that humans find meaning in the world by exploring it through their own use of language. Many creative writers testify that they don't know what they're thinking until they start writing about it. Many professional writers would say the same. This is what the English novelist E.M. Forster had to say: 'How do I know what I think until I see what I say?' In an essay in *The New York Times Book Review* Joan Didion, the American writer, once said: 'Had I been blessed with even limited access to my own mind there would have been no reason to write' (1976).

When people write about something, they understand and learn it better. That's why it's called the writing–thinking–learning connection. By exploiting this interdependence between writing, thinking, and learning, you will be able to use writing as a tool to more effectively think, learn, and communicate, both at university and in the workplace. Writing creates ideas. We get to know the world through language. We write to find out what we want to say. Writing is epistemic: it constructs/creates knowledge. As the American scholar T.Y. Booth explains:

> The assumption that composing is primarily or essentially a matter of getting clearly in mind what we want to say, and then finding the words which will recall those meanings and make them available to others, is possibly the single most serious obstacle for most people all through the composing process. (1986, p. 455)

When we start to put words on the page or on the screen, we discover what we are really thinking much more clearly than when we mentally visualise our topic before we write. We think about what we have learned and learn about how we think, which makes the whole process circular and generative.

> The relationship between observing and writing is not a one-way traffic: the more acutely and passionately one observes, the more there is that feels worth recording, yes; but conversely the more one becomes committed to such writing, the more active—as a consequence—one's observings become ... The world that is verbalized is more interesting potentially than the world that remains unverbalized. (Fulwiler, 1987, p. 37)

Each element—thinking and learning—is both a cause and an effect of the other. Therefore, start to appreciate writing as an essential key to unlocking thinking and learning.

How does writing bring about learning?

1. Writing gives concrete form to ideas.
2. Pursuing an idea through writing requires us to think in a focused way.
3. Writing out thoughts allows us to move beyond the trivial and immediate to the more complex and significant.
4. Rewriting demands an internal monologue on the ideas under consideration about phrasing, connections, 'signposts', inclusions, exclusions, and structure.

Two well-known writers have this to say: Stephen King notes that 'Writing is refined thinking' (2001, p. 131), and Oscar Wilde is alleged to have said, 'If you cannot write well, you cannot think well; if you cannot think well, others will do your thinking for you'.

Keeping a journal

One way to make thinking and learning central to your writing and to exploit their connection is to keep a journal/notebook/log/diary/day book—what was once called a 'commonplace book' and even more quaintly, a *vade mecum*. Many professionals keep a journal in the form of a field notebook in which they record observations, notes of conversations, reflections on actions they have carried out, articles and books they have read, insights they have reached, etc. Management Professor Nancy Adler headed an article in *Harvard Business Review* with the title 'Want to be an outstanding leader? Keep a journal' (2016). She believes that 'Writing online doesn't provide the same benefits as writing by hand' and urges her readers to 'buy a real journal'. She's such a strong believer in the value of a hand-written journal that she has designed one for sale. Many people are just as fervent about the benefits of an online journal.

In her Christmas Day message in 2013, Queen Elizabeth II urged everyone to keep a journal as a record of their lives. Keeping a journal is valuable for you as a writer because it will enhance your writing–thinking–learning processes and, of course, supply you with material for your ongoing writing.

Creating and maintaining a journal will allow you to:
- be introspective and self-aware and gain perspective on your thoughts and feelings by clarifying your thoughts
- hold a private conversation with yourself
- practise writing by experimenting with different styles
- stimulate your imagination and keep your mind open
- harness your creativity, such as when you write in a stream-of-consciousness manner
- speculate and brainstorm
- keep a record of to-do lists, fragments of text, particulars, thoughts, observations, incidents, and events that you can come back to later with no fear about forgetting anything
- remain organised and focused
- keep sight of your past accomplishments and milestones
- develop a sourcebook of materials such as snippets of writing, images, videos, websites, etc. from which you can extract material to share with others later, perhaps in blog posts (see Chapter 10).

Many medical professionals and institutions have also endorsed journalling as a method to achieve cathartic release and quieten the mind by managing overwhelming emotions and thereby reducing anxiety and stress. There is no doubt that writing can be therapeutic: just remember the last time you wrote a complaint letter and then didn't send it.

In a post on the website grammar.about.com labelled '12 reasons to keep a writer's diary', columnist Richard Nordquist quotes famous writers on the benefits of keeping a diary. The novelist and essayist Virginia Woolf called her diary a 'capacious hold-all' (Olivier, 1977). The poet Sylvia Plath said: 'As of today I have decided to keep a diary again—just a place where I can keep my thoughts and opinions when I have a moment. Somehow I have to keep and hold the rapture of being seventeen' (Connors & Bayley, 2007). And those of us who spend way too much time pootling around daily on the internet can identify with the reason advocated by literary critic Northrop Frye for keeping a daily diary: 'Meeting my own conscience at the end of the day may cut down on my dithering time' (Denham, 2001).

A double-entry journal—that is, a journal in which you reflect in a meta-entry on what you have written previously—is particularly valuable. You initially write on the right-hand page of your journal, and later comment on the facing left-hand page. (See example in Figure 1.1.) When you reread earlier entries, you can expand on your learning, achieve perspective, remember and take stock of where you have been, synthesise, self-evaluate, and delight in your progress. The nineteenth-century American novelist Nathaniel Hawthorne said: 'You'll be surprised to find on re-perusing your journal what an importance and graphic power these little particulars assume'. In *The Importance of Being Earnest*, Oscar Wilde has a diary enthusiast in Gwendolen, who says: 'I never travel without my diary. One should always have something sensational to read in the train'.

Figure 1.1 illustrates the double-entry journal of the Australian writer Mary-Rose MacColl.

Writing educator Ann Berthoff (quoted in Fulwiler, 1987) calls the double-entry journal a 'dialogue journal' and says that writing in a journal provides the readiest means of carrying out what I.A. Richards called an *audit of meaning*.

> Writing as a way of knowing lets us represent ideas so that we can return to them and assess them. Keeping a journal is the best habit any writer can have; indeed, most real writers probably couldn't function without their notebooks, whatever form they take or however they are kept. Notebooks can serve as cradles, which is the way Henry James characterised his jottings—scraps of conversations, speculations about one image or

Figure 1.1 A double-entry journal

another, sketches of characters, plot ideas, etc; notebooks can serve as shorthand records or detailed accounts. Of what? Of observations—and observations of observations; recollections, remembrances, things to be remembered—memoranda; things to be returned to—*nota benes*; things to be looked up—ascertainable facts; notions to be puzzled over. Keeping a notebook is a way of keeping track of the development of ideas, as well as their inception and origin, of monitoring a work in progress. (p. 11)

Inspiration for journalling

To get you started on keeping a journal, you might like to write an entry discussing the ways in which writing is like running or dancing or boxing or painting or cooking, or any other activity you can think of (particularly one you enjoy). The novelist Haruki Murakami has written about writing and running in a *New Yorker* article, 'The running novelist' (2008), and Ferris Jabr (2014) has a wonderful essay in *The New Yorker* about why walking helps us think. The novelist Neil Gaiman has written about writing and cooking while talking about writing the short story 'A Study in Emerald' (2006). Gaiman says 'Writing's a lot like cooking. Sometimes the cake won't rise, no matter what you do, and every now and again the cake tastes better than you ever could have dreamed it would'.

In an essay titled 'Cooking dumb, eating dumb', Nahum Waxman, who owns a fabulous cookbook shop on the Upper East Side of Manhattan called Kitchen Arts & Letters, says that he dreads being asked by customers if the recipes in a cookbook 'work'. He tells them that it is they who must work. He says that his customers 'must think, must apply their intelligence and judgment to ideas and to the materials that will be turned into a dish' (1996). He could well be talking about some of the potential pitfalls of writing when he goes on to say that customers

> need to bring their own good sense to cooking—their ability to understand variability in ingredients, to recognise error in a written text, to acknowledge their own tastes and preferences, to not let themselves be intimidated by the food arbiters into dreary cooking-by-numbers.

You could add to this list of suggestions one of the key tenets of writing and editing advice: 'first you make a mess and then you clean it up'. There is a section, Further Reading, towards the end of this book that contains suggestions for material that may provide topics for reflection. You may be motivated to follow up on some of these by writing about them in your journal. When you are ready, go back and reflect on your earlier entries. This is where your double-entry journal comes into play: use your original entries to self-evaluate your personal and writing progress.

Features of journals

Because journal entries can be self-reflective, speculative, and experimental, written in the rhythms of everyday speech, you may use colloquial diction, first-person stance ('I'), loosely structured and meandering sentences, and informal punctuation. However, if you subsequently use material from your journal in academic or professional contexts, you'll need to adhere to more formal conventions.

If you use journal entries as the basis for later blog posts, as I suggest in Chapter 10, here are the criteria to aim for:

- content that's interesting, engaging, and appropriate for readers (be aware of cultural differences)
- content that speculates, poses problems, raises questions, challenges or informs and is based on authentic, credible, and authoritative research
- structure that's logical, coherent, cohesive, and focused
- style that's energetic, compelling, and concise
- sensitively crafted humour to avoid offending readers who don't share your sense of humour
- correct grammar, spelling, and punctuation.

Writing as a problem-solving process

Many people lack confidence in their writing and see the process as a painful chore, but if you treat it as a thinking–learning problem-solving process and put into practice the strategies that I advocate in this book, you will come to find writing pleasurable. Being able to produce writing worth reading will guarantee your success in your studies at university and in your subsequent professional and personal life.

Writing is judged on how successfully it communicates with its intended readers. How do you ensure that your readers can act on the information provided in your documents? Your writing needs to say something. It needs to make things happen. Writing is not just getting things down on paper; it's getting things into the minds of other people. Readers read to understand, to learn, to remember, or to be entertained. So, aim for a reader-centred dialogue, not an egocentric writer-centred monologue.

All communication rests on rhetorical relationships, that is, the relationships between:
- the purpose of the document
- the content of the document—its substance and argument
- the writer
- the reader
- the genre of the document—its structure and style
- the context of the document (when and where it will be read)
- the consequences of the document—its reception and any response it evokes.

Identify and analyse the problem, situation, or exigency to be addressed by the document, its subject, purpose, readers, and context, by using the heuristic for professional writing that I developed, shown in Figure 1.2. This heuristic is based on the journalist's heuristic of the five Ws and an H, spelled out so neatly in the opening lines of a Rudyard Kipling poem:

> I keep six honest serving-men
> (They taught me all I knew);
> Their names are What and Why and When
> And How and Where and Who.

To use the heuristic, you need four levels of knowledge:
1. topic/content knowledge
2. knowledge of the genre conventions of your document
3. rhetorical awareness, sensitivity, and sophistication
4. metaknowledge—that is, knowing what you know about the principles of writing, along with your repertoire of strategies.

Who	will write it? On their own behalf? On their superior's behalf? (in the workplace)
To whom?	Who is the reader?
What	does the reader need to know? method of reading will they use? (surface/skim or deep reading) does the writer need to say?
Why	does it need to be written?
Where	will the material come from? will it be written?
How	will it be organised, formatted, designed, checked, signed off, printed, and distributed?
When	is the deadline?

Figure 1.2   The heuristic for professional writing

Getting started

How do you start to write?
- Exploit the writing–thinking–learning connection by keeping it in mind at all times.
- Use predetermined headings and subheadings in templates, if available.
- Recognise that it's easier to correct than to create. 'Satisfice' (make do) on a first draft (also known as a 'zero' or 'discovery' draft).
- Use WIRMI (what I really mean is). WIRMI is the strategy to use to talk to yourself when you can't immediately express yourself in the formal style that your document requires. For example, in a job application you might use WIRMI to write *I know if you gave me this job I could do it*, and subsequently 'translate' that into *I believe that my qualifications and experience make me an appropriate applicant for this position*.
- Avoid premature editing. Elbow reminds us that our 'editorial instinct is often much better developed than [our] producing instinct' (1973, p. 25). He goes on to say that 'Producing writing, then, is not so much filling a basin once, but rather getting water to keep flowing *through* it till it finally runs clear' (p. 28).
- So, value iteration (looping and recursivity), not linearity: writing is rewriting.

Producing writing worth reading

What is writing 'worth reading', and how do you produce it? How do you write what needs to be written to achieve the results you want—that is, rhetorically appropriate and effective texts?

There's a knack to producing writing worth reading. It requires sharp rhetorical cutlery. However, there are no absolute laws of composition. Each principle of writing may be flouted to solve a particular problem in a specific piece of work. The key question that a writer should apply to a page is the question: 'Does it work?'

To begin with, though, you need to have a compendium of reliable practices and explicit strategies that will unequivocally lead your reader to your intended meaning. You need to be your own best reader and editor, which requires competence and confidence—what psychologists call 'self-efficacy'. The 'just-sounds-better-that-way' approach just won't do. In a world awash with swathes of unedited writing, well-edited material has a higher currency than ever. (Editing is discussed in Chapter 11.)

Habitual, immersive practice in writing will build an instinctive self-efficacy, which will lead to the kind of pleasurable writing familiar to experienced writers when they are intellectually engaged in writing tasks.

Aim for:
- writing that's riveting (compellingly captures and holds your reader's attention), tight (concisely encapsulates what you mean and makes every word count), and smart (logically conveys the hierarchical structure of your ideas, by linking them explicitly and leading your reader down the reading path that you design)
- writing that's original, vital, exuberant, stylistically innovative, and engaging
- writing that conveys specific, significant, relevant, current, accurate, comprehensive, authoritative, and honest information that is clear, coherent, structured (ordered), focused, and simple—writing that provides 'a momentary stay against confusion' (Frost, 1939).

What characterises good writers?

They:
- know why they are writing and what their readers hope to find
- know what they know and what they don't know about their topic
- can draw on their large repertoire of writing strategies and principles and know what works
- prefer simple, direct expression of ideas
- satisfy the reader's need for information, not their own need for self-expression
- know the rules, but also know when to break them for effect
- exhibit syntactic clarity and rhetorical sensitivity and sophistication
- present work that has been meticulously edited and proofread.

The last word

To conclude this chapter, I'd like to emphasise that writing is hard and takes a long time. A helpful tip when you are writing a document over several days is to 'park on the downhill slope'. In other words, stop writing for the day at a point where it will be easy to get going again in your next writing session. There is not one, correct, easy writing process to follow when preparing documents. There are no shortcuts, even for very experienced writers.

Richard Nordquist devotes a column 'Pros on prose: The best advice on writing' (2015) on grammar.about.com to some further advice about writing: write one inch at a time (similar in meaning to taking one step at a time); finish your first draft; write with authority; and *Sitzfleisch!* (*Sitzfleisch* is a word of German origin that means 'The ability to endure or persist in an endeavour—to sit through it'.) So, to summarise: hang in there and put in the time to finish your writing task.

Activities

1. Watch on YouTube my video interview with Geoffrey Pullum (2014) about the upsurge of writing with the rise of the internet, listed in the Further Reading list, and/or watch 'The history of English in 10 minutes', also on YouTube, and respond by writing in your journal about any aspects that interest you.

2. Comment in your journal on whether you can identify with writing educator Peter Elbow's (1998) statements below about 'writing with power'.

> Writing means getting power over words and readers; writing clearly and correctly; writing what is true or real or interesting; and writing persuasively or making some kind of contact with your readers so that they actually experience your meaning or vision.
>
> But writing with power also means getting power over yourself and over the writing process; knowing what you are doing as you write; being in charge; having control; not feeling stuck or helpless or intimidated. I am particularly interested in this second kind of power in writing and I have found that without it you seldom achieve the first kind. (1998, p. 1)

3. Reflect on your knowledge about and experience of writing and comment in your journal about whether the following statements are myths about writing that need to be dispelled.
   - Writing simply involves transferring thoughts from the mind to the paper or to the screen.
   - The writing process must begin at the beginning and follow on through to the end in a linear, left-to-right fashion.
   - Writing should be right the first time.
   - There is a standard, step-by-step writing procedure that, if followed, ensures good writing.
   - Writing is speech plus handwriting, spelling, and punctuation.
   - A writer is a gifted individual—born, not made.
   - You must have something to say in order to write.
   - Writing is easy.
   - The world of work is routinised, and the writing it needs is largely formulaic, so there is no room for the infusion of a personal voice.
   - Form and content are separable (what you say can be separated from how you say it).
   - Writing is an artificial, academic exercise with little application to the real world.
   - Writing is always a sedentary, silent, solitary activity.
   - Good writing is always correct writing.
   - There are so many different types and styles of writing that you have to be an expert to use them all, and most people will never have to use that many anyhow.
   - Every teacher or boss has their own way of writing that you will have to learn, and you'll have to unlearn everything you've ever studied before.
   - If you didn't get a good writing background in primary or secondary school, it's too late for you now!

4. Do you have any writing rituals as idiosyncratic as those followed by some famous writers?
   - Robert Frost avoided daylight.
   - Charles Dickens couldn't write without his china monkey.
   - Friedrich Schiller kept rotten apples in his desk and his feet in ice-cold water.
   - Marcel Proust wrote in a cork-lined room.

- James Jones said: 'As long as I don't get too drunk, I can write anywhere'.
- Agatha Christie apparently wrote in a large Victorian bathtub.
- Edith Sitwell liked to write lying down in an open coffin.
- James Joyce, Marcel Proust, and Truman Capote also liked to lie down to write, while Virginia Woolf and Ernest Hemingway preferred to stand up.
- Several writers have written in sheds, including Roald Dahl, Dylan Thomas, and Philip Pullman.
- Percy Bysshe Shelley and Jean-Jacques Rousseau wrote bareheaded in the sunshine.
- Vladimir Nabokov liked to write in his car.
- Gertrude Stein liked to write in her Model T Ford while parked in a Parisian street. (Burnham, 1994; Isard, 2015)

5. What is your reaction when you are asked to do some writing? Why? Can you remember when you first started to feel that way? Reflect on a time when writing worked for you. What form did it take? What processes did you follow? (Where? When? How?) Explore your metaknowledge; that is, reflect on what you have learned about writing. If you had to pass on your best advice about writing, what would it be?

2

How reading works

> Read in order to live.
> GUSTAVE FLAUBERT

Why read?

There's no shortage of endorsements from writers on the value of reading. Most of the quotes below apply to fiction, but many can also be applied to nonfiction. Flaubert isn't the only one to have advocated reading as a necessity for living.

> 'A reader lives a thousand lives before he dies,' said Jojen. 'The man who never reads lives only one.'
> GEORGE R.R. MARTIN, *A DANCE WITH DRAGONS*, 2011

> To acquire the habit of reading is to construct for yourself a refuge from almost all the miseries of life.
> W. SOMERSET MAUGHAM, *BOOKS AND YOU*, 1940

> People say that life is the thing, but I prefer reading.
> LOGAN PEARSALL SMITH, *AFTERTHOUGHTS*, 'MYSELF', 1931

> Reading enriches your life in a way that isn't just pleasure—it actually educates you and makes you understand other times, places and ways of thought.
> WRITER JOHN CAREY, IN AN INTERVIEW WITH MATTHEW REISZ, 2014

Whether we're reading a novel, a biography, or for that matter a book about orchids, we seek an elusive combination of pleasure, utility and intellectual stimulation, something to pique our curiosity and engage our minds.
BOOK CRITIC RUTH FRANKLIN, 2005

The greatest gift is a passion for reading. It is cheap, it consoles, it distracts, it excites, it gives you knowledge of the world and experience of a wide kind. It is a moral illumination.
WRITER AND CO-FOUNDER OF *THE NEW YORK REVIEW OF BOOKS* ELIZABETH HARDWICK, 1985

And here's a further observation, by non-fiction writer Verlyn Klinkenborg (2009), who suggests that, although we generally read silently, reading aloud is valuable because it 'recaptures the physicality of words. Our idea of reading is incomplete, impoverished, unless we are also taking the time to read aloud'. In Chapter 11, I advocate reading aloud as a very valuable strategy to use when you are proofreading.

How does reading help writing?

Reading and writing are intimately connected in an osmotic relationship. The novelist Francine Prose says: 'Like most—maybe all—writers, I learned to write by writing and, by example, by reading books' (2006, p. 2). William Giraldi says: 'There's no such thing as a skilful writer who is not also a dedicated reader' (2015). Alan Bennett's touching novella *The Uncommon Reader* (2007) is based on the belief that the right book at the right time can ignite a lifelong habit and create a true booklover.

In a review of the book *So Many Books, So Little Time: A year of passionate reading,* Motoko Rich (2007) quotes its author, Sara Nelson, who is editor-in-chief of the trade magazine *Publishers Weekly*. Nelson says that 'why people read what they read is a great unknown and personal thing'. Rich comments that 'part of what draws people to books can now be found elsewhere . . . television shows like *The Sopranos* and *Lost* can satisfy the hunger for narrative and richly textured characters in a way that only books could in a previous age'. Video games also contain strong and complex narratives.

Rich has a point, but if you want to learn to write well, immerse yourself in reading. Wide reading, particularly of authors who write well, will help you to absorb a great deal about the craft of writing—about word choice, sentence structure, patterns of paragraphs, punctuation, rhythm, etc. The more you know about style (see Chapter 3) and grammar and syntax (see Chapters 4 and 5), the greater your pleasure in reading.

At the beginning of every new writing class, I pass on to my students Henry James's advice in *The Art of Fiction* (1884): 'Try to be one of those on whom nothing is lost'.

Find writers whose work you admire and read their work, paying conscious, sustained attention to their techniques and effects. Look up new words in a dictionary. Take notes. Try to analyse what makes a piece of writing resonate with you. Writers such as Alan Bennett (2007) and Tim Parks (2014) advocate reading with a pencil in hand. Transcribe by hand sentences and passages that you admire. Imitate. Emulate. (There is a difference.) Respond to your extracts and analyse them in your double-entry journal (see Chapter 1).

If you're already confident about your writing competence, reading syntactically challenging writing can be enlightening, pleasurable, and exhilarating.

Here are some key ways in which reading can help your writing that complement those offered by the authors of the opening quotes of this chapter:

- Reading expands your vocabulary.
- Reading exposes you to different writing styles.
- Reading helps you to subconsciously absorb the rules of syntax, grammar, style, and punctuation.
- Reading helps you to subconsciously absorb genre conventions, and the principles of effective structure and document design.
- Reading gives you increased insight and inspiration.

Some potential disadvantages that creative writers might experience are worth being aware of:

- You might spend too much time on reading and not enough on writing.
- You might become intimidated by great writing produced by others.
- You'll see only the finished product and not how it was created.
- Imitating or emulating another writer's style won't necessarily help you to become more creative, and could limit the development of your own style.

Writing for your readers

It goes without saying that you need to 'write for your reader'. Robert Graves (1944) urged writers to imagine a reader looking over their shoulder when they sat down to work. It certainly helps your writing when you can visualise the actual reader of your work. It would be great to have movies of people's minds as they read your work (Elbow, 1973, p. 77).

Of course, writing can never fully anticipate its reading. Your reader is not clairvoyant, and what's on the page or on the screen is not necessarily the message that the reader will construct. It's pointless saying to a reader who has misconstrued your message: 'It's there in black and white'. Readers 'receive' a document by composing it for themselves. They don't necessarily just interpret an unequivocal message.

Studies of reading by researchers in many fields have shown that people do more than passively absorb data; they actively structure data to construct meaning for themselves. When people read, they call on schemata—mental representations of their previous experience of situations, events, and actions. So, readers use pre-existing knowledge, opinions, and beliefs to interact with and process texts.

Reading is often an act of re-creation, with meaning created somewhere in the interaction between writer, text, reader, and context. As we saw in Chapter 1, language does not simply provide a transparent window on reality. Language constructs reality. Language is epistemic, not merely communicative; that is, it is part of the process by which we create knowledge.

The late David Foster Wallace (2012) told his writing students that the most important thing for them to remember was that 'someone who is not them and cannot read their mind is going to have to read this'.

When we say that a text is 'readable', what do we base our judgement on? Whether it is:
- legible (for the reader)?
- aesthetically attractive (to the reader)?
- interesting (to the reader)?
- understandable (to the reader)?
- able to be acted upon (by the reader)?

All of these criteria are essential, but the final criterion is crucial if we are reading 'to do' rather than reading 'to learn'. Reading 'to do' would include, for example, teaching ourselves how to build a website by following a set of instructions, or responding to a letter from the Taxation Office requesting extra payment. Reading 'to learn' would include reading a textbook to understand concepts. Reading a literary text for pleasure would be different again.

Theories of reading range from formalist theories adhered to by the New Critics from the 1930s to the 1960s, which proposed that written texts contain some determinable coherent meaning put there with the author's discernible intention, through to contemporary theories that claim that the only meaning locatable in a text is that which is put there by the reader. The most extreme example of this theory is expressed in Roland Barthes's 1967 essay 'The Death of the Author', in which he asserted that 'the reader writes the text' and 'in the text only the reader speaks' (1984, p. 151).

The New Critics subscribed to a version of the theory of reading espoused more than two millennia earlier by Plato (1963), who uses Socrates as his spokesman in the following statement:

> Writing . . . has this strange quality about it, which makes it really like painting: the painter's products stand before us quite as though they were alive; but if you question them, they maintain a solemn silence. So, too, with written words: you might think they spoke as though they made sense, but if you ask them anything about what they are saying, if you wish an explanation, they go on telling you the same thing, over and over forever. (p. 69)

Stanley Fish, in his widely cited book *Is There a Text in This Class?* (1980), questioned New Criticism's effort to locate literary meaning in the formal features of the text and proposed the concept of 'interpretive community'. Fish argues that interpretation is not the art of construing but the art of constructing (p. 327). Interpretations are made, not just by the reader as an individual in cooperation with the text and the writer, but also by the reader in cooperation with the institutions in which they are embedded.

Fish's point is illustrated well by Hermione Lee, who wrote in her celebrated 1996 biography of Virginia Woolf:

Virginia Woolf's story is reformulated by each generation. She takes on the shape of difficult modernist preoccupied with questions of form, or comedian of manners, or neurotic highbrow aesthete, or inventive fantasist, or pernicious snob, or Marxist feminist, or historian of women's lives, or victim of abuse, or lesbian heroine, or cultural analyst, depending on who is reading her, and when, and in what context. (p. 769)

Contemporary reading theorists now accept that meaning does not reside exclusively in texts, as the New Critics claimed, but is rather located somewhere in the interaction that occurs when readers process texts in specific contexts. Alberto Manguel (2010), who has written extensively about reading, says that 'every text is, in an essential sense, an interactive text, changing according to a particular reader, at a particular hour, and in a particular place' (p. 195). The effective transmission of meaning is achieved when the writer's intentions are congruent with, rather than disparate from, the reader's expectations and inferences.

Organisational theorist and management professor John Van Maanen (1988) sums up contemporary reading theory in the following passage:

Writing is intended as a communicative act between author and reader. Once a manuscript is released and goes public, however, the meanings writers may think they have frozen into print may melt before the eyes of active readers. Meanings are not permanently embedded by an author in the text at the moment of creation. They are woven by the symbolic capacity of a piece of writing and the social context of its reception. Most crucial, different categories of readers will display systematic differences in their perceptions and interpretations of the same writing. (p. 25)

It helps, of course, not to have the kind of idiosyncratic style that Gertrude Stein had. Her distinctively original style provoked one journalist greeting her in New York in 1934 into asking: 'Why don't you write the way you talk?' She replied: 'Why don't you read the way I write?' (Stein, 1971, p. 9). If you are curious about Stein's unique style, read the wonderful essay 'Poetry and grammar' (1971), in which she describes her feelings about various punctuation marks. Unlike the iconoclastic Stein, we cannot ask our readers to read the way we write. Reading theory has taught us that they will read the way they read.

As Van Maanen says: 'Writers are the privileged readers of their own texts and are, within limits, the only ones who can speak with some advantage and special authority on their own intentions and textual assumptions' (1988, p. xv). Readers do not have this advantage, so deciding what to write and how to say it depends entirely upon whom you plan to tell it to. Just remember that you cannot fully anticipate readers' reactions to a text, even when you try to write so that you cannot possibly be misunderstood.

Before you set out to write a formal document in the workplace, or a job application, first consider the kind of documents that you like to receive: ones that get to the point, that are coherently structured, and that concisely communicate the content needed to get the job done. In a professional context, rarely do people write merely to inform. Most of the time they write so that their readers can act on the information provided.

You won't usually be able to ask your readers for their reading preferences, though in many organisations page limits and style requirements for certain documents are specified. Managers may say to you that they want 'no more than a page'. Recruitment consultants may request that you respond to the selection criteria in no more than two pages, even in cases where the criteria themselves take up two-thirds of a page. Granting bodies may provide templates for proposals that are set up to accept only a certain number of characters, including spaces. They also usually specify typeface and type size.

In literary contexts, it is often necessary to adhere to word limits, particularly in literary competitions for flash fiction, short stories, and novellas. There are dozens of contests worldwide for creative writers—for poems, scripts, short stories, novellas, novels, etc. Almost without exception, they specify word counts.

In formal, professional contexts, you will need to consider your readers'
- education—level, field of study, their existing theoretical, practical, and/or technical knowledge
- experience—academic, professional, organisational, managerial, technical
- familiarity with the subject—if they are very familiar with it, they may get bored; if feeling threatened, they may become hostile

- attitude towards the subject—positive, neutral, or negative
- expectations and needs of the document—for example, new information, instructions, recommendations. Advice in education, health, and legal contexts? Does the document fulfil their content and genre expectations (see Chapter 8)?
- motivation to read—how interested/motivated are they?
- urgency—how pressing is the need for information? How quickly can you provide the information while ensuring that it is accurate and comprehensive?
- context—the environment in which they will be reading; possible distractions, noise and interruptions; their emotional state.

Reading in the workplace

Workplace messages are often sent without enough prior thought. Email messages are notorious in this regard (see Chapter 10). At the university where I was teaching, I once received two email messages within a few days of each other with the same subject line: 'Missing trolley'. The two emails are reproduced as Figures 2.1 and 2.2.

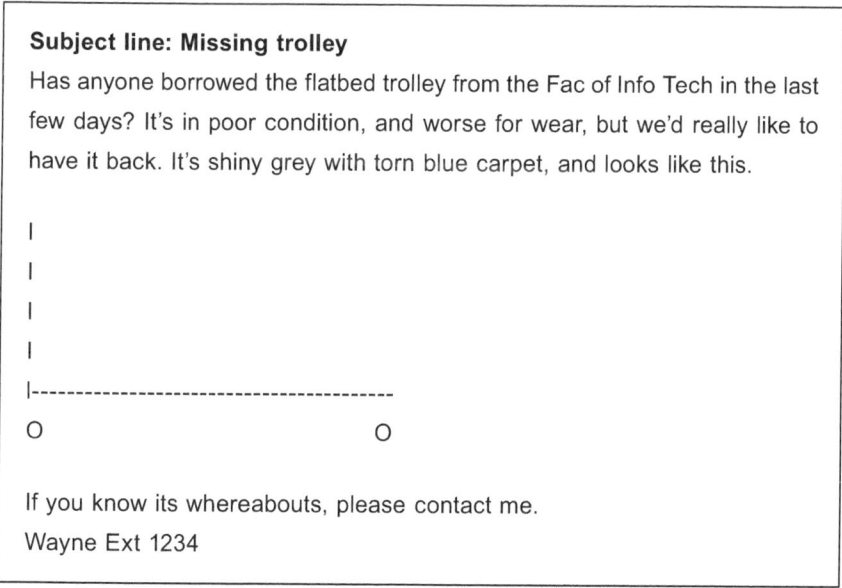

Figure 2.1 Missing trolley 1

> **Subject line: Missing trolley**
> A trolley has gone missing from W101 on Monday 28 July.
> It is a red trolley with pneumatic tyres, and belongs to an external contractor.
> Could the person responsible please return said trolley ASAP to Kathy Ext 2498.

Figure 2.2 Missing trolley 2

It's often difficult to predict how many potential readers you have with a particular message, but the writer of the second email clearly made no effort to consider who might read her rather blunt message about the 'said' trolley. On the other hand, it's difficult to be certain whether the writer of the first email consciously considered his readers, either. However, I think most readers would be more inclined to respond to Wayne's heartfelt message and be on the lookout for his trolley, particularly because they could see how fond the writer was of the trolley and how much trouble he had taken to illustrate it.

Figure 2.4 is an example of a message that sounds as though the writer, Michael, an events coordinator, has considered his readers, but does he succeed? He sent out a letter to apologise for an invitation that the company had previously sent out. As so often happens, the apology didn't rectify the original problem by clarifying the message, and in fact did further damage by being sloppily written, unless the unique double comma after 'apology' was intended to emphasise the sincerity of the apology. The original invitation is shown as Figure 2.3, and the letter of apology as Figure 2.4.

Is Michael apologising for assuming that everyone has a partner that they'd like to bring to the dinner? Is he apologising to people who don't have a partner? Is he apologising for not naming partners? Does he not want anyone to bring a partner? Would Fiona, or any of his readers, be any the wiser?

> HillEnd Marketing Services Limited
> Requests the company of
> Fiona Anderson & Partner at the Inner Circle Dinner
> at the Mayfair Hotel on Friday 28 July at 7 pm.

Figure 2.3 The invitation

> Oops! Fiona, when we centralised most of our administration to Head Office last year we achieved some big results.
>
> But . . . it looks as though we dropped the ball on the most important issue. Over the next two weeks we are celebrating our success with our special people—YOU.
>
> As you know, we have organised a special dinner to show that we care. We sent you a special invitation asking you to join us as our guest . . . and then, disaster! We demonstrated the impersonal nature we all suspect of a Head Office. We asked you and your . . . uumm . . . your . . . er . . . partner!!! . . . to dine with us.
>
> We're sorry.
>
> Please accept our most sincere apology,, for this unforgivable lapse in our usually high customer-focused communications. We have taken steps to ensure that it will never happen again.
>
> As I am responsible for all events including Business Sessions, Seminars, Conferences and Conventions the buck stops with me.
>
> Michael

Figure 2.4 The letter of apology

Context

Readers need a context.

On 30 October 1938, Orson Welles's Mercury Theatre players broadcast an adaptation of H.G. Wells's novel *The War of the Worlds* on the Columbia Broadcasting System radio network in New York City. During the broadcast, which took the place of the usual dance-band program, Welles presented news bulletins (which were in the playscript) reporting that New York City was currently being invaded by Martians. Many listeners who hadn't tuned in from the beginning—and therefore lacked context—panicked. There were stories about people fleeing across the Hudson River to New Jersey. *Radio Days* (1987), Woody Allen's lovely autobiographical movie about the golden age of radio, includes a scene in which Woody's aunt is out on a date when her beau turns on the car radio after the broadcast has started and, hearing about the supposed invasion, jumps in his car and flees, leaving her stranded.

One of my students, who published a (street) fashion magazine, wrote this sentence about a female designer: 'Her twentysomething clients like wearing retro-style clothes'. It never occurred to my student that not all of her readers would have the cultural knowledge that the term 'thirtysomething' had first appeared as the title of a television show some years earlier, and had subsequently come into common usage to refer to people in a particular decade of life (e.g., *a thirtysomething man*). This example illustrates how, when a reader processes a text, the message is not necessarily in the text/words themselves, but somewhere within the interaction of content, writer, reader, and context. It didn't occur to the writer of the article that the term could be misunderstood as the number of clients who were on the designer's books. It is always a good idea not to assume that your reader will share your cultural background and frames of reference.

In a fascinating *New Yorker* essay, revered writing teacher John McPhee (2015) discusses how context and frames of reference operate and how quickly they evolve from currency to obsolescence. McPhee suggests that writers look for allusions, references, and images that have some durability. He relates an anecdote from the *New York Times* journalist Frank Bruni, who was teaching a writing class in which they were discussing an essay that repeatedly invoked Proust's madeleine. Marcel Proust was one of the most influential French novelists of the twentieth century. In the first volume of his novel *In Search of Lost Time*, his narrator dips a madeleine (a tiny shell-shaped sponge cake) into warm tea, an action that triggers a memory from his childhood, as details of his aunt's house and its surrounding streets flood into his consciousness. As the discussion progressed, Bruni realised that almost none of the students understood what the madeleine signified, or for that matter 'who this Proust fellow was'. Bruni wondered whether we are losing our 'collective vocabulary', and asked: 'Are common points of reference dwindling?'

This is a generational thing. As I was writing this book, I was constantly aware of the wide age and cultural-interests span of those who would read it. Another reminder came from an unexpected source. Seeing a photo on Facebook of a friend of mine in a none-too-flattering hat, I sent her an email message: 'Where did you get that hat?' She took my message literally and offered to buy one for me from the shop at the beach where she had bought hers. I didn't mean her to infer that. I assumed—and we should all know how foolish it is to assume anything—that she would immediately remember the comical old English music-hall song that starts: 'Where did you get that hat? Where did you get that tile [slang for "hat"]?' She hadn't.

So, although it will be difficult to foresee the way in which your readers will experience and process your words, try to keep in mind potential misreadings.

Structuring writing for reading

When you write and design documents, you need to present a guided tour, a 'reading path', that helps readers to move through and 'interpret' the text. The opening often makes or breaks a message. Try to structure the reading in an unobtrusive, 'natural' flow so that the reader has no trouble following the 'reading path' that you create.

Remember, readers are not absorbent sponges. They will actively construct their own meaning, so consider their KAN—knowledge, attitude, and needs (Petelin & Durham, 1992, pp. 16–17). Producing coherent, well-structured writing in the academy and the workplace is achieved by:

- using textual features such as a foreword or preface, a table of contents, a title, an abstract or summary, and headings and subheadings that preview and clarify the structure of the document
- providing an 'advance organiser', for example, *This report deals with the history of the project and analyses the progress to date*
- structuring coherent, well-punctuated, and unambiguous sentences
- structuring coherent and cohesive paragraphs with a topic sentence to introduce a paragraph (where appropriate), and a summary sentence to conclude a paragraph (where appropriate)
- presenting an appropriate sequence of ideas (when you are editing, check this against a retrospective outline)
- using different levels of headings (major and minor headings) as signposts/cues to indicate levels of significance (sometimes you can use predetermined headings, if it's a document that is commonly produced in your organisation)
- using distinct, repeated patterns (not undeveloped, random ones)
- using parallel structure for coordinate elements in headings, within lists (such as in this list), and within sentences, wherever possible

- making it as easy on the reader as possible by linking different sections of a text using connecting words/transitional expressions/'cohesive ties' (see Chapter 5 in the section on paragraphing, where I list and explain what linguists call 'cohesive ties')
- providing useful redundancy, for example, repeating the same information in the summary, introduction, and conclusion of an essay or paper
- anticipating and addressing potential pitfalls and areas of confusion for readers, for example, troubleshooting steps in a set of instructions such as in a recipe book
- including visual representations such as pictures, graphs, tables, and infographics to illustrate complex concepts and phenomena, which has become increasingly popular in many document contexts because some readers can process graphic communication more quickly than words
- using appropriate typography and layout to enhance the text
- concluding the document by summarising and making recommendations, where appropriate.

Reading critically

As a writer, you need to try to be the best reader of your own documents, but this is very difficult. I'll cover revising, editing, and proofreading in Chapter 11, but, in the meantime, you can test yourself as a reader of this book. First, consider the following key dimensions and decide whether this book satisfies your genre expectations (see Chapter 8) in relation to:
- content—what it says
- structure/framework—how it's organised/sequenced
- style—how it says what it says
- format/layout—how it looks
- mechanics—is it flawless?

Now, ask yourself specifically:
- What is the aim of this book?
- Why are you reading this book?
- Who are the key intended readers of this book?
- Is the approach to the subject matter appropriate for the readership?
- Are you reading this book as a paperback or as an ebook?

- What kind of reading does this book invite? Chronological reading? Skim-reading? Close reading?
- How is this book organised/structured? (See Chapter 7)
- How is this book designed and presented? (See Chapter 7)
- What generic 'textbook' conventions such as exercises and references does this book feature?
- Have you read similar books? If you have, how does this book compare with them?
- How do you intend to use the information in this book?
- Who do you think the writer is? What kind of 'voice' comes through? Is the address direct or has the writer adopted a persona? (See Chapter 3)
- Is the writer an authority on the topic, with an appropriate background and qualifications?
- What perspective/framework informs the writer?
- Is there any evidence of bias in this book?
- Is the content trustworthy, fair, and sufficient?
- Is the reasoning sound?
- How practical or useful is this book?
- Does the book have an index?
- Is the material in the book up to date?
- Has the book been published by a reputable publisher or by a 'vanity' press?

You can apply these questions (suitably modified) to other books that you read. In Activity 6 at the end of this chapter, I invite you to write a review of the book, and provide some more information about what a book review might include.

Two other aspects of reading that are worth noting are readability formulas and speed reading.

Readability formulas

During the 1920s in the United States, a movement in education known as the Scientific Movement began setting standardised tests in schools to measure students' achievements. To predict the difficulty levels of written texts for students, readability formulas were devised that supposedly correlated two variables—sentence length and word length—with readability.

However, the 'readability' of a text is not something that can be measured. The determinants of readability are much more involved than this kind of measurement. Ease of reading depends on how interested your readers are in what you have to say, how motivated they are, how enticing and understandable your writing is, and whether readers can act on your documents if they need to. Not all short words are familiar, for example, *erg, ilk, lien*, and *tort*. Short, familiar words can be used to express an unfamiliar concept, for example, a *sunk-cost*. The purpose of the document, content of the message, word order, grammar, sentence structure, and design are not taken into account by these formulas. As well as these factors, readability goes beyond words and sentences to the coherence of paragraphs and beyond.

So don't be tempted to apply 'mathematical' readability formulas, such as the ones included in some software, to your documents. Verbal (from the Latin word *verba*, meaning 'word') meaning can't be quantified. Reading research has consistently discredited these formulas over the past 60 years. (If you need to convince anyone about the unreliability of readability formulas, see further discussion in Petelin & Durham, 1992, pp. 24–7.)

Speed reading

The rates at which readers read are determined by the kind of knowledge they need to acquire. Many people scan and skim business documents, picking up information from headings and dot-point lists. This contrasts with the way that people closely read texts to gain knowledge and the way in which people read for leisure. At the other end of the speed spectrum there is the painstakingly slow rate at which meticulous proofreading gets done.

It was announced in April 2015 that a start-up company in Boston had designed an app that promises to help users to read faster by saving them the trouble of moving their eyes. The app streams words directly onto the screen one at a time, using a technology called 'rapid serial visual presentation', and the developers claim that 'anyone can improve their reading speed and even work their way up to the top setting—1,000 words a minute'. Detractors worry about the trade-off between reading speed and comprehension, but there are many proponents of speed reading. Check out the app at spritzinc.com.

The last word

Following the advice presented in this chapter for producing readable workplace and academic writing will contribute substantially to your readers' reception of your writing.

When it comes to your own reading, the research on online reading versus reading on paper reports mixed results. To date, it's clear that digital texts are intangible and ephemeral; they haven't yet replicated the tactility of paper. In his well-received book *The Shallows: What the internet is doing to our brains*, Carr (2010) argues that our reading is being undermined by digital technologies that are turning us into scanners, skimmers, 'surfers', and shallow readers. In discussing 'deep reading', he quotes the research of Maryanne Wolf, who says that in reading online we sacrifice the facility that makes deep reading possible (quoted in Carr, p. 122). On the Oxford University Press blog, Naomi Baron, author of *Words Onscreen: The fate of reading in a digital world*, argues that 'What computer technology wasn't designed for is deep reading: thoughtfully working through a text, pausing to reflect on what we've read, going back to early passages, and perhaps writing notes in the margins about our own take on the material. Here is where print technology wins' (2015).

Baron reports on research that she carried out with young adults in four countries. She asked them on which reading platform they found it easiest to concentrate: hard copy, computer, tablet, e-reader, or mobile phone. Hard copy was the choice of 92 per cent of her participants.

There are many books about reading for people who love reading. See the list in Box 2.1. There are also hundreds of blogs about reading.

BOX 2.1   **Books about reading for those who love books and reading**

Bennett, A. (2007). *The Uncommon Reader: A novella*. London: Faber.

Birkerts, S. (1994). *The Gutenberg Elegies: The fate of reading in an electronic age*. New York: Fawcett.

Corrigan, M. (2005). *Leave Me Alone, I'm Reading: Finding and losing myself in books*. New York: Vintage Books.

Fadiman, A. (1998). *Ex Libris: Confessions of a common reader*. New York: Penguin.

Hill, S. (2010). *Howard's End is on the Landing*. London: Profile Books.
Jacobs, A. (2011). *The Pleasures of Reading in an Age of Distraction*. New York: Oxford University Press.
Lesser, W. (2002). *Nothing Remains the Same: Reading and remembering*. Boston: Houghton Mifflin.
Manguel, A. (1997). *A History of Reading*. London: Flamingo.
Manguel, A. (2010). *A Reader on Reading*. New Haven: Yale University Press.
Nelson, S. (2003). *So Many Books, So Little Time: A year of passionate reading*. New York: G.P. Putnam's Sons.
Pearl, N. (2003). *Book Lust*. Seattle: Sasquatch Books.
Pearl, N. (2005). *More Book Lust*. Seattle: Sasquatch Books.
Pennac, D. (2010). *The Rights of the Reader*. London: Walker Books. (Gallimard: Paris, 1992).
Prose, F. (2006). *Reading Like a Writer: A guide for people who love books and for those who want to write them*. New York: HarperCollins.
Quindlen, A. (1998). *How Reading Changed My Life*. New York: Ballantine.
Schwartz, L. (1996). *Ruined by Reading: A life in books*. Boston: Beacon Press.
Spacks, P.M. (2011). *On Rereading*. Cambridge, MA: Harvard University Press.

Activities

1. Read the quotes about the value of reading at the beginning of this chapter. Which most resonate with you and why? Discuss your responses to the quotes as an entry in your journal.
2. Do you think that the amount of reading that you do has affected your writing ability? Do you think that those who say that you can't be a skilful writer if you aren't a dedicated reader are overstating their case? Discuss as an entry in your journal.
3. Comment in an entry in your journal about whether you agree with the comments made by Carr, Wolf, and Baron that I have reported in The

Last Word about the difficulty of engaging in 'deep reading' when you read onscreen.
4. Questions for readers who read fiction for pleasure:
   - What are you reading at the moment (other than this book)?
   - When is your favourite time to read?
   - Where is your favourite place to read?
   - What are your favourite kinds of books?
   - What is your favourite bookshop?
   - What are your three 'desert-island' books?
   - What is the first book you can remember reading?
   - What is your favourite children's book?
   - Who is your favourite fictional character?
   - Is there a book you couldn't finish?
   - Do you have a comfort book that you reread?
   - Which book do you love that not enough other people know about?
   - Which author do you most admire and why?
   - Who are your two ideal fictional dining companions?
   - Do you have a favourite film of a book? If so, what is it?
   - What book would you like to see filmed?
   - Which book changed your life?
   - What book are you looking forward to reading?
   - Is there a book that you think you ought to read?
5. Some people reread certain books yearly, for example, each of Jane Austen's six novels. Stephen Fry (like many others, including me) rereads P.G. Wodehouse books every year. I also reread Madeleine St John's four novels every year. Do you agree with the statement: 'No book is worth reading that isn't worth rereading'? Use your responses to this and the questions in activity 4 above to write a paragraph in your journal about the value of rereading.

    If you want to follow up on this phenomenon, read the articles 'The pleasures of rereading' by Tom Lamont and 'Rereading: Authors reveal their literary addictions' by Chris Fenn, both in *The Guardian* on 8 April 2012.
6. Using the prompt questions earlier in this chapter on assessing the value of this book and the further points in the rubric below, write a review of this book.

Most high-quality published reviews will include details about the book's format, publisher, place of publication, price, availability, and an appropriate selection of the following elements:

- an intriguing headline that indicates the reviewer's evaluation of the book
- an opening sentence that reveals the reviewer's judgement of the attraction or otherwise of the book for a reader
- a summary of the book's argument or contents
- for a work of fiction, observations about the plot, structure, characters, style, dialogue, and presence of humour
- evidence that the reviewer has read the book with a critical eye
- information on the author's previous publications and their authority to write the book
- the reviewer's opinion clearly distinguishable from fact
- short extracts to illustrate a point or to substantiate the reviewer's opinion
- all the reviewer's claims substantiated
- evidence of the reviewer's broader reading on the book's topic
- comparisons between this work and others previously published in the genre or on the same subject
- errors of fact, gaps in the material, irrelevancies, deficiencies in proofreading, inconsistencies, infelicities of style, and triumphs or otherwise of design.

3

How words work

> Every utterance is deficient—it says less than it wishes to say.
> Every utterance is exuberant—it conveys more than it plans.
> — JOSÉ ORTEGA Y GASSET

Using words well

In this chapter, I'll cover the concept of style at the word level with suggestions about how to use words well to enhance your writing.

In Chapter 1, I emphasised how crucial the quality of your writing is to success in your professional and personal life. Your writing quality depends heavily on your choice of words. One key factor that determines excellent writing style is how well your choice of words matches your readers' expectations, and that depends on who those readers are. In formal writing—for example, at university and in the workplace—you'll need to adhere quite strictly to the conventions of academic and professional writing. If you are writing creatively, you have a much wider choice in relation to word choice and can be as imaginative and idiosyncratic as you like. That said, you may also be somewhat creative in some workplaces, where there's been a strong movement to embrace the 'narrative turn'.

In recent years, social scientists have come to appreciate what political, religious, and military figures have long known: that stories (narratives, myths, or fables) constitute a uniquely powerful currency in human relationships (Gardner, 2011, p. 40). Organisational story telling has become prominent in some workplaces, where it's been seen as a powerful technique.

How word-aware are you? Do you relish words? Do you consider yourself to be a wordsmith? Do you take pleasure in crafting sentences, in reading the stylish sentences of others? Do you recognise how your handling of words can help you to produce clear, economical, precise, logical, and compelling writing? Words, saturated with values and symbolic power, are your greatest tools. Read, read, read! Write, write, write!

Although it's usually not a good idea to use a foreign phrase that readers might not know, there is a French expression that encapsulates what you should aim for: *le mot juste*, the perfect word. In his article 'Draft no. 4' (2013b), John McPhee relates how his eighth-grade teacher, Miss Bartholomew, told her class that 'Gustave Flaubert walked around the garden for days on end searching in his head for *le mot juste*. Who could forget that?' McPhee certainly didn't. He went on to become a highly revered writing teacher at Princeton University and has been a contributor to *The New Yorker* magazine for more than 50 years. Your readers will never wonder why you didn't use a more appropriate word when you consistently use the intensely right word.

English is tricky, though. Sometimes a word that means something in one context means the opposite in another: for example, *cleave*, which can mean 'to cut' or 'to adhere to'; and *wise*, as in *a wise man* and *a wise guy*, where *a wise man* is a complimentary description and *a wise guy* is a negative description. Sometimes a word or term and its opposite (its antonym) can mean much the same thing: for example, *slim* and *fat* are antonyms, but *a slim chance* and *a fat chance* both mean that there's little chance of something happening.

Language is fluid and flexible, not static. The fabric of English is constantly changing. New words (called neologisms or coined words) such as *selfie* (and *ussie* for a group selfie) enter the language and, once they become popular and widely used, may be added to dictionaries. It's quite difficult to find true neologisms. When I was writing this chapter the neologism *Brexit* had been coined to express the potential departure of the United Kingdom from the European Union. The children's book writer Dr Seuss invented the term *nerd*. The American talk-show host Stephen Colbert coined *truthiness* to use when your intuition, opinion, or perception indicate that something seems to be true, although logic and facts may be absent. It was word of the year for NBC in 2005.

Some words that have been around for a long time take on new meanings, for example, *zombie*, which is used to name a computer taken over by hackers. Words coming into common use since the rise of the internet (itself a new word) have included *avatar, hashtag, meme, trolling*, and many more.

Mansplaining, which takes place when an over-confident and insensitive person explains something to someone else in a patronising manner, was *Macquarie Dictionary*'s word of the year in 2015. It was not a popular choice. (The Oxford Dictionaries' word of the year for 2015 wasn't even a word; it was an emoji, of a face crying tears of joy.) In 2016, Facebook launched a set of 'graphicons' for users to express their responses to posts on the Facebook site. Sometimes what we think is a new word has been around for some time before it reaches critical mass. *Selfie* was the Oxford Dictionaries' word of 2013, though it was coined in Australia in the early 1990s. The word *twerking* isn't new, either; it was also coined in the early 1990s, in New Orleans. Nor is the initialism *OMG* new: it was first used in a letter to Winston Churchill in 1917. *Unfriend* apparently goes back to 1659. The neologisms *blogosphere, twittersphere, webinar*, and *webisode* are all portmanteau words, that is, words formed from parts of other words.

What are some of your favourite words? I love *evanescent, ineffable, ineluctable, redolent*, and *resonate*, though I don't get to use them often. The Merriam-Webster dictionary site has a list of people's favourite words.

Do you have any pet-peeve words and expressions, an aversion to particular words that's called logomisia? Do any words make you wince when you see or hear them? I wince when I see *actionate, factoid, redact, relatable*, and *utilise*. (See the article by Lucy Ferriss in Further Reading about the word *relatable*.) And how about the fairly recent appearance on the political and business scene of *agile*, which has apparently been in use in software circles for many years, but has now migrated to politics, where it is ubiquitous? YouTube has many clips on 'most hated' and 'least favourite' words.

If English is your first language, you have never looked up in a dictionary most of the words that you use. The etymology of words is often fascinating. Check in a dictionary for the Latin origins of *procrastination, promiscuous*, and *supercilious* to see what roots they evolved from. Knowing that *supercilium* is the Latin word for an eyebrow will help you remember the meaning of *supercilious*. Or, how about *eureka*, *hoi polloi*, and *kudos*, which we have borrowed from the Greek language.

One of my students, Jessica Miller, wrote the following response to the essay-starter 'I like words':

> I like words. My favourite word is 'wainscoting'. It refers to the wooden panelling at the foot of the walls in a room. I like it because it is dark, knobbly and intricate sounding. It calls to mind the echoing corridors and heavy iron doorknockers of the gothic mansions that were so frequently the settings of the books I read in my childhood. The language of Architecture is full of words such as wainscoting—parapet, balustrade, eaves—all of them so precise and antiquated. I like the word 'tilt'. I think it strikes exactly the right balance between precision and playfulness. 'Gullible' is wonderful in the stumbling and endearing way it rolls off the tongue and 'jaunty' is, in my experience, the perfect adjective to use when describing someone wearing a red hat.
>
> My favourite Scrabble words, much as I hate to impart them to anyone, are 'quill' and 'leonine'. I will also always have a soft spot for 'knoll', the word that I used to great effect when I was seven, during my family's painful annual car trip to Broken Hill, to win a particularly competitive round of 'I Spy'.

In May 2015, Collins added 6500 words to the 276,000 words that were already in its *Scrabble Dictionary*.

Here's an irresistibly persuasive job application that uses words to great effect. The author was Robert Pirosh, who was looking for work as a screenwriter in Hollywood in 1934.

> Dear Sir:
> I like words. I like fat buttery words, such as ooze, turpitude, glutinous, toady. I like solemn, angular, creaky words, such as straitlaced, cantankerous, pecunious, valedictory. I like spurious, black-is-white words, such as mortician, liquidate, tonsorial, demi-monde. I like suave 'V' words, such as Svengali, svelte, bravura, verve. I like crunchy, brittle, crackly words, such as splinter, grapple, jostle, crusty. I like sullen, crabbed, scowling words, such as skulk, glower, scabby, churl. I like Oh-Heavens,

my-gracious, land's-sake words, such as tricksy, tucker, genteel, horrid. I like elegant, flowery words, such as estivate, peregrinate, elysium, halcyon. I like wormy, squirmy, mealy words, such as crawl, blubber, squeal, drip. I like sniggly, chuckling words, such as cowlick, gurgle, bubble and burp.

I like the word 'screenwriter' better than 'copywriter', so I decided to quit my job in a New York advertising agency and try my luck in Hollywood, but before taking the plunge I went to Europe for a year of study, contemplation, and horsing around.

I have just returned and I still like words.

May I have a few with you?

Robert Pirosh

He got a job at MGM as a junior writer, served in World War II in Europe, then went on to write for the Marx Brothers. In 1949 he won an Academy Award for his script for the film *Battleground*. My source for Pirosh's clever letter is a widely admired collection of letters, *Letters of Note*, edited by Shaun Usher.

Taking words seriously: style, voice, and tone

Three central concepts in word usage are style, voice, and tone, with their related concepts of ethos and persona.

Style

Style defies definition, to some extent, but is generally judged on a writer's choice and command of words and syntax (sentence structure), which I cover in Chapter 4. The poet Samuel Taylor Coleridge once said that the infallible test of a perfect style is 'its untranslatableness in words of the same language without injury to its meaning'. He also said: 'Prose is words in the best order'. The poet Matthew Arnold put it another way: 'Have something to say and say it as clearly as you can. That is the only secret of style'. The novelist W. Somerset Maugham (quoted in Williams, 1995) also advocated clarity:

> There is nothing to be said against lucidity, and against simplicity only the possibility of dryness. This is a risk well worth taking when you reflect how much better it is to be bald than to wear a curly wig. (p. 152)

The *New Yorker*'s plea to 'Read something that means something' is a superb example of a simple and lucid sentence. A further example of simplicity and lucidity in professional writing is this press release from *The Spectator* when it launched a new magazine with not one wasted word:

> *The Business* is the new weekly magazine devoted to business, from the publishers of *The Spectator*. Bold, concise, and ruthlessly relevant, *The Business* is the only magazine that covers global business and finance from London, the world capital of international business. With its sharp insights, the ability to break global scoops, and its prescient overview of business trends and market conditions, *The Business* is essential reading for those who want a head start on the coming week.

Raymond Chandler (quoted in Fisher, 2006), writer of detective fiction, had this to say about style:

> The most durable thing in writing is style, and style is the most valuable investment a writer can make with his [*sic*] time. It pays off slowly, your agent will sneer at it, your publisher will misunderstand it, and it will take people you have never heard of to convince them by slow degrees that the writer who puts his individual mark on the way he writes will always pay off. (p. 84)

A creative writer with an unparalleled command of style is P.G. Wodehouse, widely regarded as the most accomplished humorous writer of the twentieth century, and whose work is the source of more than 1750 quotes in the *Oxford English Dictionary*. Indeed, Wodehouse's influence reaches into 21st-century popular culture: Michael Deacon (2013) has suggested that in the TV series *Game of Thrones*, the sprawling fantasy adapted from George R.R. Martin's novels, the canny matriarch Olenna Tyrell bears a remarkable resemblance to Bertie Wooster's Aunt Dahlia, sharing her 'magnificent imperiousness, toying sarcasm, [and] brisk dismissal of waffle and flummery'. *The Code of the Woosters* (1938) contains probably Wodehouse's most famous *bon mot*: 'He spoke with a certain what-is-it in his voice, and I could see that, if not actually disgruntled, he was far from being gruntled'.

Voice

Your voice in writing is what creates your relationship with your reader: what 'comes through' about you through your writing, how you present yourself to your readers. Your readers 'hear' your voice and construct your character. Voice is what makes a writer distinctive.

How would you describe your voice in any writing that you have done? Is your voice authoritative, reassuring, avuncular, sincere, humble, opinionated, knowledgeable, idiosyncratic?

How did the purpose of your writing affect the voice that you were aiming for? Hugely, surely. Do you visualise your reader when you write? As I mentioned in Chapter 2, that's a very helpful strategy.

Tone

Tone is what creates the effect of your message on your reader. Tone murmurs—or sometimes shouts—between the lines. It is always subjective, that is, open to different interpretations by different readers. However, most readers share a sense of whether a communication is cold or friendly, condescending or sincere. Peter Elbow (1973) suggests talking about your writing as though you are talking about the weather. Is your writing foggy, sunny, gusty, cold, clear, crisp, drizzling, or muggy? Is it breezy? Witty? Dry? Droll? Bemused? Wry? Poetic? Dramatic?

Do you think that your readers feel informed, pleased, motivated, bored, patronised, intimidated, or irritated when they read your messages?

How would you feel if you received any of these less-than-friendly messages that I have collected over the years?

> Please refrain from unnecessary correspondence.
>
> Your reply has been noted. [This could sound menacing.]
>
> Inquiries concerning the above-mentioned should be directed to the 'below-named'/the 'undersigned'.
>
> Please advise if you wish to debate this, as I need to know.
>
> If you require us to retain the contractors as suggested, your prompt response would be appreciated as the consultancies are due to expire in the near future and both contractors are considering their options.

You should aim to make an emotional connection with your reader, but you can't assume that they'll cooperate with you. Avoid any attempt at sarcasm or irony, as they can be misconstrued. Beware of taking a reader's cooperation for granted. People can be put off by assumed intimacy, for example, 'Be a doll and read on'. Ask yourself: what sort of person does my reader think I am as they read my words? Humour can also backfire.

Some time ago, I received the following message from a prospective writing tutor: 'I'm writing to express my interest in tutoring with you next semester. I think I'd do a damned fine job and I'm great to have around. I hope to hear from you soon'. Would you have hired this cheeky person? Do you think that I did? Yes, I did hire this fellow, despite his seemingly 'impertinent familiarity', because I knew him. He had been a clever and witty student who had gone on to a stellar career as a writer. I knew that he would do a great job; I knew that the students would love him. And they did!

Some time afterwards, I received a message from another prospective writing tutor whom I did not know and whom I had never met. He ended his letter as follows: 'I presume you will do me the courtesy of an interview'. Did I interview that person? No, I didn't. I had no inclination to meet, let alone appoint as a writing tutor, a person with so little idea of appropriate tone.

Ethos and persona

As with style, voice, and tone, ethos and persona are concepts related to how writers represent themselves textually. When we evaluate a writer's authority, intelligence, competence, and integrity, we also evaluate their character and credibility, which fall under the rubric of ethos. **Ethos**, a Greek word, means character, which is achieved through the writer's authoritativeness, their moral character, and their trustworthiness. Academic and workplace writers need to convince their readers that they know what they're talking about and that their documents contain accurate, comprehensive, and trustworthy information. For Aristotle, an orator's ethos was a rhetorical strategy employed by an orator whose purpose was to inspire trust in his audience. So, your ethos rests in your audience's trust in what you write.

The word **persona** is the Latin word for a mask. It refers to the narrator of a work, usually identified with the author.

So, persona is the role that writers create for themselves. It is a concept more common in creative and journalistic writing than in academic and professional writing.

In the following extract from a 2005 article by Jim Hoberman, who had a 30-year career as film critic at *The Village Voice*, he takes on the persona of TM (Teenage Me), casting himself as 'a teenage cinéaste' who 'falls in love with the *Voice*'s film pages'.

> Not exactly trekking to the one-room schoolhouse six miles across the tundra but a schlep nonetheless for the Teenage Me to find the one newsstand in Flushing (and later, Binghamton, New York) that carried *The Village Voice*. The paper ran many interesting things, to be sure, but (for the TM) the big must-reads were Jonas Mekas's 'Movie Journal' and Andrew Sarris's 'Films in Focus'. How else to know what was happening?

Choosing words wisely

Let's move on now to other specific word-choice concerns at the nitty-gritty level. You need to be aware of the following aspects of word choice to ensure that you choose *le mot juste* in all your writing, whether it be academic, professional, journalistic, or creative.

Abstraction and concreteness

Avoid abstract words such as *aspect, element, facility, factor, item,* and *resource*, unless you anchor them to specific concrete entities. *We installed a new facility in the office last week* lacks concrete detail. It is far better to write: *We installed a new photocopier in the office last week*. Concrete words allow your reader to clearly visualise what you are talking about. I once attended a conference where the hotel listed a room as 'a one-bedroom efficiency'.

Academic terms

Terms such as *précis* and *synopsis* are regarded as old-fashioned in the professional workplace, as well as in the academy, so avoid them. Both words mean *summary*. You can use *abstract* if you are referring to the summary in a published paper.

Acronyms and initialisms

An acronym is generated when the initial letters of a phrase form a pronounceable word, for example, *ASIO* for the Australian Security Intelligence Organisation. An initialism is generated when the initial letters are individually spelled out, for example, *the CIA* (Central Intelligence Agency) and *the FBI* (Federal Bureau of Investigation). Some acronyms and initialisms are widely known, for example, *FAQ* (frequently asked questions) and *FYI* (for your information). However, other terms may not be familiar to some readers, for example, *BAE* (before anyone else), *FOMO* (fear of missing out), and the not exactly intuitive *TANSTAAFL* (there ain't no such thing as a free lunch). *LOL* emerged decades ago as an initialism for 'little old lady', then morphed into 'lots of love', then became 'laughing out loud'.

Use only those acronyms and initialisms that your readers will be familiar with and use only those that are necessary. Don't introduce an acronym/initialism that then doesn't appear in your text. Some acronyms and initialisms are used to denote different entities, for example, *SME* can mean subject matter expert or small to medium enterprise. Always write them out in full the first time you use one, with the acronym or initialism in brackets. After that you can use the acronym/initialism in the text.

Acronymfinder.com is a searchable database with more than five million acronyms, abbreviations, and initialisms. Categories include business and finance, information technology, and slang and pop culture.

Allusion

An allusion is a reference, usually indirect, to a person, place, or event—real or fictional. In Chapter 2, I referred to the situation that Frank Bruni experienced of 'lost frames of reference' when his students were unfamiliar with Proust's madeleine. It is important that your writing evokes only allusions that your readers will be familiar with. A classical allusion is an indirect though not accidental reference to a Greek or Roman legend. The following review cleverly uses a classical allusion. It was written by one of my students, Richard Newman, responding to a task to review a cultural event such as a film, play, or art exhibition. In an inspired, surprising twist, because the assignment did not require the students to use an allusion, Richard adopted Homeric style to review the Bundall farmers' market at the Gold Coast Turf Club, held every Sunday from 7 am till 12 noon.

> **Book XVI: In which Odysseus and his crew brave the fabled temptations of a weekend Farmers' Market**
> There were only a few signs, and a faint, sour smell, of horses, as gourmets temporarily replaced gamblers in the Gold Coast Turf Club's grounds. Sunday morning's Farmers' Market was, however, emptying wallets as rapidly as the races. Odysseus warned his crew. 'These places are all exactly the same. You've fought hard, sacked a towering city, for those coins; don't be tempted by fudge samples, or by fruit and veg we can get back in Ithaca. I won't have my men cheated, nor softened into gluttons'. As the Greek king spoke, a tray of fat red apples caught his eye. 60 cents each; he'd sneak back for those.
> An unlikely siren, his greasy beard thick and belly sizeable, lunged into view with the first offer of free food. Cautious souls feared a trap, but hunger brutishly won out, and generous samples of thick butter chicken—a floury triangle of naan peeking from each styrofoam cup—were passed around. The stall's jars of intriguing chutney and paste were selling at $20. Each. Markedly less generous.
> The crew strode on, dodging prams driven like fleeing chariots and sausage-clutching toddlers. 'Fat Sausage' was the rather candid name of the stall responsible. Odysseus liked to think, but could not be sure, that other ingredients were involved. One toddler was being force-fed a gigantic strawberry. If he did not choke, he would grow to carry a heavy spear.

An allusion is a figure of speech—an expression that uses words in a distinctive way. Figures of speech do not use words in their literal, denotative sense. There are hundreds of figures of speech that writers can use to achieve specific effects. The figures of speech that I cover in this chapter, apart from allusion, are analogy, oxymoron, simile, and metaphor. Figures of speech are usually regarded as the province of creative writing, but they are often present in academic and workplace writing.

Americanisms and Britishisms

If you are writing for an international audience, you need to be aware of the many differences between North American and Australian/British terms, for example, *candy/sweets, check/bill, cookie/biscuit, elevator/lift, faucet/tap, sidewalk/footpath.* Australia doesn't yet accept the North American *gotten* rather than *got*, particularly in writing. Ben Yagoda has collected a list of Britishisms that have been adopted in America; his website is listed in Further Reading for this chapter.

There are also many differences between North American and Australian/British spelling, for example, *catalog/catalogue, center/centre, check/cheque, defense/defence, gray/grey, honor/honour, mold/mould, organize/organise*. Remember that you have no licence to change the spelling of proper names. If you write about the World Trade Center in New York City, or the Document Design Center in Washington, DC, leave the spelling as is.

Americans always spell the word *practice* with a *c*, whether it's a noun or a verb. In Australia and Britain, *practice* is spelled with a *c* when it functions as a noun and an *s* when it functions as a verb or verbal. For example:

I'll do my piano **practice** *(noun) when I get home today.*

I usually **practise** *(verb) every afternoon, as I am a* **practised** *(past participle of the verb functioning as an adjective) professional.*

The word *licence* follows the same convention in Australia and Britain (Americans write *license*, going the opposite way to their spelling of *practice*).

Analogy

An analogy is an extended comparison that clarifies by illustration, for example, *Building an extra lane on the freeway to alleviate traffic congestion is like going on a diet by loosening your belt.* Stephen Fry once said that *Books are no more threatened by Kindle than stairs by elevators.* Analogies can be very effective in making a point in your writing.

Arcane/esoteric words

When writing for the general public, avoid using words that your reader may need to look up in an unabridged dictionary, for example, *quotidian* (meaning 'daily'). When I was writing this chapter, a British election had just been held. Reading an article about the election in *The New Yorker* by one of my favourite writers, the film critic Anthony Lane, I came across a word that I had never seen before, *psephology*, so I looked it up. It comes from the Greek word for pebble, which the Greeks used as ballots, and means the scientific analysis of past elections. I enjoyed learning a new word, but it's not necessarily a good idea to use an obscure word unless you use it in a context that helps to supply the meaning.

Archaic and obsolete words

Avoid archaic and obsolete expressions such as those I have often seen in workplace documents and students' essays, or your readers may fear that you have not moved on since the nineteenth century. These words and phrases are pompous and outmoded: *amongst, heretofore, if paid timeously, perusal, pursuant to, the said document, the undersigned, we deem it advisable, we hereby acknowledge*, and *whilst*.

In reporting on the one piece of advice that he received about his university writing style, Geoffrey Pullum relates how his professor, after reading his first 'embarrassingly pompous screed', told him: 'You write like an 18th-century clergyman'. Pullum says: 'I could see that he did not intend this as praise, so I stopped doing it' (2013).

Biased language/loaded words

Try to write objectively rather than exhibit bias, for example, *We use only our own experts because they are the best in the business.* You might see a sentence such as this in a business proposal, though it reads more like marketing material. Loaded or emotive words are those that elicit in the reader an emotional response that may or may not be intended by the writer. The two sides of the abortion debate deliberately use loaded words: *pro-life* and *pro-choice*. Loaded phrases such as *rabid supporter* have negative connotations. When you are editing your academic or workplace writing, check to see that you haven't unintentionally used biased or loaded words.

Buzzwords

Journalist Lucy Kellaway (2015) describes these expressions as 'the brainlessly upbeat language of the contemporary workplace'. She highlights *Does that resonate with your radar?* and *to action forward* as being particularly obnoxious, and chooses her favourite blurb: 'As brands build out a world footprint, they look for the no-holds-barred global POV that's always been part of our wheelhouse'. Also see the article by Emma Green (2014) on the origins of 'officespeak'.

Box 3.1 contains a list of words and expressions I've come across that you should avoid, if you can, in workplace writing, but which will give you ammunition if you want to take part in 'buzzword bingo', played by staff in office meetings when they deposit buzzwords on a bingo board and tick them off on the board each time a colleague uses one.

BOX 3.1 **Buzzwords**

While most buzzwords are clichés (see below) because they are not as fresh and original as they once were, note that I have italicised a few buzzwords in the following list because I would classify them as 'garden-variety' clichés that are also used in more general contexts.

24/7
agile
at elbow
at the end of the day
back in the day
back to the drawing board
ballpark figure
benchmark
best-in-class
best-of-breed
a big ask
bite the bullet
blue-sky thinking
cascade up
coalface
deliverables
drill down
the elephant in the room
enablers and barriers
explore every avenue
eye-opener
few and far between
finger on the pulse (of the corporate heartbeat)
game changer
game plan
gap analysis
give/put in 110 per cent
the go-to person
going forward
granularity
greenlight
iconic
inevitable delay
it's early days
jump the shark
knife and fork it
lean in
level playing field
low-hanging fruit

mission critical	skin in the game
my ask of you	solution-driven
the object of the exercise	swallow the frog
on steroids	synergy
out of the box	take it to the next level
paper over the cracks	*through thick and thin*
paradigm shift	tipping point
the pointy end	too-hard basket
push back	touch base
push the envelope	triage
put your thumb on the scales	upskill
quick and dirty	value proposition
quick win	*viable alternative*
rainmaker	what's your take on this?
reach out	win–win
results-driven	window of opportunity
revenue-driven	work–life balance
ring-fenced	world class
scalable	*the writing's on the wall*
shape shifter	zero-sum game
shift the dynamic	

Clichés

A cliché is a hackneyed or cloying expression that has been over-used to such an extent that it has become stale. Clichés are regarded pejoratively by most people. 'It is generally accepted that critics and readers covet the fresh, the original, the novel, while condemning the conventional, the tired, the trite, and the over-used' (Petelin, 2010b, p. 14). There's no objective test for identifying clichés, but often it is easy to predict what is coming next when you see, for example, the word *inevitable*. You know that the next word will be *delay*. In contrast with Kellaway's remonstration about buzzwords, journalist Hephzibah Anderson (2012) says that clichés deserve to live on because their informality and familiarity put people at ease. She praises the 'sturdy truthfulness and comforting ancientness' of clichés. So, it may be acceptable to use clichés in certain contexts where their familiarity can be comforting and they can help to persuade a reader to a particular point of view.

Coined words/neologisms

In formal writing, avoid coined words such as *clickability*, *presenteeism* (showing up for work even when sick for fear of losing one's job), *thinkability*, and *twofer* (unless you are writing marketing copy).

Colloquialisms and slang

Colloquialisms (from the Latin verb *loquor* meaning 'to speak') are casual expressions that you should avoid in formal writing. Confine colloquialisms and slang expressions to speaking and creative writing. Colloquialisms—for example, *a cop-out, whatever*—are more widespread and less exclusive than slang, which is the particular argot of a distinct group. Here are some examples of Australian slang: *blokey, done like a dinner, don't come the raw prawn with me, shoot through like a Bondi tram, silly as a two-bob watch, too crook to take a sickie*. Here's an example of an American slang term, *dogfooding*, that was used to refer to the testing of software to iron out the kinks: 'Dude, they should have spent more time dogfooding that app!'

Confusable words

Getting words confused will erode your credibility, so go through the list in Box 3.2 and check in a dictionary any of the distinctions that aren't clear to you.

Geoffrey Pullum (2015) has written a delightful column, 'Comprise yourself', on the misuse of the word 'comprise' (see Further Reading).

BOX 3.2 Commonly confused words

activate/actuate	alternate/alternative
admission/admittance	ambiguous/ambivalent
adverse/averse	appraise/apprise
advice/advise	arrant/errant
affect/effect	assign/attribute
allude/elude	assume/presume

attain/obtain
bail/bale
baited/bated
blatant/flagrant
bloc/block
born/borne
cache/cachet
carat/caret/carrot
cereal/serial
charted/chartered
cite/sight/site
complacent/complaisant
complement/compliment
compose/comprise
constant/continual/
    continuous/incessant
criticise/critique
cue/queue
decent/descent/dissent
decide/determine
delegate/relegate
deprecate/depreciate
desert/dessert
deserve/merit
diffuse/infuse/suffuse
discreet/discrete
discrepancy/disparity
disinterested/uninterested
dual/duel
effective/effectual/
    efficacious/efficient
elegy/eulogy
eminent/imminent/immanent
emulate/imitate
expedient/expeditious

extant/extinct
evoke/invoke
faint/feint
fandango/farrago/fiasco
faze/phase
fictional/fictitious
flare/flair
flaunt/flout
flaw/floor
flounder/founder
formally/formerly
font/fount
forbear/forebear
forego/forgo
foreword/forward
hear/here
historic/historical
hoard/horde
home in/hone
imply/infer
incidence/incident
insidious/invidious
instance/instant
invaluable/valuable
lead/led
leant/lent
lightening/lightning
literally/figuratively
luxuriant/luxurious
magnate/magnet
manner/manor
meat/meet/mete
militate/mitigate
mnemonic/pneumonic
Moorish/moreish

oral/verbal
pair/pare
palatable/palpable
palate/palette/pallet/pellet
paramount/tantamount
peace/piece
peak/peek/pique
pore/pour
practicable/practical
precede/proceed
principal/principle
prise/prize
rack/wrack
raise/raze
rap/wrap
regime/regimen
reign/rein
reluctant/reticent
riffle/rifle
scupper/scuttle
sewage/sewerage
simple/simplistic
sole/soul
sort/sought
spasmodically/sporadically
specious/spurious
stationary/stationery
straightened/straitened
strategic/tactical
substantial/substantive
tack/tact
throe/throw
tended/tendered
tenant/tenet
vain/vein
want/wont
while/wile
wreak [havoc]/wreck

Connotation and denotation

Denotation—that is, the dictionary meaning of a word—is the explicit and direct meaning. A connotation is the meaning (indirectly) suggested by the word. Compare the denotation of the word *mother* as 'female parent' with the connotations that the word evokes for different people. Be conscious of the connotations of words when you are writing and editing.

Debasement/transformation of words

Several words whose meanings have widened and/or weakened are *curate*, as a verb, now no longer confined to exhibitions; *fascist*, now often used to mean merely bossy; *feral*, now meaning wild; and *parse*, now no longer confined to grammar. Professor Anne Curzan (2014) amusingly relates the way in which the word *perfect* has become the response of choice in inappropriate situations. I certainly find it disconcerting when ordering a meal in a restaurant to have the waiter respond with 'Perfect' to each of my choices. Other words with degraded meanings include *artisanal, embed, evolve, iconic,* and *robust* (see the 2013 article by John McWhorter in Further Reading). I advise against using such words in their degraded meanings, for example, *These figures need careful parsing.* There are often perfectly good words that will do the job. *Scrutiny* or *analysis* would be better. (Parsing in its correct, grammatical sense is discussed in Chapter 5.)

Defensive/apologetic words

If you need to apologise in a formal setting for the shortcomings of a document when your work on it is deficient because of a too-tight deadline or difficulty accessing information, convey your apology in person or on the phone. Don't put it in a document that will become the permanent record. The following statements in a professional document would not inspire the reader's confidence in the writer:

> *After reading this report, I hope you find it satisfactory, though it is not as developed as it should be, due to time constraints.*
>
> *After reading our proposal, we hope you find it possible to consider us for the project.*
>
> *After seeing my qualifications, I hope you find it worthwhile to make an appointment with me.*

Dictionaries

You need to have a selection of dictionaries at your disposal. Australia's national dictionary is the *Macquarie Dictionary*. *Macquarie* is a descriptive dictionary that records usage, some of which you may be surprised to see, for example, *youse*, as in *I'll see youse guys on the weekend.*

For extended coverage, you need to have access to other dictionaries such as the free, online, most popular American dictionary, *Merriam-Webster*. OxfordDictionaries.com is a free online dictionary that constantly inserts new words. I also like the site oneword.com, which gives definitions from about twenty different dictionaries, so that you can compare them. Dictionary.reverso.net will suggest a word after you provide a meaning. And never assume that just because you've heard or used a word before, you know precisely what it means. It can be eye-opening to look up words you think you know to discover new subtleties of meaning. Use a dictionary that explains the distinctions between words with similar meanings, such as *plastic*, *pliable*, *pliant*, *ductile*, *malleable*, and *adaptable*.

John McPhee (2013b) says:

> With dictionaries, I spend a great deal more time looking up words I know than words I've never heard of—at least 99 to one. The dictionary definitions of words you are trying to replace are far more likely to help you out than a scattershot wad from a thesaurus . . . at best, thesauruses are mere rest stops in the search for the *mot juste*.

Discriminatory (non-inclusive) language

This can take the form of ageist, classist, racist, and sexist language. Any form is unacceptable and comes under the rubric of politically incorrect language. When referring to an individual, that person's gender, religion, nationality, racial group, age, or physical or mental characteristics should be mentioned only if this information is pertinent to the discussion. When referring to a person's disability, only specify it if there is a need to do so. If you must specify the disability, ensure that the person is referred to as 'having' the disability, not 'being' the disability.

The most common manifestation of discriminatory (in this case, sexist) language is the *generic he* or *she*. If you write *Every employee in the organisation enjoys his time off*, you are stating that all the employees in that organisation are male. If you write *Every employee in the organisation enjoys her time off*, you are stating that all the employees in that organisation are female. Some authors state upfront that when they use *he* they mean it to include *she*, but disclaimers such as this are unacceptable. Others alternate their use of *he* and *she*, but this draws attention to itself. The use of the term *he/she* seems to have disappeared in Australia, though not elsewhere.

Often, the solution is to make the sentence plural: *All employees enjoy their time off*. Another solution is to use the singular 'they', which has been a source of contention in the United States for decades. There has been a recent shift to accept it in some circles there (Nunberg, 2016), with the American Dialect Society making it its word of the year for 2015. An American airline is trying so hard to adopt the singular 'they' that it sent my husband this message: 'Roslyn Petelin has selected you as their companion this year'. I had forgotten that my name was a gender-neutral name like 'Drew' or 'Evelyn'. (The English novelist Evelyn Waugh, known as he-Evelyn, was married to Evelyn Gardner, known as she-Evelyn.) Australia has used the singular 'they' in most professional contexts widely and happily for more than 30 years.

The most recent advances in politically correct language are the inclusion of an option to record your gender status on sites such as Facebook and the registration of students' choice of gender pronoun on university sites. In addition, the online version of the *Oxford English Dictionary* is considering adding *Mx* as a new honorific for those who are uncomfortable with assignment to a particular gender. Britain appears to be leading the way here. In an article in *The New York Times* on 7 June 2015, 'Me, myself and Mx.', Katherine Rosman reported that

> the honorific has already made headway in Britain. About a year ago, the Royal Bank of Scotland, for instance, began to instruct its employees to offer customers the option of selecting Mx. when filling out paperwork at local branch offices. The move was made, said Marjorie Strachan, the head of inclusion for the bank, to respond to requests made by bank employees and customers.

I also discuss the issue of non-sexist language in the section on pronouns in Chapter 5.

When it comes to specifying relationships, many alternatives have been suggested. Some are acceptable, some are not, while others are intended only to amuse. Here's a list: *spouse, wife, husband, partner* (sometimes specified as *life* or *business*), *significant other* (though *sother* never caught on), *companion, lover, friend, de facto, common-law wife* or *husband, my better half, the missus, the boss, the little woman, her indoors,* and *she who must be obeyed*. The final two featured in the British television shows *Minder* and *Rumpole of the Bailey*, respectively.

Doublespeak

Doublespeak is euphemistic language carefully designed to mislead. A *career-associate scanning professional* sounds better than a shelf stacker in a supermarket. A *domestic executive* is a fancy term for housewife. As is *sobriety-deprived* for drunk, or *vertically challenged* for short.

In the United States, the 2003 federal law that relaxed regulations on air pollution was called the *Clear Skies Act*. William Lutz once identified more than a hundred doublespeak alternatives used by companies to 'sack' workers, including *de-hire, de-recruit, deselect, de-staff, idle indefinitely, non-retain, re-future, select out,* and *uninstall*. HSBC UK *demised* nearly 900 managers in 2013.

Equivocation

Equivocal literally means 'equal-voiced'. The following expressions exemplify equivocation: *tends to stem from, I sort of maybe probably did know that, I think perhaps that might tend to have stemmed from the sort of thing that maybe someone might think is okay. Newish, youngish,* and *slowish* are further examples. Unlike doublespeak, equivocation is not necessarily designed to mislead. It's used to avoid being direct or even blunt, but ends up sounding wishy-washy.

Euphemism and dysphemism

Euphemisms make things sound more pleasant than they are, for example, *quantitative easing* sounds more responsible than *printing money*. Describing someone as being *economical with the truth* sounds better than calling them a liar. A McDonald's burger sounds better on an *artisanal roll* than on a bun. Dysphemisms make things sound nastier and more offensive than they are, such as describing an elderly woman as an *old bat* or an elderly man as an *old codger*. As with doublespeak and equivocation, avoid both euphemisms and dysphemisms in your writing.

Expletives

I'll cover grammatical expletives in Chapter 5. Here I am referring to the expletives that mostly consist of four letters. Expletives should never be used in formal writing, but creative writers and journalists can take advantage of their shock value and power. The journalist Giles Coren sent an email loaded with expletives to his subeditors at *The Times* newspaper on 25 July 2008, after they had changed 'a nosh' to 'nosh' in the final sentence of a restaurant review that he'd written. If you are curious, you can find the email easily on the internet. I haven't heard about editorial interference with any of his reviews since then.

Foreign expressions

Generally avoid using foreign expressions in your writing, although I must say that I prefer the French word *protégé* to the recent arrival *mentee*. It's a good idea to be familiar with commonly used terms such as the following, all of which are Latin and all of which I've seen in business documents, particularly when I've consulted to law firms: *ad nauseam, annus horribilis, bona fide, carpe diem, ceteris paribus, circa, infra dignitatem, modus operandi, ne plus ultra, per se, persona non grata, prima facie, quid pro quo, sine qua non, status quo, via,* and *vice versa*. English borrows words from many other languages too, including French, German, and Yiddish: for example, *au courant, avant la lettre, ça va sans dire, cause célèbre, chutzpah, fait accompli, manqué, mensch, outré, passé, sangfroid, savoir faire, schadenfreude, shtum, spiel, über,* and *vis-à-vis*.

Idioms

Idioms are particularly tricky for English as an additional language (EAL) speakers, because knowing the meaning of the individual words won't necessarily help them to understand the meaning of the phrase—such as in the classic case of a recent migrant to Australia who, asked to 'bring a plate', arrived at a barbecue with just an empty plate.

Be careful not to use idioms that may confuse EAL speakers. Check on idiomsite.com for a list of idiomatic expressions, such as *a drop in the bucket, a piece of cake, at the drop of a hat,* and *Can I have a word?*

Intensifiers

These are qualifying words that are meant to intensify by emphasising. *Very* is probably the most common intensifier; it is very often used to intensify very pedestrian statements. Many weasel words and expressions are used as intensifiers. Check for those listed in the discussion of weasel words later in this chapter.

Jargon and gobbledygook

Appropriate jargon (or 'shoptalk') can be an effective shorthand if all your readers are familiar with it. There are many classes of jargon, such as *bureaucratese, computerese, corporatese, cyberspeak, journalese, legalese, medicalese, menuspeak, officialese, reviewerese,* and *technocratese.* We have all been to restaurants that would once have had 'potatoes, boiled' on the menu, but now have 'Idaho potatoes with butter and a touch of cream, whipped to perfection'.

The 'jargon club' is an effective way to exclude readers. There's a famous case of this practised by P.T. Barnum, the American circus owner and well-known huckster. People loved the exhibits in his American Museum in New York so much that they were lingering for hours, making it impossible for newcomers to be admitted. To move them on, Barnum placed signs near the exit that said 'This Way to the Egress'. Many customers thought that an egress was some exotic new animal, rather than the Latin word for *exit*. They followed the signs, only to find themselves unhappily outside the building and needing to pay again to get back in.

Jargon is a constant worry for workplace writers because of the mixed readership of many documents: executives, specialists, technicians, and the general public. This is where appendices and glossaries come in handy.

A related term is *gobbledygook*: this is text that's unintelligible or meaningless because it's so wordy, larded with unfamiliar jargon, and characterised by circumlocution (structured in a long-winded, roundabout way). See if you can untangle the example of gobbledygook below:

> 'Container', in relation to an investigational medicinal product, means the bottle, jar, box, packet or other receptacle which contains or is to contain it, not being a capsule, cachet or other article in which the product is or is to be administered, and where any such receptacle is or is to be contained in another such receptacle, includes the former but does not include the latter receptacle. (Clause from the UK *Licensing Act 2003*, Department for Culture, Media and Sport)

Malapropisms

This term is derived originally from the French phrase *mal à propos* (poorly placed). It is the name of a character in Richard Brinsley Sheridan's 1775 comedy of manners, *The Rivals*. Mrs Malaprop's bungled attempts at erudite speech led her to declare one gentleman 'the very pineapple of politeness!' and to say of another, 'Illiterate him . . . from your memory'. The Australian television characters Kath and Kim were notorious for their malapropisms, such as Kim's 'I want to be effluent and practise serial monotony'.

Malapropisms undermine the authority of your writing. In an article in 2014 about the proposed new airport at Badgerys Creek in Sydney, a reporter mentioned 'a relatively modest and small group that would have some affectation'. Did the reporter mean 'effect'?

The San Remo Hotel in San Francisco highlights its 'turn of the century decorum'. On the UK version of the television show *The Apprentice*, one of the contestants talked about 'appealing to the female genre'. Other examples that I have noted include 'What are you incinerating about me?'; 'a Dorian of the theatre'; 'a logo that amplifies modernism and professionalism'; 'It's not as if the English language is frozen in aspen' (though it is pretty cold in Aspen); and 'As we approach the footy finals, I can emphasise with the players'. The singer Justin Bieber recently said: 'I was detrimental to my own career'. I think we can guess that Justin meant 'instrumental', but maybe not. A former prime minister of Australia used the term 'suppository of wisdom', rather than 'repository'. We can also guess what most of the other malapropisms should have been (decor, gender, insinuating, doyen, exemplifies, aspic, empathise).

Note that there needs to be a tinge of humour for an expression or word to be labelled as a malapropism, and it needs to be a real word. Richard Lederer has a hugely amusing post on malapropisms on his verbivore.com site, including this fine example: 'If you wish to submit a recipe for publication in the cookbook, please include a short antidote concerning it'.

Metaphors and similes

These figures of speech can add colour and impact to your writing. A metaphor makes an implicit comparison between two things. A simile makes an explicit comparison between two things. *Slicker than a slug on ice* and *tighter than two coats of paint* are similes—they compare two otherwise dissimilar things. 'Life is like a box of chocolates' was the famous simile at the heart of the 1994 film *Forrest Gump*.

A metaphor also compares two things, but states that one thing *is* another, for example, *You are an angel*. A mixed metaphor occurs when one image becomes ridiculously tangled with another, as when a politician says: 'All I ask is a straight-down-the-middle fair crack of the whip'.

A president of the Australian Law Reform Commission once wrote about a budget that 'has removed the bottom-line teeth from the Commission'. Other examples include 'We need to replace the dead wood with new blood', and 'The business model that lifts all boats remains elusive'.

Negative expressions

Whenever possible, avoid using negative expressions, such as *bar, decline, exclude, fail,* and *reject*. When your message content itself needs to be negative, try to create a positive tone to mollify your reader without resorting to equivocation, euphemisms, doublespeak, or weasels.

Unless you have a good reason, also avoid double or multiple negatives, which are usually difficult for a reader to unravel. For example, a reader is going to have to think twice about sentences such as *This assumption does not seem inexplicable, Your reader is never unsure, It hardly went unnoticed,* and *I was not uninvolved with the process.*

Don't universally avoid the double negative, however, because it can have a subtle meaning. *It is not uncommon* is not equivalent to *It is common.*

Nouning and verbing

Nouning occurs when verbs (or other parts of speech) are used as nouns (for example, a big *ask*, a *solve*). Verbing occurs when nouns (or other parts of speech) are turned into verbs (for example, an airline reporting that it *directionalises* its ad responses to its website, or a company that helps you to *architect* your Web presence). Although this phenomenon has become more prevalent and acceptable over the years with verbs such as *incentivise* (from *incentive*) and *liaise* (from *liaison*), I'd avoid extreme examples of it, such as in a newspaper headline I noted: 'How to *readify* students for work'.

Nuance

A nuance is a shade of meaning. Can you detect the 'shades of meaning' that distinguish these similar words: *aggravate, annoy, chafe, grate, irk, jar, nettle, peeve, rile, upset,* and *vex*? How about *balderdash, humbug, piffle,* and *poppycock*? Always try to use the most appropriate shade of meaning in your word choice.

Oxymorons

An oxymoron is a figure of speech in which there is an apparent contradiction in terms. It occurs when you take two things that contradict each other and join them. Examples in workplace writing include a *mandatory option*, an *exact estimate*, a *genuine imitation*, or a *definite maybe*. In *The Great Gatsby* (1925), F. Scott Fitzgerald talks about 'ferocious indifference' and 'magnanimous scorn'. Oxymorons can be powerful in creative writing, though in workplace writing they usually indicate equivocation. Check the website oxymoronlist.com for other examples.

Polemical language

This is 'soapbox language', as in *All students should learn to code, Everyone should be able to read statistics*, or *Everyone in business should do an MBA*. Avoid it.

Portmanteau words

A portmanteau word is a word such as *advertorial* or *guesstimate* that is composed of sections of other words. Another example is *satisfice*, a blend of *satisfy* and *suffice*. This is a heuristic that was coined by Herbert Simon in 1957 to mean making a judgement that is good enough, given cognitive and situational constraints. It's a useful heuristic to remember when writing your first draft. Satisfice (make do) with the draft and go back later to refine it. (See further discussion in Chapter 11.)

Puns

A pun is a play on words. Copywriters in advertising agencies often use puns. A famous example is the slogan that the Saatchi brothers generated for a United Kingdom Conservative Party election campaign poster in 1979, challenging the incumbent Labour government. The poster showed a snaking line of people queuing for the unemployment office under the words: 'Labour isn't working'. The slogan was credited with winning the 1979 national election for the Conservatives, led by Margaret Thatcher, and was voted the best poster advertisement of the twentieth century by the trade magazine *Campaign*.

Newspaper articles also often use puns, for example, Ben Yagoda's 2014 article about punctuation, 'The commas suit ya'.

Redundancy/tautology

Both of these terms refer to the use of unnecessary words in expressions such as *audible to the ear*, *cooperate together*, a *manual recount by hand*, *parochial issues of a purely local kind*, *rectangular in shape*, *recur again*, and *the underlying subplot*. Look out for these and other redundant phrases at the editing stage and adjust them to eliminate the redundancy.

Spelling

English spelling rules aren't always reliable. The rule about *i* before *e* except after *c* doesn't work in this commonly cited sentence: *It's i before e, except when there's a feisty heist on weird foreign neighbours reinventing protein at their leisure*. As I said earlier in this chapter, English is tricky. All of the following words end in *-ough* but are pronounced differently: *although, enough, hiccough, plough, through*. You can use a spell-checker (but don't rely exclusively on it) and a dictionary to help with your spelling, but be aware of commonly confused words such as *discreet/discrete* (see Box 3.2).

Thesaurus syndrome

Thesaurus syndrome, sometimes known as 'elegant variation', comes into play when you recall what one of your early teachers told students about varying their language use to avoid boring their readers. This is not good advice for writers. If you use *company, corporation, firm*, and *organisation* in one document to refer to the same entity, you will confuse your readers, as you will by discussing an upcoming *assignment, job, program*, and *project*, and by addressing a key *condition, facet, feature*, and *issue*. If you use the terms *opening, position*, and *vacancy* in a letter to an unsuccessful job applicant, they may be glad that you didn't hire them.

James Kilpatrick, quoted in Safire and Safir (1992), gives the following advice:

> Have no unreasonable fear of repetition . . . The story is told of a feature writer who was doing a piece on the United Fruit Company. He spoke of bananas once; he spoke of bananas twice; he spoke of bananas yet a third time, and now he was desperate. 'The world's leading shippers of the elongated yellow fruit,' he wrote. A fourth banana would have been better. (p. 206)

However, note that all my examples of the thesaurus syndrome are nouns. Verbs are a different matter. I have listed variations to verbs in the section on CVs in Chapter 8 and in the section on reporting research in Chapter 9.

Verbosity

Verbosity equates to wordiness and pomposity. Are you the sort of person who prefers to *purchase from an emporium* rather than *buy from a shop*? Would you describe Kylie Minogue as *a diminutive Antipodean chanteuse* or *a short Australian singer*?

Verbose writers use *facilitate* instead of *ease*, *utilise* instead of *use*, *initial* instead of *first*, *prioritise* instead of *rank*, *ascertain* instead of *find out*, *endeavour* instead of *try*, *transmit* instead of *send*, *fabricate* instead of *build*, *each and every* instead of *every*, *at such time as* instead of *when*, *parameters* instead of *variables*, *make enquiry regarding* instead of *enquire* (or *ask*), *for the purpose of* instead of *for*, *in order to* instead of *to*.

I have been unable to find a source for the following passage, which I first came across many years ago and which can now be found on many websites, but with no reliable identification of its author.

> In promulgating your esoteric cogitations and in articulating your superficial sentimentalities and amicable philosophical or psychological observations, beware of platitudinous ponderosity. Let your conversational communications possess a clarified conciseness, a compact comprehensibleness, coalescent consistency, and concatenated cogency. Eschew all conglomerations of flatulent garrulity, jejune babblement, asinine affections. Let your extemporaneous descantings and unpremeditated expatiations have intelligibility and veracious veracity without rhodomontade or thrasonical bombast. Sedulously avoid all polysyllabic profundity, pompous prolixity, psittaceous vacuity, ventriloquial verbosity, and vaniloquent vapidity. Shun double entendre, prurient jocosity, pestiferous profanity, obscurant or apparent.
>
> In other words, talk plainly, briefly, naturally, sensibly, purely, and truthfully. Keep from slang, do not put on airs, say what you mean, mean what you say, and DON'T USE BIG WORDS.

Weasel words

The concept of weasel words is a contested one. Many key dictionaries and Google define weasel words as words or statements that are intentionally misleading. However, I believe that many writers use weasel words unintentionally, which results in meaning being sucked out of their writing in the way that a weasel can suck the innards out of an egg without breaking the shell. There's debate about the origin of the term, with *The New York Times* tracing it back to 1879, the year that Theodore Roosevelt (1916) said he'd got it from 'Bill Sewell's brother'.

Weasel words are often used as qualifiers, intensifiers, and 'fillers', and will weaken your speech and writing. (There was a suggestion that a candidate for the prime ministership of Australia lost an election because every time he spoke to journalists he opened his remarks with the phrase 'speaking frankly'.) Unless you use them deliberately, believing that they are adding weight to your writing, generally avoid them as much as you can. See Box 3.3.

BOX 3.3 Qualifying words to avoid

absolutely	fully
actually	fundamentally
apparently	generally
arguably	highly
as it were	in essence
basically	in fact
certainly	literally
clearly	merely
comparatively	naturally
definitely	notably
duly	obviously
eminently	possibly
entirely	presumably
essentially	quite
evidently	rather
extremely	really
frankly	seriously

simply	up to a point
somewhat	veritably
to be honest	very
totally	virtually
truly	wholly
ultimately	with all due respect

Spoken communication

Those of you concerned about correct spoken communication in academic and professional contexts should be careful to avoid the mispronunciation of words identified by Harold Scruby that he calls 'Waynespeak'. You can find this lexicon in his little book called *Waynespeak* (1987). 'Wayne words' are words and expressions that are frequently mispronounced, for example, *advocado, anythink (nothink, somethink), astericks, dateth, deteriate, ecksetera, expresso, fillum, haitch, libree, perculator, pronounciation, stastistics*. (Note that I have spelled them all wrongly to illustrate how they are mispronounced.) These are Australian variations on standard spoken English, but there are equivalents in other countries. Daily Writing Tips, a very useful North American website, has a list of '50 incorrect pronunciations that you should avoid'.

Another widespread mispronunciation is of the word *the* in front of a word beginning with a vowel. Many people pronounce *the* as a neutral sound rather than sounding it out as *thee* (as in *tea*). It's *thee orange*, not *thuh orange*.

The last word

The advice in this chapter can be summarised as follows:
- Choose your words carefully. Aim for inventiveness, clarity, grace, wit, succinctness, spareness, subtlety, order, precision, and control in your writing, keeping in mind at all times your readers and their expectations of the generic conventions of the documents that you are presenting them with.

- Avoid muddy, turgid, opaque, clichéd, and verbose writing.
- Acquire a rich and ample vocabulary—your repertoire of words—but not a penchant for polysyllables. Take the advice that Wikipedia states appeared in print at least as early as 1959, when it was used as a section heading in a NASA document: 'eschew obfuscation; espouse elucidation'. Introducing new words (and associated concepts) into your vocabulary will increase your skill as a writer, but make sure that you can discriminate between nuances of meaning and that you are conscious of the words' contextual meaning, their spelling, and their pronunciation.
- Use figures of speech such as analogies, metaphors and similes—James Wood in *How Fiction Works* (2009) says that they create a 'little explosion of fiction' (p. 202). Some of the most colourful figures of speech in the Australian political arena have been those delivered by former prime minister Paul Keating. His best-remembered simile is probably 'As flash as a rat with a gold tooth' to describe a snappy dresser. His best-known metaphor was his putdown of a high-profile politician whom he regarded as a lightweight. Keating posed the question 'Can a soufflé rise twice?'

Activities

Answers are at the back of the book.

1. Read the two articles cited below, which discuss the choices that govern what is included in the *Macquarie Dictionary*. Do you agree that you may need to supplement the *Macquarie* with other dictionaries, as I've suggested in this chapter? Write a paragraph in your journal analysing the articles below and discussing your responses to them. There are several other relevant articles in the Further Reading for this chapter.
    a) Susan Butler. (2014, 12 August). 'Why "youse" deserves its place in Australia's national dictionary'. Retrieved from *The Guardian*.
    b) Chad Parkhill. (2014, 11 August). 'What even is Australian English? An interview with the editor of the *Macquarie Dictionary*'. Retrieved from junkee.com.

2. Read the following message sent by a bookshop and select the word below that best describes the paragraph's style.

> We acknowledge with many thanks the receipt of your esteemed order of the 26th ultimo. We have already placed an order with the publishers for your book and will send it along to you as soon as it is to hand.

archaic   authoritative   esoteric   ambiguous

3. Read the following passage and select the word or phrase below that best describes the problem with this paragraph.

> When I went to the meeting, I took the leaflets that my team had prepared, because I wanted to show my colleagues which flyers our team wanted to use. We had worked hard to produce pamphlets because we were aware that another organisation had used brochures very successfully. My colleagues agreed at the meeting that the booklets that my team had prepared were appropriate for our customers.

buzz expressions   hyperbole   colloquialisms   thesaurus syndrome

4. Read the following sentences and choose the word below that best describes the problem in all of them.

> The chicken was roasted and left bacteria-tauntingly warm.
> When I saw your ad, I said: 'Hey! That's my job!'
> Judging from my career so far, I believe that I should get this job.
> Can you just chuck me into a Tuesday night tutorial, PLEASE?
> Some companies make artificial yoghurt to fool customers.

archaic   inappropriate tone   abstract   ambiguous

4

How sentences and form-class words work

To be, or not to be.
That is a sentence fragment.
Whether 'tis nobler in the mind to suffer
the shame of not being able to identify the parts of speech,
or to take a lead pencil against a sea of comma misuses,
and by opposing, end them. To punctuate, to correct
forever more, and by correct to say we end
the heartache, and the thousand natural mistakes
that can be attributed to poor grammar, devoutly wished to be
    corrected!
To punctuate, perchance to give meaning: ay, there's our
    grammarian's purpose.
For in that pursuit of meaning, what errors may come
when we have shuffled over to the grammar exam?
Shifts in tense and mood must give us pause—there's a thing
that makes calamity of keeping sentences consistent.
Who would bear the misuse of case forms,
the subjective, objective, and possessive—both singular and plural?
Intransitive and transitive verbs, participles, gerunds, and infinitives,
verb phrases, verbal phrases, and phrasal verbs.
The patient merit a worthy grammarian takes,
when they might just want quiet, and to not make

known the difference between coordinating and correlative
    conjunctions,
or to grunt and sweat over a conjunctive adverb.
But that dread of something not quite right,
in a confusing sentence, in its very words,
makes the grammarian return, it puzzles their will,
and makes them rather fear those ills on the page
than fly to fellow grammarians who they think may know.
Thus fear of being wrong makes cowards of us all.
Is it a problem with the voice—active or passive?
Is this word able to take a comparative and superlative form?
With this in regard, the current turns us awry,
and we lose the thrust of action ... Soft now,
I gaze at my grammar textbook, and try to remember everything;
may all the grammar sins be remembered.

'HAMLET'S SOLILOQUY: GRAMMAR STYLE', MEGAN PORTER

Why study grammar and syntax?

This chapter is about how sentences and form-class words work, topics that are covered by the terms **syntax** and **grammar**. Grammar is the underlying system of rules of a language. When you study what's acceptable (Standard English) and what's not acceptable (non-standard English), you're studying grammar. Syntax describes the way in which words relate to one another in a sentence, the arrangement and interrelations among words—in other words, the structure of the sentence.

The stronger your grasp of sentence structure, the better your writing will be. Grounding your writing in grammatical rules and syntactical principles will allow you to structure coherent sentences and cohesive paragraphs. Understanding syntax and grammar provides you with a metalanguage, that is, a language to talk about language.

In Chapter 3, I covered the principles of effective writing at the word and phrase level. In this chapter and the next, I'll introduce you to the traditional parts of speech—what contemporary linguists call 'word classes'—and explain how to understand the function of each word in a sentence.

Glamour is probably not the first word that you think of when you hear the word *grammar*, but a philosopher and editor at the University of Queensland, Professor Fred D'Agostino, talks about the 'glamour of grammar' in a wonderfully evocative talk that notched up more than 20,000 views on YouTube after it was posted in July 2014. He explains how both *glamour* and *grammar* are derived from the Greek word *grammatikos*, meaning 'of letters', which covered the whole of arts and sciences. In the Middle Ages, *grammar* meant 'learning', which, in the popular imagination, included a knowledge of magic—or 'glamour'. So, grammar has origins that are glamorous and magical. If you'd like to listen to D'Agostino (2014), you will find the video clip listed in the References.

It's quite usual for people to speak and write correctly without knowing the explicit rules of grammar. So, when you're studying grammar, you're studying what you may already instinctively know. If you are a native speaker, you have an intuitive grasp of grammar because you've been using it since you first started to talk, but having a formal knowledge of the rules so that you can apply them to your writing will give you greater control over your writing and editing. No one starts at zero. Your intuitive sense of grammar will help you to write, but you need to be able to pinpoint what makes a piece of writing work or not work. Knowing the rules of grammar can give you greater power over your writing and make you into a confident and accomplished writer.

The novelist Philip Pullman (2002) says:

> Taking care of the tools means developing the faculty of sensing when we're not sure about a point of grammar . . . Sometimes we're told that this sort of thing doesn't matter very much. If only a few readers recognise and object to unattached participles, for example, and most readers don't notice and sort of get the sense anyway, why bother? I discovered a very good answer to that, and it goes like this: if people don't notice when we get it wrong, they won't mind if we get it right. And if we do get it right, we'll please the few who know and care about these things, so everyone will be happy.

British journalists Dot Wordsworth and Harry Mount have been very outspoken about the value of grammar. Dot Wordsworth (2012) says: 'It's cruel not to teach grammar to children . . . Grammar sets them free. No one would think it a kindness to give a teenager a car without teaching her to drive, and that includes the rules of the road. Or as Alexander Pope observed: "True ease in writing comes from art, not chance, / As those move easiest who have learned to dance"'.

Harry Mount (2013) says: 'Grammar is the skeleton on which language is built; and it's an extremely flexible skeleton. Know your grammar and you can produce every kind of fantastic verbal construction and—this is the crucial bit—be understood'.

The basis of grammatical awareness is sentence sense, and this comes with reading. Poor writers cannot or do not read their own writing accurately or perceptively. They lack a reader's perspective. As I advocated in Chapter 2, you need to read widely. Wide reading, particularly of authors who write very well, will help you to absorb a great deal about grammatical, syntactical, and punctuation patterns and the craft of writing. Find a piece of writing that you admire and try to analyse why it works. The more you know about grammar and syntax, the easier that will be.

If you are at school or university, you know how important your standard of writing is to your academic progress. When you move into the professional workplace, you'll see that it, too, requires the use of Standard English, the world's lingua franca. English is the main language in more than 60 countries; it is used all over the planet in academic and professional communication.

Standard English is the set of standards that professional experts have agreed upon while also acknowledging that language constantly changes. The rules for Standard English are defined by the ways in which educated people use it, but English is not strictly codified in the way that the French language is. English has no body equivalent to the 400-year-old Académie Française, a council of revered experts on the French language.

Many employers react strongly against the use of non-standard English in the workplace because they believe that errors erode the credibility of the organisation. You'll exponentially enhance your employment prospects and career mobility if you write well.

Descriptivism and prescriptivism

There are two groups of grammarians: descriptivists (many of whom have been trained in linguistics) and prescriptivists (many of whom have been trained in traditional grammar). **Descriptivists** describe how language is used and how it changes. **Prescriptivists** prescribe how language ought to be used.

Professor Geoffrey Pullum, a linguist who is a world authority on grammar as the co-author with Rodney Huddleston of *The Cambridge Grammar of the English Language* (2002), and who blogs regularly on *Lingua Franca* on *The Chronicle of Higher Education* site, is one of those who resist the dichotomy. He is quoted as saying that 'We grammarians who study the English language are not all bow-tie-wearing martinets, but we're also not flaming liberals who think everything should be allowed. There's a sensible middle ground where you decide what the rules of Standard English are, on the basis of close study of the way that native speakers use the language' (Chivers, 2014).

I agree with Pullum. In this chapter I set out the basic grammatical rules of Standard English as required in any formal written context. In creative writing, these rules don't need to be followed so closely, but creative writers can benefit just as much as academic and workplace writers from understanding how grammar and syntax work. An understanding of grammar and syntax helps writers to produce logical prose that expresses the hierarchical structure of ideas, economical prose that says exactly what is meant, and compelling prose that holds a reader's attention.

Traditional grammar

Traditional grammar, which relied on prescriptive rules relating to nine 'parts of speech', is the grammar that was taught for around 2000 years, though, as Professor David Crystal comments in an interview that I filmed with him at the Oxford Literary Festival in 2014, for a few decades—from the 1960s up until the 1990s—to his dismay, grammar was absent from most writing classrooms. There is a link to the video in references. Another eminent professor who laments the decline of grammar teaching is Professor John Frow, who calls the decline 'a calamity' (2007, p. 1627).

Traditional grammar prescribes rules and follows what some people call the 'doctrine of mechanical correctness'. While most people acknowledge the importance of presenting error-free writing in academic and professional contexts, we must accept that language practices change constantly. For example, don't follow the old-fashioned advice based on Latin grammar that forbids splitting an infinitive verb, usually with an adverb (*to **boldly** go*), or ending a sentence with a preposition (*What did you do that for?*). These rules were based on the fact that all Latin infinitives are expressed as one word—for example, *amare* means 'to love'—and that Latin prepositions are always placed before the noun, as in *ad infinitum* (literally, 'to infinity'), so can never appear at the end of a Latin sentence.

There are lots of other rules that you might remember from school, such as not starting a sentence with *and*, *but*, or *because*, but these are what some grammarians call 'bogus', 'phony', or 'zombie' rules. See the articles by David Marsh (2013) and Steven Pinker (2014) listing these rules and explaining why it's okay to break them. In 2014, Weird Al Yankovic released an album, *Mandatory Fun*, which featured the song 'Word Crimes' (to the tune of the song 'Blurred Lines'). The song relied on his knowledge of seventeen prescriptivist rules (called shibboleths), and he was subsequently widely pilloried for doing this by those in the descriptivist camp.

The 'real' rules of grammar

You need to understand the 'real' rules of grammar so that you know when it's acceptable to break them. Much of the material in this and the next chapter covers the real rules of grammar. Joseph Williams (1995) lists seven rules 'whose violation would generally brand one as a writer of non-standard English'. Williams suggests avoiding:

1. Double negatives. *The engine had hardly no systematic care.* (*The engine had hardly any systematic care.*)
2. Wrongly formed verbs. *They knowed that nothing would happen.* (*They knew that nothing would happen.*)

3. Double comparatives. *This way is more quicker.* (*This way is quicker.*)
4. Adjectives for adverbs. *They did the work real good.* (*They did the work really well.*)
5. Pleonastic subjects (more than needed). *The man he said.* (*The man said.*)
6. Incorrect pronouns. *Him and me will study the problem.* (*He and I will study the problem.*)
7. Subject–verb disagreement. *They was ready to begin.* (*They were ready to begin.*) (p. 190)

The American poet and Pulitzer Prize winner Carl Sandburg nicely exemplified non-standard grammar when he amusingly claimed: 'I never made a mistake in grammar but one in my life and as soon as I done it I seen it'. Traditional grammar was based on nine parts of speech, which appear in Figure 4.1.

Figure 4.2 shows a sentence that uses all the parts of speech in their traditional function, that is, doing their usual job. You may worry that I have started the sentence in Figure 4.2 with 'And'. But, as I said above, there's no rule to say that you can't do that.

Noun (a naming word)	*a* **chance**
Pronoun (a noun substitute)	***their*** last chance
Verb (a doing or being word)	they ***lost*** the chance
Adjective (a word describing nouns or pronouns)	***fat*** chance
Adverb (a word describing adjectives, verbs, or other adverbs)	a ***very*** slim chance; she danced ***divinely***
Article (definite = *the*; indefinite = *a/an*)	*a* good chance
Conjunction (a joining word)	a slim chance ***and*** a very slim chance
Preposition (a word that positions)	***at*** the dance
Interjection (an exclamation)	***Wow!*** (What a dance!)

Figure 4.1 The traditional parts of speech

And	the	good	goblin
CONJUNCTION	ARTICLE	ADJECTIVE	NOUN
apparently	noticed	me	in
ADVERB	VERB	PRONOUN	PREPOSITION
the	crowd.	Gosh!	
ARTICLE	NOUN	INTERJECTION	

Figure 4.2 Sentence demonstrating the traditional parts of speech

Word classes

A group of linguists who rose to prominence in the 1960s argued that traditional grammar could not always be relied upon to analyse written texts. This is because many words can function as several different parts of speech.

Take the word *face*, for example. In the sentence *That's such a happy face*, it works as a noun. But in the sentence *I can't face that mountain of work*, the word *face* is functioning to describe an action, and is therefore part of a verb phrase. In yet another example, *Let's schedule some face time*, it is functioning as an adjective that describes the kind of time.

You can see from these simple examples that we can't categorically identify a word as a particular part of speech until we see it in its context in a sentence. Many words can multitask, doing different jobs in different sentences. The function of a word in a sentence—that is, its role and its relationship to other words in the sentence—always determines its part of speech in that sentence.

Linguists have examined the way words work in sentences and divided their roles or functions into two groups: form-class words and structure-class words (see Figure 4.3).

The **form-class words**—sometimes called 'open' or 'lexical' words—contribute content-meaning to the text and comprise the central subject matter in dictionaries.

The **structure-class words**—sometimes called 'closed', 'grammatical', or 'function' words—contribute grammatical-structural meaning to the text. That is, they signal the relationships between words in a sentence and function to make a text cohesive. They work rather like glue or mortar that connects the bricks of the form-class words to each other.

I'll cover the form-class words, as well as sentences, in this chapter, and the structure-class words, along with paragraphs, in the next chapter. The interjection, the ninth part of speech, doesn't fit into either class.

Form-class words	Structure-class words
nouns	pronouns
verbs	determiners (includes articles, as in traditional grammar)
adjectives	conjunctions
adverbs	prepositions

Figure 4.3 Word classes

Syntax

The rules of grammar govern what is acceptable in Standard English. The rules of syntax (sentence structure) govern the relationships of words, phrases, and clauses in a sentence.

Word

Each word in a sentence can be labelled as a particular part of speech according to its function in the sentence. Each word can have only one label at a time. A word cannot be labelled as a particular part of speech outside its context; for example, the word *time* can function as several different parts of speech, as in the following sentences:

> *Please fill out your **time** sheet.* (adjective)
> *It's **time** to go.* (noun)
> *Let's **time** this activity.* (verb)

Phrase

A phrase is a coherent string of two or more words (a word cluster) that does not contain a finite verb. That is, there is no subject–verb relationship. For example, *to love reading, favourite books, loving books, considered clever*. The list below illustrates different kinds of phrases.

- **Absolute phrase** (self-contained phrase): ***Her eyes tired after reading for hours,*** *Jane stopped for tea.*
- **Appositive phrase** (explains, describes, defines, identifies, or restates the noun): *Corinne Bailey Rae,* ***the singer,*** *has released a new album.*
- **Noun phrase** (names something): ***The state of affairs.***
- **Adjectival phrase** (describes something or someone): *a **ten-year-old** child.*
- **Adverbial phrase** (describes how an action is performed): *We read the letter **extremely carefully**.*
- **Prepositional phrase** (states when or where something happened): *We dined **after the film**.*

I'll cover two other kinds of phrases, **verb phrases** and **verbal phrases**, in the section of this chapter on verbs.

Clause

A clause is a string of words (a group of related words) containing a finite verb and its subject. There are two kinds of clauses.

An **independent** (main, principal) clause makes sense and can stand alone as a sentence. It has a finite verb. For example, *I love reading.*

A **dependent** (subordinate) clause does not make sense when it stands on its own. For example, *Because I love reading.*

A dependent clause will often have a marker word (a subordinating conjunction) introducing it, such as *after, although, because, before, unless, until, when, while.* When it stands on its own (as in the example above), it's called a **sentence fragment**.

The sentence

A sentence is an arrangement of words, phrases, and clauses that starts with a capital letter and ends with a full stop, question mark, or exclamation mark, unless its first word has a quirky spelling such as iPod, of course. A grammatical sentence follows grammatical rules. It contains a finite verb and expresses a coherent thought or thoughts through the relationships of the words. It can stand by itself and make sense.

A **finite verb** is a verb that relates to a subject, which may be assumed (can be 'understood'). For example: *I am happy. I read.* ***Read!***

As I explained above, when a sentence does not make sense on its own, it is called a **sentence fragment**. For example, 'To be, or not to be' is a sentence fragment because it has a verb (used twice, in fact) that is not finite (*to be* is an infinitive), but 'That is the question' is a complete sentence because *is* is a finite verb that relates to the word *that*.

A fragment can be a dependent clause (*When he was only 50*); a subject without a predicate (*James Cook*); a phrase (*Explorer James Cook*); or a single word (*Cook*).

Fused sentences and comma-splice sentences are ungrammatical sentences, they occur frequently.

The sentence above is an example of a **comma splice**. If you remove the comma, you have a **fused** (or **run-on**) **sentence**. You can often eliminate a comma splice by inserting a full stop or semicolon between the two clauses: *Fused sentences and comma-splice sentences are ungrammatical sentences; they occur frequently.*

In Alan Bennett's *A Life Like Other People's* (2010), he gives a wonderful example of a comma splice when his cousin Florence writes in a letter: 'Frank died last week, haven't we been having some weather?' Bennett remarks: 'Seldom can a comma have borne such a burden' (p. 162).

The four main sentence structures

There are four main sentence structures: simple, compound, complex, and compound-complex.

Simple sentences contain one independent clause, in which the subject names the source of the action and the predicate tells what happens. See Figure 4.4.

Compound sentences contain two or more independent clauses joined by a) a semicolon or b) a coordinating conjunction such as *for, and, nor, but, or, yet, so*. (These conjunctions can be remembered by the mnemonic FANBOYS; see further discussion in Chapter 5.)

James Cook died; however, his sailors survived.
*James Cook died **and** he was widely mourned.*

Subject (names)	Predicate (tells)
James Cook (actor)	*died* (action).
John (actor)	*bakes* (action) *cakes* (acted upon).
Reading to toddlers (activity)	*contributes* (action) *to their literacy* (acted upon).
I (actor)	*thank* (action) *you* (acted upon).
Jane (actor)	*acted* (action) *strangely* (manner of action, or 'how').

Figure 4.4 Simple sentences

Complex sentences contain one independent clause and one or more dependent clauses, either at the beginning, in the middle, or at the end of the sentence.

When he was only 50 (dependent clause), *James Cook died* (independent clause).
James Cook, when he was only 50, died.
James Cook died when he was only 50.

The three sentences above demonstrate another way in which sentences can be classified by their structure: **loose** or **periodic**. Loose sentences provide their key message at the beginning. Periodic sentences save their punchline till the end.

These can be categorised respectively as left-branching (LB), mid-branching (MB), and right-branching (RB) sentences.

When he was only 50, James Cook died. (LB; periodic)
James Cook, when he was only 50, died. (MB; periodic)
James Cook died when he was only 50. (RB; loose)

Compound-complex sentences contain two or more independent clauses and at least one dependent clause.

When he was only 50 (dependent clause), *James Cook died* (independent clause) *and he was widely mourned* (independent clause).

Although he was relatively young (dependent clause), *James Cook died* (independent clause), *and he was widely mourned* (independent clause) *because he was a great sailor* (dependent clause).

Sentence-structure problems

Potential sentence problems include 'is-ness', 'and-ness', and 'of-ness' (terms I coined to describe sentence problems caused by overuse of parts of the verb 'be', the conjunction 'and', and the preposition 'of'), misused modifiers, lack of parallel structure, and mixed or shifted constructions.

Avoid **is-ness**, which occurs when you rely on the weak verb *is* or other parts of the verb *be* (*am*, *are*; *was*, *were*). For example, *The intention of the tax office **is** to audit their records* could be written much more directly as *The tax office intends to audit their records*. In the rewrite the weak verb 'is' has been replaced with the verb that the nominalisation ('heavy' noun) 'intention' is derived from. See below for an explanation of nominalisation.

Avoid **and-ness**, an overreliance on *and*. For example, *Proposals are to be submitted in duplicate, **and** enclosed in a sealed envelope, **and** endorsed with a reference number, **and** lodged at the address below.* This sentence can be rewritten much more directly as *Submit your proposal in duplicate, to the address below, using a sealed envelope clearly marked with the reference number.*

Similarly, avoid **of-ness**, the overuse of *of*. Williams (1995) presents the following sentence: 'Our lack *of* knowledge about local conditions precluded determination *of* committee action effectiveness in fund allocation to those areas in greatest need *of* assistance' (emphasis added). He eliminates the instances of 'of' and rewrites it as follows: 'Because we knew nothing about local conditions, we could not determine how effectively the committee had allocated funds to areas that most needed assistance' (p. 17).

There are three kinds of **misused modifiers**: dangling or hanging; misplaced; and ambiguous or squinting.

To contain the epidemic, *the area was sealed off.*

In the sentence above, the unattached, hanging, **dangling modifier** modifies something to which it is not logically related. The modifier has nothing sensible to modify in the sentence. Rewrite the sentence as *To contain the epidemic, the city sealed off the area.* Or, *The city sealed off the area to contain the epidemic.*

As a young child my grandmother used to read me the best stories.

We can guess that the grandmother used to read stories to the writer when the writer was a young child, but that's not what the above sentence says. The **misplaced modifier**, *as a young child*, wrongly attaches to the grandmother. Rewrite the sentence as follows: *When I was a young child, my grandmother used to read me the best stories.*

We failed entirely to understand how serious the problem was.

As readers, we cannot be sure whether the **ambiguous/'squinting' modifier** *entirely* is referring to the failure or the understanding. Clarify by moving the modifier: *We entirely failed to understand* or *We failed to entirely understand.*

When you have parallel concepts, you need parallel (coordinate) syntax, particularly in dot-point lists. Notice how the third dot point below breaks the **parallel structure** set up by the first two.

This department:
- *ensures that all safety rules are followed*
- *performs regular checks on equipment*
- *its primary focus is on maintaining the highest standards of compliance.*

Rewrite as follows:

This department:
- *ensures that all safety rules are followed*
- *performs regular checks on equipment*
- *maintains the highest standards of compliance as its primary focus.*

A mixed sentence or shifted construction occurs when a writer changes course within the sentence, which results in a mismatch between the beginning and end of the sentence. In the sentence *In all his efforts to please others got him into trouble*, for example, you can feel how awkward the construction is. You can correct the problem by changing the sentence to *All his efforts to please others got him into trouble* or *In all his efforts to please others, he got himself into trouble.*

Form-class words

I'll now move on to a discussion of the form-class words: verbs, nouns, adjectives, and adverbs.

Verbs

As Karen Elizabeth Gordon says in her marvellously imaginative grammar book *The Deluxe Transitive Vampire*, 'The verb is the heartthrob of a sentence' (1984, p. 40).

Verbs can express an **action**, an **occurrence**, or a **state of being**:

*I **ate** my lunch.*
*Something **happened**.*
*I **am** happy.*

Verbs can link. **Linking (copular) verbs** link a **subject** with a **complement**, which describes or explains the subject, restates it, or describes its state of being. They include verbs of the senses—*see, hear, taste, smell, feel*—and verbs such as *appear, be, become, grow, prove, remain, seem, stay,* and *turn* (when they refer to a state or condition).

I (subject) ***remain*** (linking verb) *confident of their ability* (complement).

Linking verbs connect their subject with their complement (i.e., what completes them), which has the same 'case' as their subject, that is, subjective case. (See discussion of case below under nouns and pronouns.)

Verbs can help. **Helping (auxiliary) verbs** combine with the base form of a **main verb**. The most common helping verbs are *be, do,* and *have.*

*I **am*** (auxiliary verb) *going* (main verb) *to San Francisco. I **do** love it there. I **have** gone there often.*

Modal auxiliary verbs combine with the base form of a main verb to suggest a condition such as an ability, advisability, intention, necessity, possibility, or permission that is not expressed by the main verb in the sentence. The modal verbs in English are *can/could, may/might, must, shall/should,* and *will/would.* Then there are the **semi-modals** *be able to, have (got) to, need to, ought to,* and *be supposed to.* These days, however, *shall* is regarded as archaic, and is best avoided. Instead of 'shall':

- when giving permission, use *may*
- when recommending a course of action, use *should*
- when indicating the future, use *will*
- when something is fact, use *is*
- when stating a legal obligation, use *must*
- when communicating policy, use *must, required, have to,* or *need to.*

Finite verbs can be **transitive** or **intransitive**.

Transitive verbs need a **direct object** in the form of a noun or a pronoun to complete their meaning; they can also have an **indirect object**.

*I read **the book** (direct object) to **the class** (indirect object).*

Verbs used **intransitively** don't need an object to complete their meaning. They are complete in themselves. The verbs in the following sentences are used intransitively because they have no object, but all of them apart from 'seem' can be used transitively as well.

*Ice **melts**. Let's eat! He **felt** confused. It **seemed** ridiculous. The joke **grew** stale.*

For example, *They grew angry* (intransitive) but *They grew cabbages on their farm* (transitive). *That toddler melted my heart. Let's eat that cake. I felt the cold in Canada.*

Verbs can be **finite** (*I read the book*) or **non-finite** (*to read*). (See the following discussion under 'Verbals'.)

Verbals

Non-finite verbs are classed as **verbals**, of which there are three kinds: **participles** (present and past), **gerunds** (verbal nouns), and **infinitives**.

A **participle** is added to a helping verb to make a verb:
- **present** (always ends in -*ing*): *I am **cooking** dinner tonight.*
- **past** (often ends in -*d*, -*ed*, -*en*, or -*t*): *I have **cooked*** (past participle) *dinner tonight. My friend has **built** a shed. We have **broken** our promise. He had **held** a party.*

Participles can also function as adjectives: ***Bored*** (past participle functioning as an adjective) *students need extra work to do. The **writing** room* (present participle functioning as an adjective).

A **gerund** (verbal noun)—always ends in -*ing* and always functions as a noun: ***Cooking*** *is a useful skill. **Writing** can be therapeutic.*

The **infinitive**—the *to* form of the verb—can function as a noun, a verb, an adjective, or an adverb; Latin infinitives consist of only one word (for example, ***amare***, to love), but infinitives in English consist of two words): ***To** boldly **go*** (verb). ***To** strictly **follow*** (verb) *a sequence.* ***To** thoroughly **integrate*** (verb) *elements of visual design.* ***To write*** (noun) *is therapeutic. These are the realities **to face*** (adjective). *The decision was difficult **to make*** (adverb).

Verb phrases, phrasal verbs, and verbal phrases

A **verb phrase** is a compound or multi-word verb that comprises a main verb and one or more auxiliary verbs, including modal auxiliary verbs. Verb phrases can take subjects, objects, or complements, and may be modified by adverbs: *The film **has started*** (subject). *I **had felt** ill* (complement). *I **would have lent** the book to them* (direct and indirect object). *I **would have been forgotten** quickly* (adverb).

A **phrasal verb** is a multi-word verb that comprises a main verb and one or more prepositions/adverbs that are integral to its meaning. Some authorities further identify a **prepositional verb**, which is also a multi-word verb that comprises a main verb and one or more prepositions that are integral to its meaning. I think that it would be simpler to label all phrasal verbs containing prepositions as prepositional verbs. According to *The Cambridge Guide to Australian English Usage* (Peters, 2007), the difference is this:

> A phrasal verb such as *turn off* can be syntactically split: ***Turn off** the light.* ***Turn** the light **off**.*

A prepositional (phrasal) verb can't be syntactically split: ***Account for*** *the consequences.* ***Consist of*** *the following choices.*

Neither kind of verb can be semantically split; that is, you need both parts to convey the sense.

A **verbal phrase** consists of a verbal (non-finite verb), plus the words modifying it:

*When **examined** carefully, the substance seemed harmless.* (past participle)

***Reading** widely will increase your knowledge.* (verbal noun/gerund)

***To do** well you'll need to work hard.* (infinitive)

Mood

The mood of a verb depends on whether it is a statement, a question, a command, or a condition:
- A statement: *I like that cat.* (**indicative/declarative** mood)
- A question: *Do you like that cat?* (**interrogative** mood)
- A command: *Be kind to that cat!* (**imperative** mood)
- A condition: *If I were that cat, I would think myself lucky.* (**subjunctive** mood)

Some people regard the subjunctive mood as antiquated or moribund. It is used for something that might happen, or could happen, or should happen, or that I wish would happen. It is used for condition, supposition, wish, demands and commands, suggestions and proposals, and statements of necessity: *If only it **were** so. Long **live** the Queen.* It usually appears in a dependent clause: *It is important that the breakdown of this figure **be** reasonable and achievable. Is* or *are* becomes *be. Am* or *was* becomes *were.* Singular verbs lose their *-s* and *-es* endings:

*I suggest that he **attend*** (subjunctive mood) *the meeting.*

*She said that she usually **attends*** (indicative/declarative mood) *that meeting.*

*The manager recommended that the offer **be*** (subjunctive mood) *open for two weeks.*

The imperative mood is an important one in the context of workplace writing. It's the clearest and most direct way to write instructions: *If you have trouble with your computer,* **turn** *it* **off** *and then* **turn** *it back* **on** *again.*

Tense

Tense relates to the time expressed by the verb and whether an action or state is continuing or has been completed. The science of linguistics recognises only past and present tenses in English because the form of the verb doesn't change to express the future but takes a modal auxiliary verb (*I go*/*I will go*). However, the *Oxford Dictionary* defines tense as 'any one of the different forms in the conjugation of a verb that indicate different times (past, present, or future) at which the action or state denoted by it is viewed as happening or existing'.

Figure 4.5 classifies twelve kinds of tenses within the three main tenses: **present, past**, and **future**. The term 'aspect' gives a perspective on the verb, indicating whether the action is complete (perfect) or is still going on (continuous or progressive). I'll cover active and passive voice in the next section.

Problems with tense can occur in the sequencing of verbs, so it is important to keep an eye on the sequence of tenses between an independent clause and a dependent clause to eliminate the error in sentences such as the following:

> Daily training improves your fitness and made (makes) you feel healthier.
>
> When players have been paid fairly, they would be (are) happier.
>
> I went shopping and had been away for several hours when my friend meets (met) me.

Voice

Voice is the property of a transitive verb that tells whether the subject acts or is acted upon; so voice is determined by whether the subject of the sentence is the verb's agent (actor or doer) or recipient (receiver).

A verb is in the **active voice** when the subject of the sentence is the doer of the act.

Tense and aspect	Active voice (third person, singular/plural)	Passive voice (third person, singular/plural)
SIMPLE (for recurring action)		
(Simple) Present	keeps/keep	is/are kept
(Simple) Past	kept	was/were kept
(Simple) Future	will keep	will be kept
CONTINUOUS (PROGRESSIVE) (for ongoing action at a precise moment)		
Present continuous	is/are keeping	is/are being kept
Past continuous	was/were keeping	was/were being kept
Future continuous	will be keeping	will be being kept
PERFECT (for completed past action leading to present events)		
Present perfect	has/have kept	has/have been kept
Past perfect (pluperfect)	had kept	had been kept
Future perfect	will have kept	will have been kept
PERFECT CONTINUOUS (for action that has been or had been or will have been going on, until now or then, but ends or has ended, or will end . . .)		
Present perfect continuous	has/have been keeping	has/have been being kept
Past perfect continuous	had been keeping	had been being kept
Future perfect continuous	will have been keeping	will have been being kept

Figure 4.5 Tenses

A verb is in the **passive voice** when the subject is acted upon. Passive voice puts the object of a transitive verb as the grammatical subject of the sentence. The passive voice will always consist of a part of the verb *be* (*am, is, was, are, were, been, being*) plus a past participle (a main verb that functions as part of the verb, not as an adjective). Figure 4.6 demonstrates the difference between active and passive voice.

If you think that a verb is in the passive voice, always look for the hidden actor, because the 'by'-agent is often not expressed; instead, it is 'understood'. If you can put *by* or *for* or *to* [*zombies*] after the verb, it's passive. Also check whether what you think is a passive verb can be converted straightforwardly into active voice. Only verbs that can be used transitively (i.e., take a direct object) can be converted into the passive.

	Subject	Verb	Object
Active voice	The client	rejected	the proposal. (direct object)
	doer/actor/agent	action	receiver
Passive voice	The proposal	was rejected	by the client. (indirect object)
	The proposal	was rejected.	(indirect object is 'understood'/'hidden')
	receiver	action	doer/actor/agent

Figure 4.6 Active and passive voice

The **impersonal passive** (with no human agency) is very common in the workplace, as is the double passive:

*It **was decided**. It **was agreed**.*
*Athletes who **are found** to **have taken** drugs **will be dropped** from the squad.* (double passive)

Use passive voice by choice, not by default. When the action is more important than the actor, use the passive voice. The passive voice can also be useful when you want to soften the tone of a message, for example, *It **has been decided*** (passive) *that your proposal cannot **be funded*** (passive), rather than *The committee **has decided*** (active) *not **to fund*** (active) *your proposal.*

A final note on verbs: Ensure that you have correctly separated verbs within word pairs in cases such as the following: **Thank you**. *I will* **follow up** *on this. I* **must have** *that report by lunchtime. I'll* **set up** *the template for you.* Words within these pairs need to be joined when they function as adjectives or nouns (see below): *Thanks for that* **thank-you** *note. Here's my* **follow-up** *report. This is a* **must-have** *book. They have a great* **set-up**.

Nouns

Nouns are naming words. They name a person (*teacher*), a place (*school*), a thing (*book*), a quality (*loyalty*), an act (*sabotage*), or an idea (*equity*).

Nouns can be **singular** or **plural**.

- For most nouns, the plural is formed by adding *-s* or *-es* to the singular: for example, *book/books, boss/bosses, Jones/Joneses* (family name).
- If there is a vowel before the *-y* at the end of a noun, add *-s* to make it plural: for example, *alley* becomes *alleys*.
- If there is a consonant before the *-y* at the end of a noun, change the *-y* to *-ies*: for example, *ally* becomes *allies*.
- Some nouns have irregular plurals: for example, *child/children, goose/geese, wife/wives*.
- Some nouns have no singular: for example, *clothes, arrears*.
- Some nouns can be counted (**count nouns**): for example, *seven little Australians, 3000 books, nine items or fewer* (not *less*).
- Some nouns can't be counted. These are called **non-count** or **mass nouns** and have no plural: for example, *anger, atmosphere, equality, equipment, etiquette, feedback, foliage, furniture, information, jargon, justice, kudos, luck, milk, potential, punctuation, spaghetti, training, underwear, weather, wisdom*. George W. Bush, former president of the United States and famous for 'Bushisms', coined a spurious plural, 'internets'. There is only one internet.
- Some nouns are plural in form but singular in meaning, so take a singular verb: for example, *athletics, economics, ethics, mathematics, measles, news, physics, politics*. *Statistics* can be singular or plural in meaning: *Statistics* **is** *a popular study option*, but *The statistics* **are** *convincing*.
- Some words have kept their Greek- and Latin-based plurals: for example, *criterion/criteria, phenomenon/phenomena, datum/data*.

These days, many people would use *data* for singular and plural, regarding *datum* as antiquated.
- Some words have both English and Latin plurals, so check the context or ask your colleagues to help you decide which to use: for example, *antennas/antennae, formulas/formulae, indexes/indices, matrixes/matrices, mediums/media*.
- The singular and plural forms of some words are the same: for example, *headquarters, series, sheep, species*.
- For measurements and figures, decide whether what you are referring to is singular or plural:

Three years **is** a long time. Six months **is** going to be plenty. (a period of three years or six months)

Forty per cent of eligible voters **are** expected to turn out. Forty per cent **is** considered to be a good turnout.

Three-quarters of the library collection **consists** of reference books.

Nouns can be **concrete** or **abstract**. Nouns are **concrete** when they name things that you can see, touch, hear, smell, or taste (*book, chair, food*). **Abstract** nouns name ideas, concepts, generalities, qualities, and trends (*beauty, justice, pleasure, wisdom*).

Nouns can be **common** or **proper**. **Common nouns** identify a general item or term (*book, house, principle*). **Proper nouns** identify a unique, specific person, location, building, event, entity, or work of art or literature, for example, Nelson Mandela, Southbank, the Empire State Building, the Oxford Literary Festival, the Queen's Trust, the *Mona Lisa*.

A proper noun always starts with a capital letter. Mignon Fogarty, the high-profile American grammar guru, says on her 'Grammar Girl' website that *the Web* and *the Internet* are proper nouns and should take an initial capital, but many other writers do not capitalise these words. *Prime Minister Winston Churchill* is capped, but *the prime minister* or *the president* should be in lower case.

Nouns can be **collective**. **Collective nouns** name groups of people, animals, plants, works, or ideas.

Collective nouns such as *a lot, audience, bunch, collection, committee, family, group, jury, majority, percentage, staff*, and *team* take a singular verb when the group or unit performs a discrete, singular action—for example, *The committee **is** unanimously opposed to this suggestion*—but a plural verb if the unit is split: *The team **are** going their separate ways after the season finishes.*

What happens to subject-verb agreement when a phrase intervenes between a collective noun subject and its verb in examples such as the following? *A **bunch** of children was/were cooking up a storm in the kitchen.* Does the verb agree with *bunch* or with *children*? *When the main **batch** of tickets is/are released, we will buy ours.* Does the verb agree with *batch* or *tickets*? In both cases, I would use the singular verbs 'was' and 'is' to agree with their singular subjects 'bunch' and 'batch', but others would use the plural.

Some writers treat *the media* as singular and others treat it as plural. There's no consensus on that one.

None can be treated as singular or plural. If you really want to specify the singular, use *not one*.

Plural collective nouns include *military*, *people*, and *police*.

Number is a collective noun that can be singular or plural:

> A number of students **are** already here. (plural)
>
> The number of students who are here **is** impressive. (singular)

Nouns can be **single** or **compound**. For example, *book*, *editor* (single); *grammar book*, *editor-in-chief* (compound).

Case

Case is the form of a noun (or pronoun) that shows the reader how the noun or pronoun functions in relation to the other words in a sentence.

Nouns can function in a sentence as a **subject**, an **object**, a **complement**, and an **appositive**. The appositive usually identifies or renames another noun nearby.

> *Madonna* (subject), *the singer* (appositive), *has given* (verb) *a concert* (object).
>
> *I* (subject) *remain* (verb) *an optimist* (complement).

Case also changes for pronouns (see Chapter 5) and the possessive form of nouns with the addition of an apostrophe: *the book's cover, the books' authors* (see Chapter 6 on punctuation).

Problems with nouns

Noun problems include **noun strings** (also known as **adjective stacks**) and **nominalisations**.

Unstring/unstack the phrases below to make it easier for your reader to process them:

> an uncertainty management heuristic
>
> a disaster victim identification specialist
>
> a property industry consultation framework

Change these to: *a heuristic for managing uncertainty, a specialist in identifying disaster victims, a consulting framework for the property industry*. Note that I have eliminated the noun strings and replaced the words *management, identification,* and *consultation* with their corresponding participles (derived from the verbs *manage, identify,* and *consult*). *Management, identification,* and *consultation* are termed 'nominalisations', which is itself a nominalisation.

A **nominalisation** is a noun derived from a verb or an adjective. Figure 4.7 shows the main nominalisation endings. The most common ending is *-tion*, pronounced as 'shun'. Some people call these terms '*shun* words' because writers should shun them and instead use the verbs or adjectives from which they are derived.

Try to convert nominalisations into verbs as often as you can. Williams (1995) gives an example of a sentence (which I used earlier in this chapter to illustrate of-ness). You can see that his sentence has several nominalisations:

> Our *lack* of *knowledge* about local conditions precluded *determination* of committee action *effectiveness* in fund *allocation* to those areas in greatest *need* of *assistance*. (p. 17)

His rewrite removes all the nominalisations (which I have italicised) in the original, apart from *assistance*:

-age (carry, not have carriage of)	-edge (know, not have knowledge of)	-ity (reciprocate, not offer reciprocity)	-ness (forgive, not extend forgiveness)
-al (approve, not give approval to)	-ence (differ, not exhibit a difference)	-ive (initiate, not launch an initiative)	-tion (acquire, not make an acquisition)
-ance (perform, not conduct a performance of)	-ery (discover, not make a discovery)	-ment (agree, not be in agreement with)	-ure (fail, not experience failure)

Figure 4.7 Common nominalisation endings

Because we *knew* nothing about local conditions, we *could not determine* how effectively the committee *had allocated* funds to areas that most needed assistance. (p. 17)

Note that there's a noun string in the original—'committee action effectiveness'—which he also removed.

Adjectives

Adjectives describe and qualify nouns and pronouns. Adjectives answer questions such as:
- which? (***New*** *challenges arose to test us.*)
- what kind of? (***Insurmountable*** *challenges arose to test us.*)

Adjectives can be **attributive** or **predicative**.

Attributive adjectives can be placed before or directly after the word that they modify: *The **part-time** teacher. A **happy** camper.* They usually come before a noun or noun phrase, but can come after: *accounts **payable**, body **politic**, city **proper**, president **elect**, proof **positive**.*

Predicative adjectives come after linking verbs such as *appear, be, become,* and *seem,* and function as a complement that qualifies the subject of the sentence. They are in the predicate of the sentence. For example: *They seemed **happy**. That teacher is **part time**.* (NB: Some predicative compound adjectives take a hyphen; others don't, for example, *He was* *sleep-deprived*, *The commute was time-consuming*, but there's no explicit rule to apply.

Participles and **infinitives** sometimes function as adjectives:

The owls stared at the **smirking** gruffalo. (present participle)

I rejected the **burnt** toast. (past participle)

The children couldn't decide which toy **to choose**. (infinitive)

Some writers display a negative attitude to adjectives. Eminent scientist and science fiction author Isaac Asimov warns writers against having a 'thick layer of fatty adjectival froth' in their work (Asimov, 1974, p. 179). Clifton Fadiman called the adjective 'the banana peel of the parts of speech' (Bauch, 2010). And Mark Twain had the following advice:

> I notice that you use plain, simple language, short words and brief sentences. That is the way to write English—it is the modern way and the best way. Stick to it; don't let fluff and flowers and verbosity creep in. *When you catch an adjective, kill it.* No, I don't mean utterly, but kill most of them—then the rest will be valuable. (Letter to D.W. Bowser, 20 March 1880; emphasis in original)

In contrast to Twain's advice, writing teacher and journalist Ben Yagoda (2004) believes that

> a resourceful and creative use of adjectives is one of the most important, if not the most important, marks of the first-rate essayist or critic. It is an indication of originality, wit, observation—indeed, the cast and quality of the writer's mind.

The French statesman Georges Clemenceau is supposed to have said to his amanuensis (a literary assistant who takes dictation): 'For you, there are only nouns and verbs; I will take care of such adjectives as may prove necessary' (Geertz, 1988, p. 60). We can only presume that Clemenceau wanted to keep the task of adding adjectives to himself.

Avoid adjectives that have become dead literary clichés: for example, **snow-capped** *peaks*, **fathomless** *depths*, **wild** *woods*, **crystal** *cascades*. Try using conventional adjectives in an unconventional/metaphorical way. In an article in *The New York Times*, John Pareles (1997) described Aretha Franklin's voice as 'creamy, loving, humble, sassy, and indomitable'.

As shown in Figure 4.8, adjectives in English can be 'marked' to indicate degree, that is, whether they are comparative or superlative.

Positive (the basic form, without comparing to any other thing)	Comparative (comparing two things)	Superlative (comparing at least three things)
happy	happier	happiest
nice	nicer	nicest
intelligent	more intelligent	most intelligent
humorous	more humorous	most humorous
noble	*either* more noble *or* nobler	*either* most noble *or* noblest

Figure 4.8 Degrees of comparison of adjectives

As shown in Figure 4.9, many adjectives form their comparative and superlative forms irregularly.

Positive (the basic form, without comparing to any other thing)	Comparative (comparing two things)	Superlative (comparing at least three things)
good	better	best
bad	worse	worst
little	less	least

Figure 4.9 Degrees of comparison of irregular adjectives

Some adjectives can be neither compared nor intensified (except perhaps for emphasis in creative writing). They are called **uncomparable**, **ungradable**, or **absolute** adjectives. They include *absolute, accurate, complete, correct, entire, eternal, exact, excellent, false, fatal, impossible, incessant, inevitable, infinite, maximum, minimum, optimum, perfect, possible, precise, preferable,* and *unique*. Do you agree that all of these adjectives are uncomparable? Can you think of others?

Sequence of adjectives in a series

When you use multiple adjectives in a sequence, you need to follow the correct adjective order. The proper order of adjectives is listed below, along with some examples for each category. This is sometimes called 'the royal order of adjectives'. However, avoid using more than two or three adjectives in front of one noun.

1. **Observations (opinion)**—*lovely, boring, stimulating*, etc.
2. **Size**—*tiny, small, huge*, etc.
3. **Shape**—*round, square, rectangular*, etc.
4. **Age**—*old, new, ancient*, etc.
5. **Colour**—*red, blue, green*, etc.
6. **Origin**—*American, Australian, Mexican*, etc.
7. **Material**—*gold, wood, silk*, etc.

Commas between adjectives?

Check to see whether adjectives are **coordinate**—that is, at the same level—and use commas where you can place *and* between the adjectives or when you can reverse their order. For example, *The small, used car. Barbie has long, curly, blonde hair.*

Adverbs

Adverbs answer the questions: when? how often? where? how much? how? in what manner? to what degree?

They can be formed by adding *-ly* to some adjectives, or can take other forms: *here, there, now, often, seldom, never, barely, scarcely, hardly*.

They can modify:
- **verbs**: *I ate* (verb) **quickly** (adverb).
- **adjectives**: *A* **wonderfully** (adverb) *scrumptious* (adjective) *meal*.
- **other adverbs**: *He speaks* **exceedingly** (adverb) **well** (adverb).
- **prepositions**: *The birds flew* **right** (adverb) *over* (preposition) *the lake*.
- **conjunctions**: *This is* **exactly** (adverb) *where* (conjunction) *I found it*.
- **phrases**: **Practically** (adverb) *to the brink of madness* (phrase).
- **clauses**: **Apparently** (adverb), *you forgot to check your references* (clause).

As with adjectives, authors have mixed feelings about adverbs. Stephen King (2001) says that 'the road to hell is paved with adverbs' but says that he 'can be a good sport about' them (p. 125). The novelist Henry James liked adverbs: 'I'm glad you like adverbs—I adore them; they are the only qualifications I really much respect', he wrote in a letter (5 January 1912).

Like adjectives, adverbs in English can be 'marked' to indicate degree, as shown in Figure 4.10.

Positive	Comparative	Superlative
badly	worse	worst
well	better	best
soon	sooner	soonest
carefully	more carefully	most carefully

Figure 4.10 Degrees of comparison of adverbs

Some adverbs, called **absolute** adverbs, cannot be compared: for example, *always, eternally, finally, first, generally, here, never, now, perfectly, rarely, singly, then, uniquely, universally*. Again, do you agree with this list? Can you think of any adverbs to add?

Avoid unnecessary qualifying and intensifying adverbs, such as *very, largely, quite, rather,* and *somewhat*. In particular, *quite* can be quite slippery. *Quite good* creates a negative vibe, whereas *quite wonderful* gives off a positive vibe. Ernest Gowers, whose book *The Complete Plain Words* (1954) was written with British civil servants in mind and has been revised and updated by his great-granddaughter Rebecca Gowers (2014), talks about 'dressing-gown' adverbs:

> Official writers seem to have a curious shrinking from certain adjectives unless they are adorned by adverbs. It is as though they were naked and must hastily have a dressing gown thrown around them. . . . The adverbial dressing gowns most favoured are *unduly, relatively*, and *comparatively*. These adverbs can only properly be used when something has been mentioned or implied that gives a standard of comparison. (1954, pp. 88–89)

Gowers goes on to say: 'Cultivate the habit of reserving adjectives and adverbs to make your meaning more precise, and suspect those that you find yourself using to make it more emphatic' (1954, p. 82).

Be careful of your placement of adverbs: *It's best to **always** get up early*. *It's **always** best to get up early*. *It's best to get up early **always***. Each has a different shade of meaning. Or consider ***just** not a pretty face* as opposed to *not **just** a pretty face*.

How many positions are there in these sentences to place the word 'only' (which can function as an adjective as well as an adverb)? *She told him that she loved him*. Or *You should read six articles this week*.

And what about the creative combinations of adverbs modifying adjectives below? Many of them appear to be oxymoronic, so provide a little kick for the reader. See if you can invent some to add to my collection. Remember that adverb–adjective combinations are usually not hyphenated.

blisteringly clever
disgracefully enjoyable
dismissively perfunctory
flamboyantly sparse [rooms]
gobsmackingly incoherent
infallibly stunning
ludicrously appropriate
madly funny

modestly conventional
nostalgically interesting
peculiarly becoming
shockingly simple
stupefyingly vulgar
swoopingly understated
unwaveringly complacent

The last word

This chapter has covered a lot of technical ground about grammar and a rationale for learning it, from the classification of sentences to the form-class words: verbs, nouns, adjectives, and adverbs. As I suggested at the beginning of the chapter, learning about grammar turns your intuitive, tacit knowledge into explicit knowhow. Grammar is hard and it takes a lot of effort to absorb its rules, but grounding your writing in grammar will pay off in your writing.

Activities

Answers are at the back of the book.

1. In your journal, use the core sentence *Sherlock Holmes waited* and the words, phrases, and clauses (with their punctuation, which you may need to adjust in some cases) in the columns below to construct as many sentences as you can. For example:

   Detective **Sherlock Holmes**, whose notoriety was getting him down, **waited**, gripping hard at his courage; however, Watson delayed his visit.

   Combining different 'chunks' of the text below will allow you to experiment, creating a variety of sentences that demonstrates your ability to coherently use words, phrases, and clauses. There are thousands of potential sentences.

   Core sentence: *Sherlock Holmes waited.*

Front position	Middle position	End position	Sentences in coordination
Detective	, whose notoriety was getting him down,	, gripping hard at his courage;	; however, Watson delayed his visit.
In the gloom,	, not far from the blaze,	and rummaged in his coat pocket;	; in fact, he would wait for the rest of the week.
Annoyed,	, the eccentric detective,	, in a state of doleful submission,	, and he was missed at Lloyd's registers.
Quietly,	, folding up the paper,	, while Watson moved the lamp,	, but the woman never turned up.
With his fingertips together,	, pale, haggard, and unkempt,	for Watson to call,	, going over the problem in his mind and rearranging the facts.

Front position	Middle position	End position	Sentences in coordination
Depressed and shaken,	, the pipe still between his lips,	for someone to speak,	, and contemplated the spotted handkerchief arranged over the woman's head.
All day,	, indifferent and contemptuous,	and stretched his long fingers.	
Chuckling to himself,	, tall and rather thin,	on the outskirts of London.	
The enigmatic	, the greatest detective of all time,	bravely.	
	, true friend of Dr Watson,	, because he was a good customer.	
	, struggling to overcome exhaustion,	for his dinner to be served.	
	, though he was impatient,	for his housekeeper to arrive.	
	, anxious to have his dinner,	for his newspaper to arrive.	

2. Read the following sentence and circle the function of the italicised phrase from the choices below.

   After inheriting a fortune, she generously contributed to charities.

   verbal phrase   appositive   verb phrase

3. Circle the transitive verbs in the following sentences.

   The story creeps to an end.
   War remains the decisive human failure.
   His eyes gleamed angrily.
   Time stretched on, indifferently.
   The stairs trembled under his feet.
   The room alarmed him.
   Her narrative grew less coherent.
   They ached with ambition.
   They finally reached the end of the road.

4. Circle the auxiliary (helping) verbs in the following passage.

   I have attached a short note to this document. While a clean uncluttered copy for submission was desired, upon final draft yesterday, errors were still found.

5. Circle any active-voice verbs in the following passage.

   Time has not permitted the production of a final, polished draft. I have edited all of the errors that were able to be located. I appreciate that this mars the presentation.

6. Circle any passive-voice verbs in the following passage.

   Time has not permitted the production of a final, polished draft. I have edited all of the errors that were able to be located. I appreciate that this mars the presentation.

7. Circle the correct answer below.

   Jack ran up the hill.

   Is 'up the hill' . . .
   a verb phrase?   a verbal phrase?   a phrasal verb?

8. Circle the words functioning as adjectives in the following sentences.

   This is a ridiculously easy test.
   The robots stared at the strange phenomenon.

Avoid unnecessary and clichéd adjectives.

A creative use of adjectives can enhance your writing.

9. Circle the words functioning as adjectives in the following phrases.

    a black cat, the city proper, the heir apparent, a gloomy outlook, the sheer richness of the material

10. Circle any of the following adjectives that are absolute (that is, cannot be compared).

    absolute, complete, equal, excellent, happy, infinite, interesting, minimum, perfect

11. Circle the words functioning as adverbs in the following sentences.

    This is a ridiculously easy test.

    I would certainly have loved to be there.

    Something had to drastically change.

    We ask you to stay safely in your seats.

    Drive safe.

12. Circle any of the following sentences that are *not* simple sentences.

    Writers write.

    Writers write books.

    Writers write books for readers.

    Writers write books, while readers read books.

    Writers are inspired to write.

13. Circle any of the following that are *not* sentence fragments.

    After going to town.

    Unless you do extra reading.

    The director addressed the meeting.

    The New York Times site.

14. What type of error does the following sentence exemplify? Circle the correct answer below.

    Gripping a pencil tightly, Sally scribbled her answers, she was running out of time to complete the test.

    comma splice   run-on sentence   sentence fragment

15. What form does the following sentence take? Circle the correct answer below.

    Whether I end up working for an organisation or whether I end up as a freelance writer, only time will tell.

    loose   periodic

16. What is the structure of the following sentence? Circle the correct answer below.

    Their dog, who was rescued from the pound, became a faithful companion to their children, who all loved him.

    compound   complex   compound-complex

17. In the following sentence, what part of speech or word class does the italicised word belong to? Circle the correct answer below.

    Sweet peas *flower* every year early in spring.

    verb   noun   adverb

18. In the following sentence, what sort of modifier does the italicised phrase exemplify? Circle the correct answer below.

    To apply for the job, his résumé had to be completely revised.

    squinting (or ambiguous)   dangling (or unattached)   misplaced

19. In the following sentence, what sort of modifier does the italicised word exemplify? Circle the correct answer below.

    People who cook for themselves *rarely* need cookbooks.

    squinting (or ambiguous)   dangling (or unattached)   misplaced

20. What do the following sentences exemplify? Circle the correct answer below.

> The purpose of this test is twofold: firstly, to make sure students understand the content. Helping students prepare for the final test is the second purpose.

is-ness   sentence fragments   lack of parallel structure

21. Which of the following sentences are truly passive? Remember that you need to have a part of the verb 'be', a past participle (and not one used as an adjective), and an agent (though the agent may be only implied).

> Room 21A is newly built and painted.
> This room is located in the new building.
> The rows of chairs are placed the wrong way.
> Here is a course of action that I believe should be taken.
> There is also a limited amount of parking.
> The building is divided into two types of seminar spaces.
> To accommodate the employees, desks are jammed together.
> There was only one thing that needed to be taken seriously.
> Restrooms are conveniently located in the building.
> The walls are painted cream.

5

How structure-class words and paragraphs work

'Preposition' at the start, then ending with a noun.
Along the flowing torrents, all custardly and brown.
Up above, the gathered clouds hooked upon the ridge.
Below, the swelling waters behind the crumbling bridge,
and then the deepest thrumming sound before a purple light
inside an orange chocolate-bar. Aloft, a rainbow kite.
Underneath, the drowning road, aside the shattered kerb . . .
(You'll never know what happens next. I cannot use a verb.)

MELANIE BAYES (POEM WRITTEN AS A RESPONSE TO THE CHALLENGE OF WRITING A 'PREPOSITION' POEM WITHOUT USING ANY VERBS)

Structure-class words, interjections, and paragraphs

In this chapter, I'll cover the structure-class words: pronouns, determiners (including articles), conjunctions, and prepositions. A fifth part of speech, the interjection, which I'll also cover in this chapter, doesn't have a grammatical or structuring function. The only structure-class words that change their form are pronouns. In the second part of the chapter, I'll discuss paragraphing.

Structure-class words

Pronouns

A **pronoun** is a noun substitute. Figure 5.1 sets out all the main personal pronouns in English, showing their **number** (singular or plural), **person**, and **case**.

Person (first, second, or third) depends on whether the person is speaking, being spoken to, or being spoken of. The concept of person also applies to things: 'it' is third person.

The **case** of a pronoun is determined by its position in a sentence and its relationship to the verb or preposition that it connects with. There are three main cases in traditional English grammar: subjective, objective, and possessive.

Number	Person	Subjective case (subject, or subject complement after a part of the verb be)	Objective case (object)	Possessive case (denotes ownership)
SINGULAR	first	*I*	*me*	*my, mine*
	second	*you*	*you*	*your, yours*
	third	*he, she, it*	*him, her, it*	*his, her, hers, its*
PLURAL	first	*we*	*us*	*our, ours*
	second	*you*	*you*	*your, yours*
	third	*they*	*them*	*their, theirs*

Figure 5.1 Case of personal pronouns

There are many types of pronouns in English: personal (including intensive and reflexive), demonstrative, interrogative, relative, indefinite, distributive, reciprocal, and expletive. Figure 5.2 below summarises the types of pronouns.

Demonstrative pronouns are used to point to *this, that, these, those,* and *such* (as subject, object, or complement):

> ***Those*** *were the best times we had.* (subject)
> *I would choose **those**.* (object)
> *The best times we had were **those**.* (complement)

Journalists often leave out a 'that'. This can contribute to ambiguity, as in the following sentence: *This is ever so disturbing, given the legislative package being pushed by the government will have practical consequences.* The sentence would be much clearer if a 'that' were inserted after 'given'.

Interrogative pronouns are used to pose questions: *who, whom* (for people); *what, where, which, whose* (for things and places).

> ***Who*** *was at the party?*
> ***Whom*** *did you see there?*
> ***What*** *was the highlight of the party?*
> ***Where*** *was the party held?*
> ***Which*** *bus did you take to get there?*
> ***Whose*** *car did you go home in?*

Relative pronouns are used to refer to an antecedent (a word that goes before) and connect it to a modifying clause: *who, whoever, whom, whomever* (for people, and for animals that have names); *whose* (for people, animals, and things); *that, which* (for animals and inanimate objects); *what* (an indefinite relative pronoun that stands for an undefined or unidentified antecedent).

> *She is the employee **who** gave me the details of the project.*
> *They'll brief **whoever** asks them.*
> *I'll write to **whom** it may concern.*
> *I'll brief **whomever** I like.*
> *I need to know **whose** proposal is the best.*
> *I know **what** they want.*
> *Here is the proposal **that** I have been working on for days.*
> *Here is my proposal, **which** I have been working on for days.*

The final two sentences in this list illustrate the difference in usage of *that* and *which*. Note that they have identical wording apart from the bolded pronouns. *The proposal **that** I have been working on* contains essential (restrictive) information; it's the one that I've been working on for days. The final sentence contains what we can call an 'aside'. It gives us non-essential (non-restrictive information) about the proposal. We are saying 'by the way, it's the proposal that I've been working on for days'. The comma before *which* is necessary to indicate that the clause that introduces it is an aside. The distinction between *that* and *which* is commonly adhered to in the United States, but not in Australia or Britain.

'That-creep' occurs when you use *that* instead of *who*: *She's the girl **that** arrived first. He's the one **that** won the prize.* Change *that* to *who* in both sentences.

Indefinite pronouns are used to refer to no one person or thing in particular, or to collective or anonymous people: *all, any, anybody, anyone, anything, both, each, either, everybody, everyone, everything, few, many, most, much more, neither, no one, nobody, none, nothing, one, several, somebody, someone, something, whoever*. Use a singular or plural verb, as appropriate.

Reflexive pronouns are used when the subject of the verb is also its object: *myself, yourself, himself, herself, itself, ourselves, yourselves, themselves*.

> I told **myself** not to worry about it.
>
> We prepared **ourselves** for the task.
>
> They prepared **themselves** for the task.

When used wrongly, a reflexive pronoun can be regarded as a 'genteelism': *She spoke to the boss and myself*. Change this to *She spoke to the boss and me*.

Intensive (emphatic) pronouns are used for emphasis: *myself, yourself, himself, herself, itself, ourselves, yourselves, themselves*.

> I **myself** witnessed the meltdown.
>
> They **themselves** took some of the blame.

Distributive pronouns are used to refer to things or people one at a time: *each, either, neither*. They are regarded as singular.

> **Each** of them trains very hard.
>
> **Neither** of them trains very hard.

Reciprocal pronouns are used to express a mutual action or relationship: *each other, one another.*

*They admired **each other**.* Use when referring to two people.
*They respected **one another**.* Use when there are more than two people.

In grammar, an **expletive** pronoun (as opposed to an expletive as an obscenity) is a construction beginning with *it is* or *there is/are*. The term comes from the Latin verb *explere*, meaning 'to fill out'. When an expletive fills the subject position in a sentence, the subject is empty of meaning. Expletives become problematic when they 'fill out' sentences that could be shorter and more direct, so, most of the time, you should avoid starting a sentence with an expletive.

Consider the following two sentences:

[It is] inevitable that grammarians will argue about some points of grammar.

When we remove the expletive *It is* and rewrite the sentence as *Grammarians inevitably argue about some points of grammar*, we have a more concise and effective sentence.

[There are] many students who have enrolled in the grammar course.

This can be rewritten more directly and concisely as *Many students have enrolled in the grammar course.*

There is an exception, which some grammarians call the 'existential expletive'. In the sentence *It is raining*, *it* is not being or doing anything. However, this is how we talk about the weather in English; the sentence cannot easily be rewritten, and is not problematic anyway.

Pronoun agreement and reference

The pronoun must agree in **person**, **number** (except in the case of the singular 'they'; see discussion later in this chapter), and **gender** with the noun that it substitutes for and refers to (its antecedent). The link needs to be close, clear, explicit (not tacit or implied), specific, and unable to be misconstrued. A pronoun must unambiguously connect with its antecedent:

Type of pronoun	Purpose/use/function	Examples
demonstrative	points to	this, that, these, those, such
interrogative	poses questions	who? whom? what? where? which? whose?
relative	connects an antecedent (a word that goes before) to a modifying clause	who, whoever, whom, whomever, that, what, which, whose
indefinite	refers to people or things in general and no one in particular	all, any, anybody, anyone, anything, both, each, either, everybody, everyone, everything, few, many, most, much more, neither, no one, nobody, none, nothing, one, several, somebody, someone, something, whoever
reflexive	used when the subject of the verb is also its object	myself, yourself, himself, herself, itself, ourselves, yourselves, themselves
intensive	provides emphasis	myself, yourself, himself, herself, itself, ourselves, yourselves, themselves
distributive	refers to persons or things one at a time	each, either, neither
reciprocal	used to express a mutual action or relationship	each other, one another
expletive	used to introduce a sentence, without adding meaning to the sentence	it, there

Figure 5.2 Types of pronouns

*The **writer** and his **father** lamented **his** ineptitude.*

Who is the inept one that the second *his* in the sentence refers to—the writer, his father, or some other person? It's impossible to tell.

Contentious pronoun issues

Two issues that are often discussed in grammar circles are the choice between *who* and *whom* and the use of a possessive noun or pronoun (or determiner—see explanation of this term below) in front of a verbal noun (gerund).

Use *who* for subjective case and *whom* for objective case.

Who *arrived this morning? To* **whom** *did they speak? Whom* is in the objective case after the preposition *to*.

Figure 5.1 clarifies this discussion.

When you have a dependent clause, whether you use *who* or *whom* is determined by the function of the pronoun in the dependent clause that it introduces, not by its function in the main clause.

The robot (antecedent) *to **whom** you've been sending flowers* (dependent clause) *is wearing his heart on his sleeve.*

*They don't know **who** made the decision.* Ask 'Who made the decision?' He did or she did, so *who* is correct.

*I'll talk to **whoever** will listen to me.* Ask 'Whoever will listen to me?' *He* will or *she* will or *they* will. So *whoever* is correct.

*Friends **whom** I rely on may be available.* Ask 'Whom may I rely on?' I may rely on *them*, so *whom* is correct.

Here's Bertie Wooster in Wodehouse's *Stiff Upper Lip, Jeeves* (1963) chastising himself for making a grammatical error:

[Spode] lowered his voice.
'I can speak frankly to you, Wooster, because you, too, love her.'
'Eh? Who?' I said. It should have been 'whom', I suppose, but that didn't occur to me at the time. (p. 108)

There's a witty video on the subject on YouTube. See Further Reading for this chapter at the end of the book.

Another contentious issue relates to the case of the possessive pronoun (or noun) used before a gerund/verbal noun (a part of a verb that functions as a noun and that always ends in *-ing*). Use the possessive case:

*They were surprised by **our** (not **us**) leaving so early.*

*They were surprised by the **parents'** (not **parents**) leaving so early.*

Non-discriminatory pronouns

A further controversial issue is that of non-discriminatory language, which I mentioned in Chapter 3. I stated that Australia had embraced the movement by widely adopting the singular 'they'. For example, *If anyone calls, **they** should ask for me.*

According to Dennis Baron (2015), gender-neutral pronouns such as *thon*, *xe*, *zhe*, and *zir* have been around for 150 years but have never been widely used. In a recent development, however, some American universities allow students to choose their preferred pronoun when they enrol. *The Washington Post Style Guide* endorses the singular 'they' (Mullin, 2015).

Determiners

Determiners are structure-class words that express grammatical-structural relationships. They precede and specify nouns and noun phrases. They indicate which particular example of the noun or noun phrase is being referred to by providing information about possession, definiteness, specificity, or quantity. Determiners, like adjectives, give information about nouns and noun phrases, but don't *describe* nouns the way adjectives do. So, determiners are not classified as adjectives. Determiners express relationships, while adjectives express attributes. NB: Some of these determiners can be classified as pronouns when they appear on their own. Figure 5.3 lists the different types of determiners.

__My__ next lecture will be on Monday.

__These__ students are excellent at grammar.

__The__ food at that café is home cooked.

In the above examples, the words *my*, *these*, and *the* are determiners because they specify which lecture, which students, and which food.

Articles	a/an, the
Demonstratives	this, that, these, those
Possessives	my, our, your, his, her, its, their
Indefinites	all, another, any, both, each, enough, either, every, few, less, many, more, most, much, neither, no, other, several, some
Cardinal numbers	one, two, three, four
Ordinal numbers	first, second, third, . . . last
Dates	The *June 2016* financial statement
Quantifiers	twice, triple, half

Figure 5.3 Determiners

In the examples below, the words *some*, *that*, and *another* are pronouns because they replace a noun:

I'll have **some**.
That was the first time I had met them.
Let's have **another**.

Prepositions

A **preposition** (from the Latin *praeponere*, 'to put before') is a word or phrase that establishes a relationship of time (*at, for, throughout, until*), place (*to, from, out of, into*), exception (*but for, besides, except*), cause or effect (*because of, on account of*), concession (*despite, notwithstanding*), opposition (*against*), or possession (*of, without*) with the noun or pronoun that usually—but not always—follows it.

A word functioning as a preposition always takes an object. The noun or pronoun following a preposition is in the objective case (see discussion of pronouns earlier in this chapter):

Let's slide **down** (preposition) *the hill* (objective case noun).
The child ran **to** (preposition) *her* (objective case pronoun).

Prepositions can function as other parts of speech. **Prepositional phrases** can function as adjectives (modifying nouns) or as adverbs (modifying verbs, adjectives, or other adverbs):

Summers spent lazily **at the beach** (adverb) were a time **for reading** (adjective).

We headed **for the island** (adverb).

Let's sit **down** (adverb).

Which one to use?
Prepositions are problematic for speakers and writers of English because they are so easy to get wrong. English has more than a hundred prepositions, and some expressions can take several different prepositions in different situations.

I have a knack **for** remembering faces.

They have a knack **of** making people comfortable.

There is a knack **to** using a corkscrew.

Evidenced in or *by*? There are no rules to help you decide. Doing a Google survey to see which one has the highest usage can help.

All of the following are examples of misused prepositions that I have noted (the correction is indicated in bold):

He is not to be mistaken ~~with~~ **for** our local rock star.

The current offer applies ~~for~~ **to** free travel on Brisbane buses.

They were curious ~~to~~ **about** where they were headed.

Final sentence ~~to~~ **of** the piece.

Typical ~~to~~ **of** diary writing.

They arrived ~~to~~ **at** the party.

Ending a sentence with a preposition
This can't be done in Latin, where the preposition always appears before the noun (*ad infinitum*), but it's not a problem in English, usually, though there are still people who object to it. To demonstrate the absurdity of the 'rule', Winston Churchill is alleged to have constructed the pompous sentence 'This is the type of arrant pedantry up with which I will not put'.

The following examples are all acceptable (if not necessarily always elegant):

> *Achievements that I am proud **of**.*
>
> *The book that I told you **about**.*
>
> *The position that they found themselves **in**.*
>
> *What are you looking **for**?*
>
> *What did you want to bring the book I didn't want to be read **to out of up for**?*

'Like'

The word *like* is acceptable as a preposition, but not as a conjunction:

> *The person in that portrait looks **like** me.* (preposition)
>
> *It happened just **like** (as) I said it would happen.* (conjunction)
>
> *You're looking around **like** (as if) you've misplaced something.* (conjunction)

In the last two sentences, 'like' is functioning as a conjunction, which is not acceptable, so it needs to be replaced by a conjunction: *as* or *as if*.

Prepositional verbs

I discussed these in Chapter 4 in the section on verbs. *The Cambridge Guide to Australian English Usage* (Peters, 2007) distinguishes between the following sentences:

> *He **ran up** a big bill.* (Prepositional verb: *ran* and *up* can't be separated. They form a distinct concept.)
>
> *He ran **up a big hill**.* (*Up* is a preposition taking *a big hill* as its object. *Ran* and *up* can be separated: *He ran at full speed up a big hill.*)

Remove superfluous prepositions in expressions such as *meet ~~up with~~*, *face ~~up to~~*.

Conjunctions

Conjunctions connect sentences, clauses, and words, providing cohesion through what some writers think of metaphorically as 'glue' or 'mortar'. A more technical term for devices that serve to make writing cohesive is 'cohesive ties'. Conjunctions provide one kind of cohesive tie. I'll cover the others in the section of this chapter on paragraphs.

There are three types of conjunctions: **coordinating**, **subordinating**, and **correlative** conjunctions (though correlative conjunctions consist of combinations of coordinating conjunctions and other words). Another connecting word that is a type of conjunction is the **conjunctive adverb**, which is the part of speech that connects independent clauses.

Coordinating (the FANBOYS—for, and, nor, but, or, yet, so)
This is a complete list of the **coordinating conjunctions**, which always connect words or word groups of the same kind, that is, nouns, verbs, adjectives, adverbs, phrases, and independent and dependent clauses.

> *I hurried to the library **and** I borrowed a book.* (independent clause + independent clause)
>
> *I hurried to the library, **but** it was closed.* (independent clause + independent clause)
>
> *I went to the library, **for** the teacher had told us to meet there.* (independent clause + dependent clause)
>
> *I hurried to the library, **or**, rather, I sauntered to it.* (independent clause + independent clause)
>
> *I went to the library **so** you don't need to go.* (independent clause + independent clause)
>
> *I hurried to the library, **yet** I still didn't get there before it closed.* (independent clause + independent clause)

Subordinating
Subordinating conjunctions connect dependent with independent clauses. They denote:
- cause or effect (e.g., *as, because, in order that, since, so that*)
- comparison or contrast (e.g., *as, as if, as though, rather than, than, whereas, whether, while*)
- concession (e.g., *although, as if, even if, even though, though*)
- condition (e.g., *if, even if, if only, provided, since, unless, when, whenever, whether*)
- purpose (e.g., *in order that, so that, that*)
- place (e.g., *where, wherever*)
- time (e.g., *as long as, before, now that, once, since, till/until, when, whenever, while*).

Note that some of these (*as*, *since*, and *while*) can be used in various contexts, so be careful to avoid ambiguity when you use them. For example, *Since it's Tuesday, I'm going to my book club.* It's not clear whether the conjunction *since* here indicates time or purpose.

Correlative

Correlative conjunctions are formed when coordinating conjunctions pair with other words; correlative conjunctions are used in pairs to link two equal (balanced) grammatical items. They can indicate:
- addition (*both . . . and*; *not only . . . but also*)
- alternative *(either . . . or*; *whether . . . or)*
- comparison (*as . . . as*)
- negation (*neither . . . nor*)
- substitution (*not . . . but*).

Ensure that the two linked items are phrased in a balanced (parallel) way:

> **Both** those who read regularly **and** those who don't can join the reading group. (balanced)

> **Not only** will they enjoy the discussion **but also** take part in the refreshments of tea and cakes that come with it. (unbalanced; rewrite as They will enjoy **not only** the discussion **but also** the tea and cakes that come with it.)

Conjunctive adverbs

Another kind of joining or connecting word is the **conjunctive adverb**. The sole use of conjunctive abverbs is to connect independent clauses separated by a semicolon. As adverbs, they describe the relation of ideas between clauses, such as:
- addition (*in addition, further, likewise, moreover*)
- cause or effect (*consequently, therefore*)
- comparison or contrast (*however*)
- emphasis (*inarguably, undoubtedly*)
- time (*at last, finally, meanwhile*).

Whereas conjunctions joining clauses always come at the beginning of a clause, conjunctive adverbs can come at the beginning, the end, or somewhere in between. In the following sentences, note the different positions of the conjunctive adverb *however*, and especially note the punctuation accompanying it:

> Education is a great leveller; **however**, it can't always be relied upon.
>
> Education is a great leveller; it can't always be relied upon, **however**.
>
> Education is a great leveller; it can't, **however**, always be relied upon.

Note that *however* functions not only as a conjunctive adverb, but can also function as just an adverb, as it does in the following sentence:

> **However** hard I try, I can't convince them of the value of reading.

Interjections/exclamations

An **interjection** is a short word or phrase that expresses passion or emotion or commands attention. Interjections rarely occur in academic or formal professional writing. Most parts of speech can serve as interjections, including nouns (*Man!*), pronouns (*Me!*), verbs (*Follow!*), adjectives (*Great!*), and adverbs (*Slowly!*).

Mark Nichol has listed 100 'small but expressive' interjections in an 'incomplete inventory of interjections' on the Daily Writing Tips site. These include the gaming acronym *WOOT* (also spelled *w00t*), meaning 'we own the other team' (in other words, we beat them). Have some fun checking them out. Even more fascinating than Mark's post, which is listed in Further Reading, is the overwhelming number of responses to it, which you might like to skim. See also Richard Nordquist's post, also listed in Further Reading, '"Oh, Wow!": Notes on interjections', on grammar.about.com.

Analysing sentences

This chapter covers the final material on grammar and parts of speech. Figure 5.4 shows how you can use your knowledge to analyse sentences by placing them into their syntactical slots and parse words by specifying their person, number, and the function that a word performs in a sentence, that is, their part of speech. Nouns and pronouns have case; verbs can be classified according to their tense, mood, and voice, and whether they are helping or auxiliary verbs, linking verbs, transitive or intransitive verbs, and finite or non-finite verbs.

Sentence	*(I)*	*thank*	*you.*	
Analyse segment/ slot/ syntax	subject	predicate		
	subject	verb	direct object	
Parse				
Person	first		second	
Number	singular	singular	singular/plural	
Part of speech	(personal) pronoun	(transitive) verb	(personal) pronoun	
Case	subjective/ nominative case		objective case	
Tense		present		
Mood		declarative/ indicative		
Voice		active		
John	***gave the cake to her.***			
subject	predicate			
John	gave	*the cake*	*to her.*	
subject	verb	direct object	indirect object	
noun	verb	determiner (article) + noun	preposition + pronoun (*her* is a pronoun in the objective case after the preposition *to*)	

Figure 5.4 Analysis and parsing

Paragraphs

Paragraphs are the blocks from which pieces of writing are built. A paragraph usually comprises a series of sentences, all relating to a main idea or topic. A good paragraph is a unified paragraph, structured so that all of its parts share the same focus, tone, and viewpoint, that is, person, as in first, second, and third person.

In his autobiography *My Early Life* (1930), Winston Churchill captured this concept when he said:

> Just as the sentence contains one idea in all its fullness, so the paragraph should embrace a distinct episode; and as sentences should follow one another in harmonious sequence, so the paragraphs must fit on to one another like the automatic couplings of railway carriages. (pp. 211–12)

Churchill was an accomplished writer. Here, he emphasises the logical sequence that good paragraphs—and, indeed, all effective writing—should take: a sentence expresses an idea; a paragraph does the same using several sentences; a piece of writing does so, too, using several paragraphs.

Paragraphs must be well planned and well structured. Most expository or analytical paragraphs in academic or professional writing begin with a **topic sentence** that states the central idea, claim, or problem that controls or guides the rest of the paragraph. In other words, it tells the reader what to expect.

The topic sentence is followed by the **body** of the paragraph, which usually consists of several sentences. The body develops or discusses what the topic sentence has stated. The body justifies the main idea, providing evidence to support or explain that idea in greater detail. This is where you, as the writer, might include data (such as facts or statistics), testimonies, anecdotes, or descriptions. In the body of a paragraph, you can describe, examine, and analyse.

The **conclusion** of a paragraph summarises what you have covered in the body of the paragraph, again in relation to the topic sentence. Good conclusions often also link to the next paragraph.

This formula is by no means set in stone, and is generally applied to paragraphs in technical, professional, or academic writing, which argue, claim, and analyse. Other forms of writing—for example, narrative, creative prose—do not necessarily require conclusions, evidence, or even explicitly stated topic sentences.

The most important points to remember are that a paragraph should be unified, coherent, and adequately developed. In other words, a paragraph should stick to one idea or purpose, follow a logical sequence, and discuss the main idea fully and adequately.

Some students learn that a paragraph must contain a certain number of sentences, but this is not a genuine or helpful rule. A paragraph should be as long as it needs to be. So, the length of a paragraph depends on its purpose. A complex idea might need a long paragraph to properly develop it, whereas a summary or a minor point of interest might need only a couple of short sentences. In some styles of writing, such as newspaper writing, a paragraph often consists of a single sentence, but it will be a sentence that tries to answer the five Ws and an H: *what, when, where, who, why*, and *how*.

When considering how long a paragraph should be, also think of your reader. A solid page of text is unattractive and overwhelming. Just as you may need to break up a sentence that's too long, you may have to break up a paragraph so that the page will not seem crowded. Paragraph breaks give your reader time to pause.

Thomas Kane (quoted in Safire and Safir, 1992) says:

> No one can say how long a paragraph should be. Subject, purpose, audience, editorial fashion, and individual preference, all affect the length and complexity of paragraphs. As a rough rule of thumb, however, you might think of expository paragraphs in terms of 120 or 150 words. An occasional short paragraph of 15–20 words may work very well; so may an occasional long one of 300. (p. 169)

Remember that paragraphs are not like pictures; your readers can't see what's there all at once. They will see what you are saying as they read. For this reason, you should carefully organise what you are going to say, and consider the best sequence in which to convey it.

For example, perhaps your argument could be neatly summarised in three points. In this case, arrange those points so that they logically and clearly flow from one to the other. Use your topic sentence to let your readers know in brief what you are going to say. This will make it easier for them to organise their thoughts as they read.

It's helpful to give information first in broad terms, and to become more specific and offer greater detail as you move through the paragraph. However, there are no fixed rules about how to order information in paragraphs. Any order that you choose will work, as long as what you have written is clear, sequential, and relates to both your topic and your reader.

Cohesion, as I mentioned in the section of this chapter on conjunctions, is the 'glue' that 'sticks everything together'. Without cohesion, a paragraph is just a list of sentences. While each sentence may be good in its own right, forming sentences into an effective paragraph means binding the sentences together. Cohesion is achieved through deliberate and effective use of punctuation, word choice, and sentence structure—using connecting and summary words, relative pronouns, and repetition. We class all of these as 'cohesive ties'.

Within a paragraph, when you are amplifying, elaborating, or reinforcing your message, you can use examples and lists. You will need to use conjunctions as transitional expressions to move between the various parts of a paragraph. Transitional expressions can contrast or qualify, continue, show cause and effect, exemplify, or summarise. In summary, you can achieve cohesion and coherence in paragraphs by expressing one focused idea and using:

- the same topic, tone, and viewpoint
- repetition of key words and phrases
- pronouns that link back to previous words
- connecting words
- summary words
- punctuation.

The last word

In this chapter, I have covered structure-class words including the many kinds of pronouns and issues related to them, determiners, prepositions, conjunctions, and interjections. I have also shown how to analyse sentences and how to achieve coherence and cohesion in paragraphs. The activities below will test your understanding of how structure-class words and paragraphs work.

Activities

Answers are at the back of the book.

1. The following three paragraphs disregard the need for a focused discussion of a topic, a consistent tone, or a consistent point of view. Read the paragraphs and write a couple of sentences in your journal about how each flouts the advice given in this chapter.

   > In this essay, your coverage of your topic is not detailed enough. You list various social media platforms but, instead of discussing their benefits, you give many examples of writers who have stopped using Facebook. Many Facebook users do tend to overshare and this can be very annoying, but maybe you should be more tolerant than those who have abandoned Facebook. They may be too busy with aspects of their lives. I have heard of people who belong to more than 100 Facebook groups. I don't know how they can keep up. Can you go back through your essay and revise it to reflect on the benefits of social media?

   > I have great pleasure in informing you that your application for a scholarship to do your PhD at this university has been successful. If you decide to accept this scholarship, which carries a generous stipend, you will need to contact us immediately so that we can make the necessary arrangements. Your allocated supervisor will then contact you to inform you about your accommodation in our student wing. And you'll have a cool time hanging out with the buddies you'll make here.

   > You will need to fill out the Application for a Visa form before you leave. Take it to your current supervisor for signing. Once this has been done, the student may make travel arrangements.

2. After reading the section in this chapter on paragraphs, answer the following quiz. There may be more than one correct answer to some of the questions.
   a) Which of the following sentences best defines a paragraph?
      i) A paragraph is an arbitrary block of text in a document.
      ii) A paragraph is a series of sentences one after the other.

  iii) A paragraph is a group of sentences relating to a central idea and appearing in a logical sequence.
b) A topic sentence . . . (tick all that apply)
  i) states the central idea or focus of the paragraph
  ii) tells the reader what to expect
  iii) develops or justifies the main idea of the paragraph in detail.
c) A well-developed paragraph should . . . (tick all that apply)
  i) contain more than five sentences
  ii) reinforce the main idea
  iii) lead the reader logically through a series of points.
d) A good paragraph conclusion should . . . (tick all that apply)
  i) remind the reader what the paragraph was about
  ii) summarise the paragraph's main points
  iii) develop a new idea that has not yet been mentioned
  iv) provide a logical link to the next paragraph.
e) In certain styles of writing, a paragraph may sometimes consist of only one sentence. True or false?
f) Pronouns, repetition, and punctuation are examples of:
  i) introductory phrases
  ii) cohesive ties
  iii) common writing errors.
g) When constructing an effective paragraph, a writer should . . . (tick all that apply)
  i) plan what they are going to write
  ii) decide on the most coherent sequence of ideas
  iii) be mindful that too many long paragraphs may overwhelm a reader visually
  iv) apply a formulaic structure no matter the type of text or idea
  v) develop the main idea by amplifying, elaborating, and reinforcing
  vi) state the main idea repeatedly without providing evidence
  vii) move abruptly from one point to the next.
h) *In conclusion, clearly, finally,* and *in short* are examples of what type of transitional expression?
  i) summarising
  ii) exemplifying
  iii) contrasting or qualifying.

i) What linking word or phrase could you *not* use instead of *likewise*?
   i)   by the same token
   ii) similarly
   iii) however
   iv) also.
j) The sentence *Grammar goblins are busy creatures: they pounce on punctuation, sort through spellings, and clear out clauses* contains . . . (tick all that apply)
   i)   an introductory clause
   ii) a pronoun linking to an antecedent
   iii) a parallel list
   iv) phrasal verbs
   v)   a compound noun
   vi) an adjective.

3. Read the passage below that I wrote about plain language and identify the 'cohesive ties' that I used to bind the sentences and the paragraphs. Just to remind you, the ties include punctuation, word choice, and sentence structure—using connecting and summary words, relative pronouns, and repetition. Coloured highlighters will help you with this exercise.

> Plain language, still called 'plain English' in the United Kingdom, has been the focus of extensive discussion, research, and legislation since the 1960s in the USA, the UK, Canada, and Australia. More recently, the plain language movement has been taken up in Europe. In Europe, France, Italy, Germany, Denmark, the Netherlands, Portugal, and Sweden have adopted plain language; other countries such as Mexico have adopted it, as well as New Zealand, Singapore, Hong Kong, and South Africa.
>
> The key principle of plain language is that the intended reader can use the document for its intended purpose. The key aims of plain language are that the reader can understand and use the document.
>
> The researcher Bryan Garner regrets that the set phrases 'plain language' and 'plain English' contain the word 'plain', because he thinks that it suggests the idea of 'drab and ugly'. However, the term has no serious competitor, so advocates of plain language need to continually explain what they mean by

it. Another researcher, Balmford, argues that the term 'plain language' is inaccurate because it places too much emphasis on words and sentences. He says that plain language involves elements of the whole document: content, language, structure, and design. No plain-language proponent would argue with his statement.

4. Correct, where necessary, the pronoun-case problems in the sentences below.
   a) I like any person who has nous.
   b) To whom should we complain?
   c) Whomever you choose for your team needs to be fit.
   d) Whom do you think you're kidding?
   e) Who do you think will win the election?
   f) My mood will determine whom I'll speak to.
   g) Want to know whom to blame for karaoke?
   h) I am she through whom enquiry can be made.
   i) Bob and me travel a good deal.
   j) He gave the flowers to Jane and I.
   k) Let's you and I go to the library.
   l) Us travellers like comfort.
   m) They provided vouchers for we passengers.
   n) They like movies more than me.
   o) Eating vegetables keeps them—John and he—healthy.
   p) Herself and me went to dinner.
   q) Susan and myself are twins.
   r) when it comes to we girls
   s) between you and I
   t) Why is the government not listening to we, the people?

5. Which preposition would you use in each of the following examples? NB: Some of these expressions may take both of the suggested prepositions; check in your preferred dictionary.
   a) I have no qualms *with/about* the project's aims.
   b) a hotbed *of/for* gossip
   c) fluent *at/in*
   d) suitability *to/for* an event
   e) take umbrage *at/to*

f) dance *to/with*
g) devastated *by/with*
h) drizzle *over/down*
i) parallel *with/to*
j) conform *with/to*
k) an aversion *for/to*
l) cater *to/for*
m) smitten *with/by*
n) adapt *from/to*.

6

How punctuation works

> Punctuation marks are the stitches that hold
> the quilt of language together.
> **THEODOR ADORNO**

> [Punctuation marks are] cues to the reader for how very
> quickly to organize the various phrases and clauses of the
> sentence so the sentence as a whole makes sense.
> **DAVID FOSTER WALLACE AND BRYAN GARNER**

> Punctuation is more than just a game for
> pedants. It's vital to convey meaning.
> **HARRY MOUNT**

Why punctuate?

Because excellent punctuation demonstrates our command of sentence structure, grammar, and style, we need to take punctuation seriously. Punctuation reveals the structure of our writing to our readers. Clear structure clarifies the meaning of our writing. You need to learn how punctuation marks reveal structure and relationships between words in a sentence and, in doing so, clarify meaning. You can have a grammatically incorrect sentence that's perfectly punctuated, but you can't have an incorrectly punctuated sentence that's perfectly grammatical. Learn to use specific marks in an informed way; study sentences in well-punctuated prose to learn the particular marks. Construct your own set of guidelines for punctuating based on the material in this chapter. At the conclusion of this chapter, Figure 6.2 presents a set of sentences that demonstrates the punctuation patterns for the main punctuation marks.

Punctuation should be there quietly doing its job, not drawing attention to itself, and consistently indicating connections between words and ideas. Each punctuation mark should convey a signal to your reader and be noticeable only to punctuation vigilantes. The American novelist Ernest Hemingway, renowned as a sparse stylist, apparently never used the semicolon, but he doubtless knew it existed. The American writer Mark Twain is alleged to have sent his publisher a page of punctuation marks for his editor to insert where needed, as a gesture of Twain's disdain for punctuation. The British playwright, poet, and iconoclast Oscar Wilde had such concern for getting his punctuation perfect that he once said he spent a morning putting in a comma, and the afternoon taking it out.

Punctuation can help us to control the pace and rhythm of our writing. However, the suggestion to insert a comma where you would pause if reading aloud is not good advice. Although a comma in writing *can* indicate where a speaker would pause, a speaker's pauses will not necessarily always coincide with a grammatically required comma, so the only time that you'll need to insert punctuation that mirrors spoken communication is when you write text to be spoken aloud, such as in speeches for administrators or politicians. Spoken and written language differ in form. Writing isn't merely 'written-down speaking'. In addition to the words themselves, speaking conveys meaning through vocal quality: tone, pitch, volume, pace, pauses, emphasis, and rhythm. Writing needs to use punctuation to help convey meaning, particularly in formal, professional writing. Creative writing often subverts 'normal' punctuation for narrative or dramatic effect, and that's fine.

Punctuation can be crucial to understanding, as Gloria Rosenthal shows in the cleverly constructed letter reproduced below (originally published in *Games* magazine in 1984). The message of the letter depends entirely on how it is punctuated. One version is a 'Dear John' letter (in World War II, many unfortunate men serving in the armed forces received such letters, telling them that their relationships were over); the other is not. Reading the two versions of the letter aloud will help you to decide whether or not they are 'Dear John' letters. Is this one?

> Dear John,
> I want a man who knows what love is all about. You are generous, kind, thoughtful. People who are not like you admit to being useless and inferior. You have ruined me for other men. I yearn for you. I have no feelings whatsoever when we're apart. I can be forever happy. Will you let me be yours?
> Gloria

What about this one?

> Dear John,
> I want a man who knows what love is. All about you are generous, kind, thoughtful people who are not like you. Admit to being useless and inferior. You have ruined me. For other men, I yearn. For you, I have no feelings whatsoever. When we're apart, I can be forever happy. Will you let me be?
> Yours,
> Gloria

Categories of punctuation marks

There are fifteen 'extant' punctuation marks (that is, those that we still use); there are some that are 'extinct', such as the punctus percontativus (⸮) to close a rhetorical question (one where the answer is so obvious as to be unnecessary), the interrobang (‽) to close a simultaneous question and exclamation (What on earth is that‽), and the dash hybrid (:—) where the dash is unnecessary. There also are a few that some punctuation aficionados would love to see come into regular use. In this chapter, I'll concentrate on the ones we still use. The Design Taxi site provides a useful infographic (see Chapter 7), 'How to use 15 punctuation marks', sorted 'in order of how much they do (and how hard they should be to learn)'.

The fifteen punctuation marks that writers regularly use are the **full stop** (or **period**), the **comma**, the **colon**, the **semicolon**, the **apostrophe**,

quotation marks, the **question mark**, the **exclamation mark**, **en** and **em dashes**, the **hyphen**, **round brackets**, **square brackets**, the **slash**, and the **ellipsis**. Some writers also regard the asterisk as a punctuation mark.

There are four main groups of punctuation marks: stoppers, linkers, intruders, and intoners. **Stoppers** include the full stop (or period) and the comma. **Linkers** include the colon, semicolon, dash, and hyphen. **Intruders** include the comma pair, bracket pair, and dash pair. The hierarchy of pairs (handles) comprises commas (for the smallest break), then parentheses, then em dashes (for the longest break).

Intoners include the question and exclamation marks. Other marks that don't fit into those categories are the apostrophe, quotation marks, the slash, and the ellipsis.

I'll cover all of these marks in turn, as well as the punctuation of lists.

The full stop

The full stop, or period, is used to signify the end of a full sentence or a sentence fragment. Alberto Manguel quotes Isaac Babel: 'No iron can stab the heart with such force as a period in exactly the right place' (2010, p. 116). It is also used to make certain abbreviations, but you need to check how abbreviations are punctuated by the people you are writing for, because usage differs in different writing arenas. Generally, you'll find that the use of full stops in titles such as *Dr* and in abbreviations such as *e.g.* and *p.m.* is diminishing.

The comma

The word *comma* comes from the Greek word (*komma*) for a cut or segment. Australian and British writers take a more minimalist approach to commas than American writers do. See Ben Yagoda's 2014 article in Further Reading, in which he claims that 'punctuational minimalism has emerged as one of the hallmarks of casual online style'.

There have been suggestions recently that the prevalence of texting and tweeting may bring about the disappearance of commas (Larson-Walker, 2014). Until that happens—and let's hope it doesn't—we need to use commas to indicate breaks in the structure of sentences. If there's no break in the structure of a sentence, don't put in a comma.

Commas have many uses:

- They're placed after an introductory sentence element: *However hard I try, I still can't get everything right. On Tuesdays, I always go to the library.*
- They prevent overreading: *The trip had been fun, for her frame of mind was always good when she headed off for a holiday.* Can you see why the comma after *fun* prevents the reader 'reading on' and thinking that the trip had been fun for her state of mind? Another example would be in the sentence *After I put my coat on, the dog knew that it was time to go out.*
- They separate independent clauses: *The steering was stiff, but the car cruised like a dream.* Notice one of the FANBOYS is used. (See Chapter 4 for the FANBOYS mnemonic.)
- They substitute for the word *and* between adjectives: *the heavy, shiny coin.*
- They set off non-essential information: *Our car, a red sedan, won.* The comma 'handles' separate out the description of the car, which is not essential to the meaning of the sentence and could be removed. In the sentence *The actor Hugh Laurie released an album,* Let Them Talk, *that was a tribute to New Orleans blues,* there are no comma handles around the actor's name because his name is essential to the sentence.

Although the comma is one of the most common and apparently unobtrusive of punctuation marks, commas can be surprisingly powerful, as the following anecdote demonstrates. The journalist James Thurber was once asked why Harold Ross, the editor of *The New Yorker*, had put a comma after 'dinner' in the sentence 'After dinner, the men went into the living room'. Thurber's answer: 'This particular comma was Ross's way of giving the men time to push back their chairs and stand up' (Truss, 2003, p. 70). Ross's comma after 'dinner' is an example of using a comma after an introductory sentence element.

Contentious commas

The comma in the phrase 'Go, set a watchman' from Isaiah 21:6 was eliminated by the late author Harper Lee from the title of her book *Go Set a Watchman* (2015). She apparently said to her publisher, who had included the comma in the page proofs of her novel: 'This is my book. And there is no comma' (Dugdale, 2015). We can only speculate on her reason for insisting that the comma be removed.

The vocative comma is used in expressions such as *Hi, friend!*, *Hello, gorgeous!*, *Good morning, colleagues!* I like to use it, but it is doubtless anathema to those writers who minimise punctuation wherever they can. It's unlikely that the absence of a vocative comma in 'Hi Alice' would create ambiguity, but commas can be essential to clarify text.

A persistently controversial comma is the one used by writers who are consistently fervent advocates of it—to separate the final *and* or *or* in a series from the item immediately before it. It is variously called the **Oxford** or **Harvard** or **serial comma**, and used when you have a series of at least three items, as in: *Remember to check your grammar, spelling, and punctuation*. The Oxford comma isn't standard in Australia, but it is sometimes necessary to use it to avoid ambiguity. You will never be wrong if you use it. I like to use it for consistency.

Robert Ritter, author of *The Oxford Guide to Style*, enthusiastically endorses the Oxford comma, which has been part of Oxford University Press style for more than a century. He says that it's commonly used by other publishers in the UK and also forms a routine part of style in US and Canadian English (2002, p. 121). The quintessential English author Beatrix Potter used the Oxford comma; I have a china mug endorsed with the sentence 'Once upon a time there were four little rabbits: Flopsy, Mopsy, Cottontail, and Peter'. You will have noticed that I am a fan of the Oxford comma and have used it in this book.

In a 2014 interview, Jessica Lahey, a reporter for *The Atlantic*, asked Stephen King: 'Oxford comma? Yea or nay?' King said:

> It can go either way. For instance, I like 'Jane bought eggs, (comma) milk, (comma) bread, (comma) and a candy bar for her brother', but I also like 'Jane raced home and slammed the door', because I want to feel the whole thing as a single breath.

However, he is incorrect here; while his first sentence contains a clear example of the Oxford comma, there's no call for it in his second sentence, because there is no series.

Misuse of commas

Be careful not to misuse commas (although you might get a free beer, as I did, if someone compiling a menu puts in an unnecessary comma, such as the one between *beer* and *batter* in the following menu item: 'Northern Reef Spotted Cod, Beer, Batter, Chips—$17').

Don't put a comma between a subject and a verb unless you insert an aside or interruption. In *The cat, sat on the mat*, you don't need that comma after *cat*, but in *Cats, who are friendly creatures, love milk*, those comma 'handles' are fine. Make sure that you have both handles, though.

Can you see why there are comma handles in the sentence *Madonna, the singer, staged a comeback* but not in this one: *The singer Madonna staged a comeback*? In the first sentence, *the singer* is an aside that's not essential to the meaning of the sentence. In the second sentence, the name *Madonna* is essential to the meaning of the sentence.

The following sentence, which was in a newly printed brochure for a hotel that prided itself on its discretion about its guest list and was a haven for publicity-avoiding celebrities, was reprinted because the management was worried that it contradicted the hotel's ethos by missing out the commas around 'as you know': 'We won't mention names, but as you know our clientele includes some of the world's most famous and discerning travellers'. The point was that celebrities relied on the fact that they could stay incognito at the hotel because the public did not know that they were staying there. The brochure was reprinted, with commas setting aside 'as you know'.

Many court cases have rested on the placement or absence of a comma. Several years ago, a Canadian company, Rogers Communications Inc., lost a case, which potentially cost it $2.1 million, when the inclusion of a comma permitted a contract that Rogers expected to be in place for five years to be cancelled after one year. The contract stated that the agreement 'shall continue in force for a period of five years from the date it is made, and thereafter for successive five-year terms, unless and until terminated by one year prior notice in writing by either party'. Rogers thought that it had locked in a five-year deal, but the comma before 'unless' allowed the deal to be scrapped with only a year's notice because the phrase 'and thereafter for successive five-year terms' is treated as an 'aside', and not as an essential part of the sentence. The company's lawyers argued that the intent of the deal trumped the significance of the comma, but they lost the case.

The colon

The colon is sometimes called an 'announcement mark'. It is 'anticipatory', because it is used to announce that an explanation, clarification, interpretation, amplification, or illustration will follow it. The colon also introduces dot-point lists and quotes, as in 'Bond: "Good morning. My name is Bond . . . James Bond"'. And here's a somewhat hyperbolic advertisement for chocolate: 'Only two things in life really matter: Dark chocolate and light chocolate'.

The colon follows an independent clause. Don't use it to separate a verb or a preposition from its object, as occurs mistakenly in the following sentences: *My favourite authors are: Madeleine St John and Dorothy L. Sayers. I am very fond of: rose and violet cream chocolates.*

The semicolon

The semicolon has two main uses.

The first is to separate closely related independent clauses that require a separation more prolonged than a conjunction such as *and*, *but*, and *or*. For example, *Speech is silver; silence is golden.*

'To write is human, to edit is divine'. Here's Stephen King again, in the acknowledgements in *On Writing* (2001). He really should have used a semicolon after 'human', because the sentence has two independent clauses. As it is, he has created a comma splice, which should be avoided in formal writing (see Chapter 4).

There was great excitement among many New Yorkers about the perfectly placed semicolon in the following sentence when it appeared on a message board in New York City subway stations in 2008: 'Please put it in the trash can; that's good news for everyone'. Louis Menand, an English professor at Harvard, pronounced the use of the semicolon by Neil Neches, the writer of the message, who has a Master's degree in creative writing, to be 'impeccable' (Roberts, 2008).

Lewis Thomas (1979), in his 'Notes on punctuation', enthuses about the semicolon:

The semicolon tells you that there is still some question about the preceding full sentence; something needs to be added . . . It is almost always a greater pleasure to come across a semicolon than a full stop. The full stop tells you that is that; if you didn't get all the meaning you wanted or expected, you got all the writer intended to parcel out and now you have to move along. But with a semicolon there you get a pleasant little feeling of expectancy; there is more to come; read on; it will get clearer. (p. 126)

The second main use of the semicolon is to punctuate listed items that are internally punctuated, for example, *Remember to check your grammar, especially agreement of subjects and verbs; your spelling, especially tricky words like 'liaison'; and your punctuation, especially your use of the apostrophe.*

The dash
The dash splits; the hyphen joins.

There are two main kinds of dash, the em dash and the en dash.

The **em dash** (—), also known as the **em rule**, is used, unspaced, as a pair to mark off a parenthetical element in a sentence (when the break is more abrupt than the use of commas or parentheses allows): *We knew that we—even with our training—were no match for them.*

It can also gather up a series of thoughts by commenting on the preceding text: *Style, pizzazz, superior cooking ability, a very nice holiday house, a love of cats—Cecilia's criteria for a flatmate were extensive.*

And it can be used to signal an abrupt change in a sentence's structure: *Of all the flowers, I still prefer the heliconia to its showy cousin—oh, but I forgot! It's your identical twin, Erwin, who's the botanist!*

A pair of em dashes is sometimes used to mark off a parenthetical element in a sentence. This is called a **dash pair**. *These three books—on presenting, interviewing, and negotiating—are helpful.*

Never use more than two em dashes in a sentence.

The **en dash** (–) is used, unspaced, in spans of figures and expressions relating to time and distance, in place of the word *to*: *1948–2016*. Or, you could write 'between 1948 and 2016' or 'from 1948 to 2016'.

It is also used to express an association between words that retain their separate identity, as in *mother–daughter relationships.*

Increasingly, a spaced en dash (–) is being used in place of the em dash in many documents. Check the preferred style of your workplace or university.

The hyphen

The hyphen is used in compound expressions to avoid ambiguity and misreading. For example, the phrase *a man eating crocodile* means a man who is eating some crocodile. However, in the phrase *a man-eating crocodile*, where *man* and *eating* form a compound, you now have a crocodile that eats people. The sentence *There were 50-odd students at the lecture* means that there were about 50 students at the lecture. Without the hyphen, the meaning is quite different, and would be rather insulting to the students.

Use the hyphen in cases such as the following: *all-inclusive, a go-between, un-Australian. A little-used car*, but *a small used car.*

A hyphen isn't used most of the time when a compound adjective comes after the noun: *a long-term plan*, but *that plan is long term*. Combinations that do call for the hyphen are *well-known player* and *fast-moving car*. However, you don't usually need a hyphen when there's a combination of adverb and adjective: *the ludicrously appropriate plan*.

In 2007, it was announced that in a new edition of the *Shorter Oxford English Dictionary* (OED) about 16,000 words had succumbed to the pressures of the internet age and had lost their hyphens. The team that compiled the *Shorter OED* dropped the hyphens after searching through more than two billion words, consisting of full sentences that appeared in newspapers, books, websites, and blogs from 2000 onwards. Rabinovitch (2007) noted, however, that 'hyphens have not lost their place altogether. The *Shorter OED* editor commended their first-rate service rendered to English in the form of compound adjectives, much like the one in the middle of this sentence'.

Round brackets (parentheses)

Round brackets are used for material that wouldn't ordinarily fit into the main thrust of a sentence but that you'd like to include regardless. If they're inserted in the middle of a sentence, then the first word is not capitalised, nor is there a full stop. For example, *Two writers (both of whom I knew) were invited to speak at the graduation ceremony.*

If the parentheses surround a full sentence, then the sentence is punctuated as normal: *We planted the Rangoon creeper cutting. (Remember that its Latin name is* Quisqualis indica.*)*

The key things to look out for in relation to brackets are to make sure you insert the closing bracket and pay attention to other punctuation that may be needed around the bracket. There's never a need to put a comma directly in front of a bracket.

Square brackets

Square brackets are used to add information to quoted text. For example, *They went from there to Balliol College [at Oxford University].*

They are also used when adding *sic* to a quotation. *Sic* (a shortened form of the Latin *sic erat scriptum*, 'thus was it written') is used to ensure that the reader knows that a mistake is not yours but is a faithful quotation of the original. The writer of 'Gladstone was a man of great importtance [*sic*]' couldn't, sadly, spell 'importance'.

If you come across an example of the 'generic he', you can draw attention to it and express your disapproval by placing [*sic*] immediately after it the first time it occurs. For example, 'A writer should always ensure that he [*sic*] carefully proofreads his [*sic*] work'. However, inserting *sic* the second time may annoy readers.

The exclamation mark

The exclamation mark should rarely be used in formal writing. However, it is useful for expressing strong feelings in dialogue, and does have a place in informal communication for interjections. *Indeed!*, *Get out of here!*, and *Surprise!* are examples of interjections.

The question mark

Make sure that question marks always follow a question. For example, *Would you please get that report on my desk by lunchtime* is a request, not a question. However, *Will you be able to finish that report by lunchtime?* is a question.

Note the distinction between a direct question and a reported question: *Why do you have such a strange attitude to punctuation?* is a direct question; *Julia asked why Gertrude Stein had such a strange attitude to punctuation* is a reported question, so you don't use a question mark after the sentence.

The apostrophe

The apostrophe has two main uses: to form contractions and to form the possessive case of nouns. Do not use an apostrophe in any possessive pronouns: *ours, yours, hers, his, its, theirs*. An apostrophe in *it's* isn't possessive. *It's* is a contraction of *it is* or *it has*.

Forming contractions

When forming contractions, do not confuse *it's* with *its*, *you're* with *your*, *they're* with *their*, or *who's* with *whose*.

Your is a possessive pronoun (or determiner), used in *your house*. *You're* is the contracted form of the phrase *you are*.

The phrase *Exploiting the situation for all it's worth* (with an apostrophe) means to exploit the situation for all that it is worth, where *it's* is a contraction of *it is*. The phrase *Exploiting the situation for all its worth* means to exploit the situation for how much you can get out of it, its worth, because *its* is in the possessive case.

Forming the possessive case of nouns

When forming the possessive case of nouns, your starting point should be working out whether you are making a singular or plural word possessive.

When making singular words possessive, add apostrophe-s, as in *the book's cover*—meaning the cover of the book. When making plural words possessive, add apostrophe-s if they don't already end in -s, such as *the children's books* (the books belonging to the children), and add only the apostrophe if they do end in -s, for example, *the players' uniforms* (the uniforms of the players). The rule also applies to surnames that end in -s. For example, *Ms Jones's car* (singular) but the *Joneses' family gatherings* (plural).

The satirical English journalist Craig Brown talks about minding his Ps and Qs when he goes carol-singing with The Pedants' Association:

> It's always pleasant to go carol-singing, or carols-singing, with The Pedants' Association, formerly The Pedants Association, originally The Pedant's Association. I first joined ten years ago with the long-term aim of attracting the requisite number of votes in order to change its title to The Association of Pedants, thus rendering the apostrophe redundant. (2003)

The apostrophe in English helps with word count. We can write *My father's brother's friend's cousin's book* (six words), while the French need to use twelve words to write the same message: *Le livre de la cousine de l'ami du frère de mon père.*

Figure 6.1 will help you to get the possessive apostrophe correct.

Singular	Possessive
employee	an employee's entitlements
apparatus	the apparatus's lifespan the lifespan of the apparatus (if you think *apparatus's* is a bit awkward)
the boss	the boss's office
the princess	the princess's tiara
Moses	Moses's sandals (this is how I would make Moses possessive) Moses' sandals (some authorities follow this practice with ancient and biblical names)
Plural	**Possessive**
the employees	the employees' entitlements
the Joneses	the Joneses' house
the princesses	the princesses' tiaras
women	women's preferences

Figure 6.1 The possessive apostrophe

The *Style Manual: For authors, editors and printers*, which is the authority for the Australian workplace, advocates adding apostrophe-s to any name ending in -s that you need to make possessive. For example, Burns's poems, Dickens's novels, and Odysseus's island (2002, p. 86).

Some years ago I saw the film *Bridget Jones's Diary* in Manhattan. I don't usually check my cinema tickets for punctuation errors, but my eye was inexorably drawn to my ticket stub, which called the film *Bridget Jone's Diary*. If you follow the practice of always using apostrophe-s to make singular words ending in -s possessive, you will never make a mistake with names of authors such as Charles Dickens when forming the possessive case.

A further issue relating to the possessive apostrophe is the leaving out of the apostrophe when there's no real claim to possession. Non-possessive nouns functioning as adjectives *describe*; they don't indicate ownership. This is the associative/attributive/descriptive/affiliative adjective in cases such as geographic names and the names of schools, writers centres, and writers festivals, where there are many cases of possessive apostrophes having been dropped. I noticed that my old school dropped the possessive apostrophe off 'Girls' some years after I had left.

When it comes to the phrase *one day's pay*, the *Style Manual* advocates leaving it in when it refers to a single instance, but advocates using the attributive form in *two years credit* and *three years leave*. I would still use the apostrophe: *two years' credit*.

Follow these styles for individual and joint possession:
- Individual—if they have an office each, punctuate like this: *Sam's and Jack's offices.*
- Joint—if they share an office, punctuate like this: *Sam and Jack's office.*
- For a compound expression, punctuate like this—possessive singular: *editor-in-chief's*; possessive plural: *editors-in-chief's*.

Never use an apostrophe to form a plural. This is called the apostrophied or greengrocer's plural, because it's very common in grocers' shops to see misspelled words such as *tomato's*. I saw an advertisement recently for a security-door company that had been selling *door's, screen's,* and *panel's*, using *supplier's* and *installer's*, for 25 *year's*. Six apostrophied plurals in one spot!

So, it's the *1980s* with no apostrophe. There is one tiny exception to this rule that will help you to avoid ambiguity and misreading. The apostrophe is inserted to separate two lower-case letters: *Please dot your i's and cross your t's. Here's a list of my to-do's.* The apostrophe is not needed for capital letters: *Mind your Ps and Qs.*

Quotation marks

Quotation marks (sometimes called 'inverted commas') have two main uses.

In documents, use single quotation marks for the titles of parts of a whole text and italics for the title of the whole text. For example, songs, journal or newspaper articles, book chapters, short poems, and episodes of a TV series are parts of a larger whole, and so are set in roman and quotation marks. Books, newspapers, and TV series are whole texts, and so their titles should be set in italics. So, Dorothy L. Sayers's short story 'The Undignified Melodrama of the Bone of Contention' (1922) comes from the book *Lord Peter: The complete Lord Peter Wimsey stories.*

In the treatment of quoted material it is common to put quote marks around single words and around direct quotes of reported speech.

The slash

The slash is used to indicate a choice between words, and normally takes the place of the word *or*. For example, *the Oxford/Harvard/serial comma.*

Slashes can also be used to indicate a line break in poetry when the poem is quoted within an essay or other text. For example, 'I wandered lonely as a cloud/That floats on high o'er vales and hills'.

The ellipsis

The ellipsis (three spaced full stops) is used to indicate an omission, such as material removed from a quote. For example: *The rituals that writers have followed include keeping rotten apples in a desk, working in a cork-lined room . . . and remaining bare-headed in the sunshine.*

An ellipsis can also indicate a pause, such as in the sentence *He wasn't . . . was he?* It can also indicate a trailing off, such as in: *I was going to . . . Never mind.*

Punctuating lists

Introduce lists with a sentence or phrase. The punctuation of the list may be determined by whether the items in the list are phrases (such as would be present in a marketing brochure or a presentation), sentence fragments, or full sentences.

If your list comprises sentence fragments, use the following style:
- no initial capital
- parallel structure for elements that are on the same level
- bullet points, with no punctuation at the end of each line
- a full stop at the end.

If your list comprises full sentences, use an initial capital letter and place a full stop at the end of each sentence.

Number and sub-number list items if you need to show sequence and hierarchy and to allow easy reference. Use 'floating' bullet symbols only if none of the above three conditions applies. Symbols such as dots, boxes, and diamonds (bullets) do not indicate hierarchy within a list.

Punctuate each list on its own merits. It is acceptable to use different conventions in different dot-point lists in a document.

Punctuation patterns

Use the model in Figure 6.2 to punctuate your own sentences.

Sentence elements	Examples
Independent clause.	*Our organisation plans to open a new service centre.*
Independent clause; independent clause.	*Our organisation plans to open a new service centre; we look forward to occupying larger premises.*
Independent clause; conjunctive adverb, independent clause.	*Our organisation plans to open a new service centre; however, we need to find a suitable site.*
Introductory phrase, independent clause.	*Some years ago, our service centre was large enough for all the staff.*
Independent clause, conjunction and independent clause.	*We expect that the shift will take place before the end of the year, but it may be later than that.*
Clause/phrase/word, inserted words, remainder of independent clause.	*Our primary role,* **as a service provider***, is to provide excellent customer service.*
Dependent clause + independent clause.	*If we cannot find other premises, some staff may need to share offices.*
Independent clause + dependent clause.	*Some staff will need to share offices if larger premises cannot be found.*
Independent clause: a, b, and c. (NB: the serial comma before *and* is optional.)	*New premises for our organisation will provide the following benefits: more space for offices, more space for training, and more space for a lunchroom.*

Figure 6.2 Punctuation patterns

The last word

As Theodor Adorno reminds us: 'Punctuation marks are the stitches that hold the quilt of language together'. Here are some final reminders for using punctuation effectively.

There are many ways to punctuate writing, and many different rules and options. You must make certain that you are knowledgeable and consistent in your use of punctuation.

Study sentences in well-punctuated prose to learn the particular marks, and familiarise yourself with how they should be used. Construct your own set of guidelines for punctuation.

Aim to punctuate to reveal structure, to clarify meaning, and to control pace and rhythm.

Remember that punctuation should quietly do its job and be visible only to those who are looking for it. Each mark should be deliberate and convey a signal to your reader to slow down or to stop.

Activities

Answers are at the back of the book.

Check out as many of this chapter's Further Reading articles as you can.

1. Do you agree with the following advice about punctuation from Robert Frost and Ernest Hemingway?

> Life is tons of discipline. Your first discipline is your vocabulary; then your grammar and your punctuation . . . Then, in your exuberance and bounding energy you say you're going to add to that. Then you add rhyme and meter. And your delight is in that power. (Robert Frost, *Life Magazine*, 1 December 1961)

> My attitude toward punctuation is that it ought to be as conventional as possible. The game of golf would lose a good deal if croquet mallets and billiard cues were allowed on the putting green. You ought to be able to show that you can do it a good deal better than anyone else with the regular tools before you have a license to bring in your own improvements. (Ernest Hemingway, letter, 15 May 1925)

2. Are you a fan of the Oxford (or serial) comma? Read articles by Curzan and Ferriss listed in Further Reading for this chapter and come up with a rationale based on your informed and considered opinion that you can write up in your journal.
3. Read the article by the Press Association (2014) along with the comments about how Cambridge City Council reversed its ban on apostrophes in place names and decide whether you agree with its decision. Write a paragraph in your journal.
4. I mentioned at the beginning of this chapter that some punctuation marks have become 'extinct'. If you are interested, check Shepherd (2011) in Further Reading. Give examples of how you would use some of these extinct exclamation marks in a sentence.
5. I also mentioned that there are uncommon punctuation marks that people would like to see used. If you are confident about your ability to punctuate, interested in unusual punctuation marks, and have some time to spare, you could read Crezo (2012) and Economist (2014) and write your thoughts in a paragraph in your journal.
6. 'End punctuation' differs from region to region, so you need to check on what is conventional in the situation in which you are writing. Read the article by Yagoda (2011) in Further Reading and consult a couple of style manuals. What is the dominant style used in Australia, the UK, and the USA?
7. Read the following inadequately punctuated sentences, then try to correct them. Can you explain why you have corrected each one? Explanations are provided in the answers section at the end of the book.
    a) That which is is that which is not is not is that not it it is.
    b) His grasp of the world of economics, found him writing for the financial pages.
    c) The lecturer asked if we had done our reading?
    d) Improvement works may affect your journey particularly at weekends.
    e) Check before you travel look for publicity at stations.
    f) The Pet Shop Boys have loads of fans including me.
    g) We suspect however that those names are pseudonyms.
    h) The food arrived however it looked inedible.
    i) Though usually happy people get sad sometimes.

j) Coincidentally several visitors arrived at the door.
k) Mary whereas her teacher had had had had had had had had had was approved by her teacher.
l) As the work pressure becomes more intense, your partner may become preoccupied apprehensive and worried about their prospects.
m) This university prides itself on its unique ability to offer students of just about every profession a balance of theory and practical experience to prepare them for careers in the real world.
n) Study may be undertaken in the fields of marketing strategic management or writing editing and publishing.

8. Test your punctuation virtuosity by correcting the following sentences, where necessary (and, in each case, explain to yourself why you have made a change).
   a) Only in recent years, have I improved my writing skill.
   b) The curtain which had been exposed to the sun was badly faded.
   c) Johnny Depp is a wonderful guy, he has so many talents.
   d) Our favourite films are: the films made by Video Arts.
   e) Please make a list of: staff eligible for leave.
   f) The software they chose had one advantage it was easy to use.
   g) She produced a large expensive glossy brochure.
   h) The comma splice is a common error, it is a fault of many writers.
   i) She said 'thank you for your help.
   j) I wish to heartily thank the members of the Working Party who within tight time constraints imposed by vacation schedules have worked constructively diligently and harmoniously on this extensive task.

9. Insert an apostrophe (or apostrophe-s) where necessary in the following phrases and sentences to convert them to possessive case. (You may have to google the terms in item (n), because these are specific entities that many of you will not be familiar with. You might also like to check on the styles used for writers' centres and festivals in the other states and territories of Australia and elsewhere.)
   a) the boys nose
   b) the mices tails
   c) Jennys books
   d) James father
   e) the mens wives

f) the ladies husbands
g) Its yours, isnt it?
h) seven weeks holiday
i) a minutes silence
j) Johns and Marys books
k) John and Mary's house
l) Sydneys beaches
m) the Joneses house
n) Brisbane Writers Festival/Queensland Writers Centre
o) the companies line of work
p) Decisions generally follow
q) Joness approach
r) Astrophysics gain is linguistics loss.
s) Whose is this book?
t) the flight schedules of QANTAS
u) the programming of SBS
v) One must choose ones words carefully.
w) There are three ls in lollipop.
x) The 1980s were good years.
y) In the 21st century, fewer writers are using ands and buts.
z) Las Vegass obvious disdain for the written word.

7

How structure and design work

> A piece of writing needs to start somewhere, go somewhere, and sit down when it gets there.
> JOHN MCPHEE

> In some respects ... words cannot compare in effectiveness with pictures.
> GARDNER, KITTREDGE, AND ARNOLD

Shaping the verbal and the visual

The art and science of integrating writing and design—shaping verbal and visual language—has come to be known as 'information architecture', a term the architect and designer Saul Wurman coined in 1975 (2001, p. 23).

In this chapter I'll cover the principles of structuring and designing. You need to know how readers process information: how they make sense of text and graphics.

Structuring

When readers are asked to assess the quality of the documents they receive, their most common complaint is that a document is poorly structured, or not structured at all. If they are reading 'to do' (that is, following instructions on how to do something), the information needs to be in a chronological/narrative/performance-based order that allows them to take the steps needed—following what is known as the 'scenario principle'. The scenario principle requires a writer to organise ideas from the perspective of the reader and around the actions that a reader/user needs to perform. If readers are reading 'to learn', the information needs to be presented in a logical, coherent hierarchy of levels that they can understand and recall.

Each time you write, you need to structure your material for your readers' needs; it must be accessible, usable, and interesting. But it is not only the reader who benefits from the structuring of the information within the text. It is essential for you as the writer to structure your information in order to fully understand your own argument. When we write, we need to work as hard as we can to make it as easy as possible for our readers to process our documents. The more work we do, the less our readers have to do. Hard writing makes easy reading.

What is structure?

Structure is the set of relationships between individual components of a document. Structuring is all about distinguishing things that are different from one another and connecting things that are related to one another.

As I explained in Chapter 1, all communication rests on the following factors, which constitute the 'rhetorical situation' (Bitzer, 1968). The rhetorical situation consists of the relationships between:
- the purpose of the document—its background
- the content of the document—its substance and structure
- the writer
- the reader
- the genre of the document—its structure and style
- the context of the document—where it's written and where it's read
- the consequences of the document—its reception and response.

Two concepts that are crucial to understanding structuring are containment and sequence.

Containment is the placing of one thing inside another. Containment creates a very strong connection between the container and the contained item. There is no doubt about whether a thing is inside or outside the container; think of a set of Russian dolls of different sizes that fit into one another. Containment also provides an explicit boundary around a group of things, signalling the implicit relationships between the contained items. Take, for example, any of the chapters in this book; various sections of text (under specific headings) are contained within each chapter.

Sequence is progression with connectedness. Sequencing establishes a relationship by putting things next to each other. A sequence can be chronological (time), such as a historical account of a period of history, or positional (space), such as a geographical account ranging across various farming regions.

A couple of other useful terms are **typology**, which is the systematic classification of types into a continuum, such as personality types in psychology, and **taxonomy**, which comprises hierarchically connected categories that are causally dependent on one another, for example, the hierarchical categories of book, chapter, paragraph, sentence, phrase, word, and letter.

The most basic structuring pattern is the one expressed by John McPhee in the epigraph (2013a) that introduced this chapter. A piece of writing needs to have a beginning, a middle, and an end. As Socrates is reported to have said:

> But I do think you will agree to this, that every discourse must be organized, like a living being, with a body of its own, as it were, so as not to be headless or footless, but to have a middle and members, composed in fitting relation to each other and to the whole. (Bizzell & Herzberg, 1990, p. 134)

In stark contrast to McPhee's and Socrates's advice, we have the bizarre list contained in

> the unforgettable Chinese encyclopedia which imperturbably divides animals into '(a) those that belong to the Emperor, (b) embalmed, (c) those that are domesticated, (d) suckling pigs, (e) mermaids, (f) fabulous beasts, (k) those drawn with a very fine camel's hair brush, (l) others, (m) those that have just broken a vase, (n) those that from a distance look like flies.' (Alberto Manguel, 2010, p. 74, quoting Jorge Luis Borges)

Wurman (1989) argues that 'manipulating finite information in various ways is crucial to critical thinking':

> Evaluation of information in . . . different terms can lead you to find the one that works best for your needs. It is the only way to discover the meanings and relationships between information. Once you've done this, you can decide which pieces are most important and which pieces are secondary. Then a possible organization almost reveals itself. (p. 3)

Wurman claims that while it may seem that the methods are infinite, there are really only five general ways to organise information in order to communicate coherently: location, alphabet, time, category, and hierarchy. He uses a hat rack as a model for understanding relationships, patterns, and connections. Although a hat-check attendant in a museum or theatre (not as common in Australia as in the UK or USA) usually puts each hat into a numbered shelf and gives the owner a correspondingly numbered ticket, for the purposes of his argument Wurman (1989) suggests that a hat-check attendant can hang hats on one of five different racks, using the mnemonic LATCH:

1. **L**ocation—country of manufacture, e.g., Australia, New Zealand, etc. [Documents classified under this heading would be travel guides, atlases, and maps, etc.]
2. **A**lphabet—e.g., Akubra, Bowler, Cap, Fedora. [Documents classified under this heading would be dictionaries, indexes, thesauruses, and style guides, etc.]
3. **T**ime—according to each guest's arrival. [Documents classified under this heading would be timetables, itineraries, programs, instructions, and historical accounts, etc.]
4. **C**ategory—e.g., feathers, ribbons, protection from weather, religious, military, etc. [Documents classified under this heading would be catalogues, reports, proposals, CVs, and brochures, etc.]
5. **H**ierarchy—continuum of magnitude, e.g., size or cost or importance. [Documents that would use a hierarchical arrangement of small to large, least to most expensive, most popular to least popular, most to least or least to most important, etc. would be a report that would end with recommendations, then conclusions.] (p. 3)

Wurman points out that

> the hats never change, but hanging them in different patterns or with different rules or on different racks can affect what we learn about them. More complex relationships may be shown when one type of organization or hat rack is combined or juxtaposed with another. Units of information may be organized by category, then arranged by location under each category. (1989, p. 3)

Before you rush into trying to order your material into an outline, understand why you are writing and what your readers hope to find.

In only the most routine and conventional documents will the structuring job be done for you and the pattern of information be determined in advance. For example, you may be asked to write a short report for which the headings are supplied, or you may want to apply for a position for which there are specific criteria that you need to address. Even in these cases, you will need to organise material within sections.

Journalists learn to write news stories to the quite strict conventional structure of the inverted pyramid. Responding to the heuristic of the 5 Ws and an H, they put the most important information in their first couple of sentences and work down to the least important information at the end of the story. This convention exists so that subeditors can cut stories from the bottom up if they need space. Social science and science papers have quite standard structures: title page, abstract, introduction, methods, results, discussion, references, and appendixes. Many workplace documents have formats that follow common conventions.

When you have the accurate, relevant, comprehensive, and up-to-date information that you know your readers need, consider Wurman's five ways of classifying it. Category ('chunk', put like with like) and hierarchy are probably the ones that you will call upon most often. Outlines can help, but, unless you have a set task with predetermined headings, it's probably not a good idea to begin with an outline that is too rigid. Written planning is not a product of thinking; it is part of the process of thinking.

Jack Selzer (1989) presents six possible arrangement strategies, most of which Wurman would class as hierarchical.

1. Writers can use first or final positions for emphasis because readers remember what comes first or last. (This is called the rule of primacy and recency.)
2. Writers can use a climactic order for emphasis by moving towards progressively more powerful information, or moving from relatively negative or neutral information to positive appeals.
3. Writers can move from the simplest to most complex, from the easiest to most difficult, from the most familiar to least familiar information (or vice versa)—an arrangement that is a partial application of what linguists call the 'given-new contract'. To fulfil this contract, the writer moves from what the reader knows already to what they do not yet know.
4. Writers can move from least controversial or surprising information to most controversial or surprising, or vice versa.
5. Writers can state a generalisation and then give evidence or arguments for it, or give reasons and evidence before the generalisation.
6. Writers can use Rogerian principles (based on the work of the psychotherapist Carl Rogers and often used in mediation) whenever the stakes are high and the case to persuade will be challenging to eliminate or reduce a reader's sense of being threatened by new or potentially challenging information. A Rogerian arrangement:
    a) introduces the problem, while conveying to the reader that their position is understood
    b) delineates the area within which the writer can accept the reader's position as valid
    c) states the writer's own position
    d) states how the reader's position would benefit if they were to adopt the writer's position. (pp. 44-7)

Physically structuring material

Structuring can be a difficult mental process. One way to make it easier is to transform it into a physical task. Never underestimate the value of the physical dimension of laying out your work. Many writers yearn for the luxury of a long, well-lit hallway lined with a shelf at a comfortable height on which they can lay out their pages. The novelist David Ireland once said in an interview that he uses luggage labels to organise his material. Other writers use Post-it notes that they can move around. The novelists Vladimir Nabokov and Robert Pirsig have related how they made extensive use of index or filing cards that they shuffled (Burnham, 1994, p. 63).

One 'physical' way of structuring material is to follow their example and put your notes onto filing cards. After doing this, sort the cards that 'seem to go together' into stacks. Prepare a 'summary' card that 'sums up' each stack. If you can't think of a statement or category that covers all the cards in each stack, take out the cards that don't fit, make new stacks for them, and write up a new card for each stack. Then lay your summary cards out in order. An obvious order may present itself, such as linear or hierarchical. Try out variations in your ordering. When you have an order that you think will work for your material, your reader, and the purpose of your document, convert your headings into a formation that you can use as an outline for your document.

The New Yorker published a brilliant essay on arranging material by John McPhee (2013a) titled 'Structure: Beyond the picnic-table crisis', which makes compelling reading. He describes how, when he was a pupil at Princeton High School, his English class had to write three essays every week that 'had to be accompanied by a structural outline', which his teacher insisted they do first. 'It could be anything from Roman numerals I, II, III to a looping doodle with guiding arrows and stick figures. The idea was to build some form of blueprint before working it out in sentences and paragraphs'. McPhee has remained grateful for this training throughout his long career as a writer. If only all teachers followed this strategy!

There are many ways of generating ideas and information and sorting them to make sense, but, in writing, all of this data has to ultimately fall into an outline structure. This is because writing is linear by nature and can best be understood if its topics can be reduced to hierarchical clusters.

An experienced writer might sometimes begin by creating a logical, sequential diagram such as a flow chart (Figure 7.1), and then expanding it in the course of writing their essay, article, or book. But most often we begin in a much more arbitrary way. Ideas and information are recorded in the order they occur to us and are connected idiosyncratically rather than logically. This is the basis of valuable strategies such as brainstorming (making no evaluation, generating the wildest ideas possible, so that you have lots of ideas to build on and modify) and free writing (writing without pausing to revise), but results in a body of information that means little to a reader if it is not structured coherently.

A mind map (Figure 7.2) and a matrix (Figure 7.3) can result in more logical sorting of information and remain in a multidirectional form. Such diagrams are invaluable for grasping complex interrelationships; however, eventually, they all need to be reduced to an outline that orders these relationships in a sequential manner.

You can outline by simply giving headings to paragraphs or whole files of similar information and then sorting each further into subcategories. Using numbering, dot points, indenting, or type-size levels helps you to identify their interrelationships. Other graphic structuring devices include issue trees (Figure 7.4) and numbered outlines (Figure 7.5).

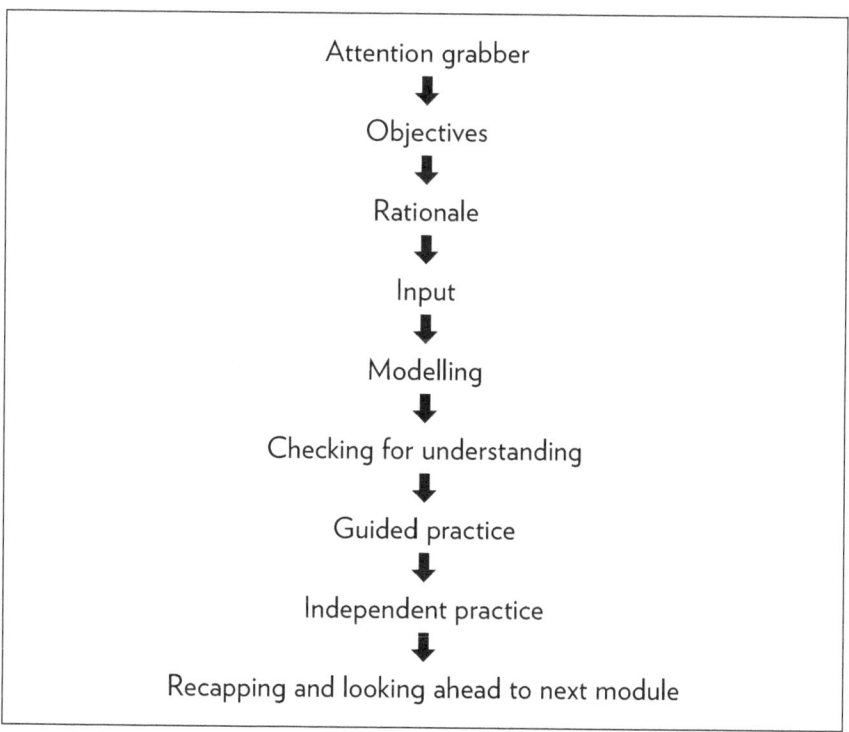

Figure 7.1 A flow chart for a module in a training program

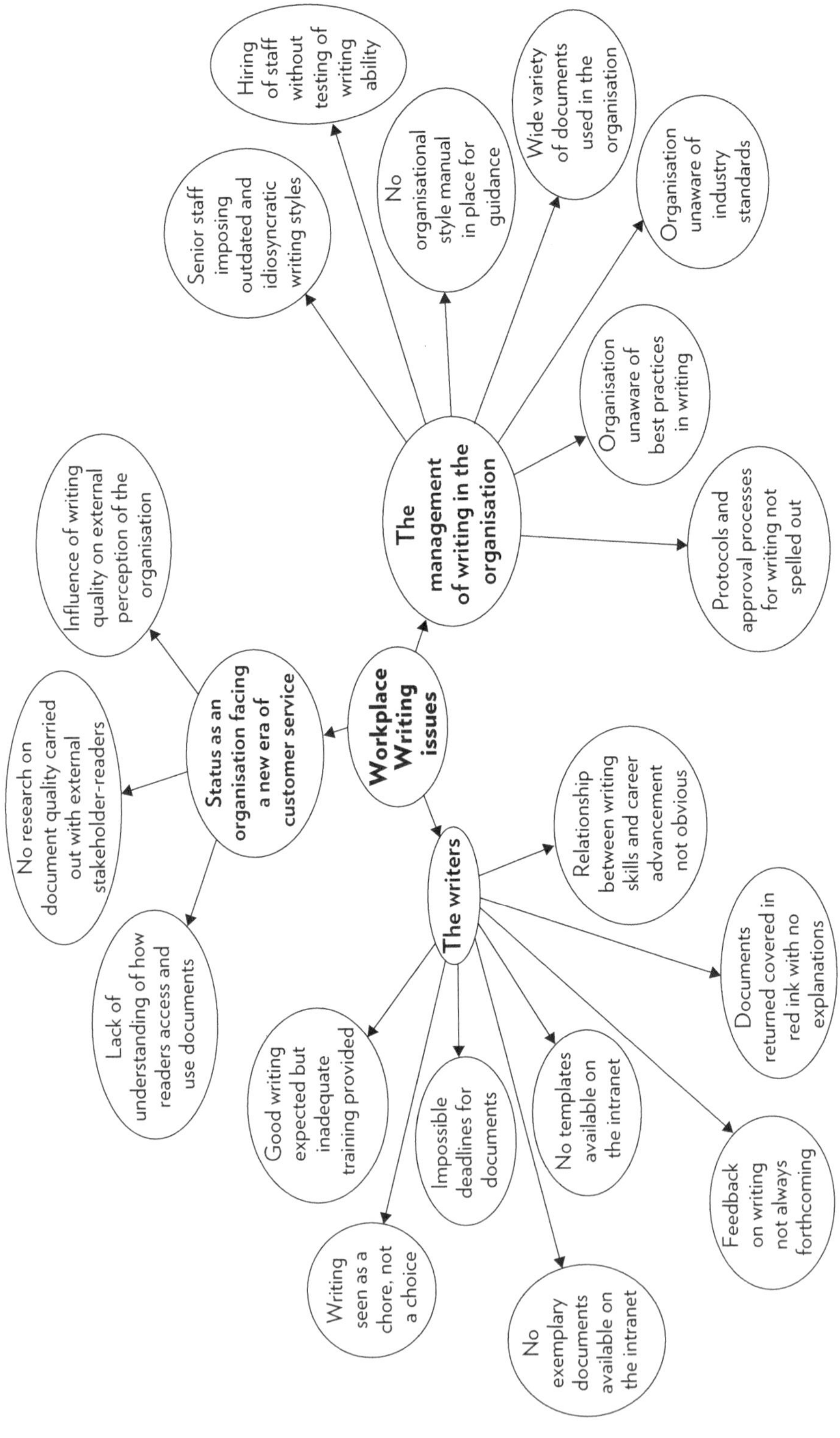

Figure 7.2 A mind map to illustrate workplace writing issues

HOW STRUCTURE AND DESIGN WORK

Factor affecting style	Academic writing	Creative writing	Workplace writing	Journalistic writing
Reader				
Reader's knowledge of topic				
Writer's purpose				
Content				
Writer's role				
Writer's stance				
Writer–reader relationship				
Language				
Tone				
Sentence structure				
Paragraph structure				
Document structure				
Presence of humour				
Presence of dramatic elements				
Title				
Documentation				

Figure 7.3 A matrix to analyse writing style

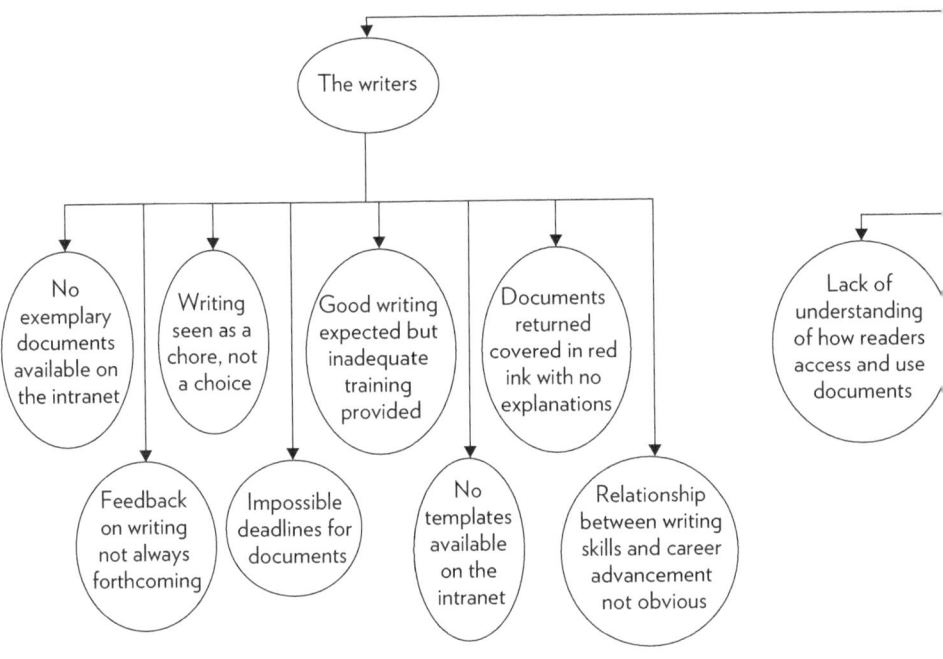

Figure 7.4 An issue tree to illustrate workplace writing issues

Outlining on a computer

Although the computer has been a superb aid to writers, one downside has been that writers often 'dump' a pile of unsorted data into a file and then try to sort it. This can be overwhelming, if not paralysing. As an alternative to using index cards, a computer is an ideal instrument for outlining because it enables you to quickly and easily shift and sort blocks of writing and assign them to new hierarchical roles. Each block in computer outlining is referred to as a 'node' and can be moved, or 'promoted' or 'demoted', by using a toolbar, using assigned keystrokes, or dragging with the mouse. Computer outlining also enables you to see

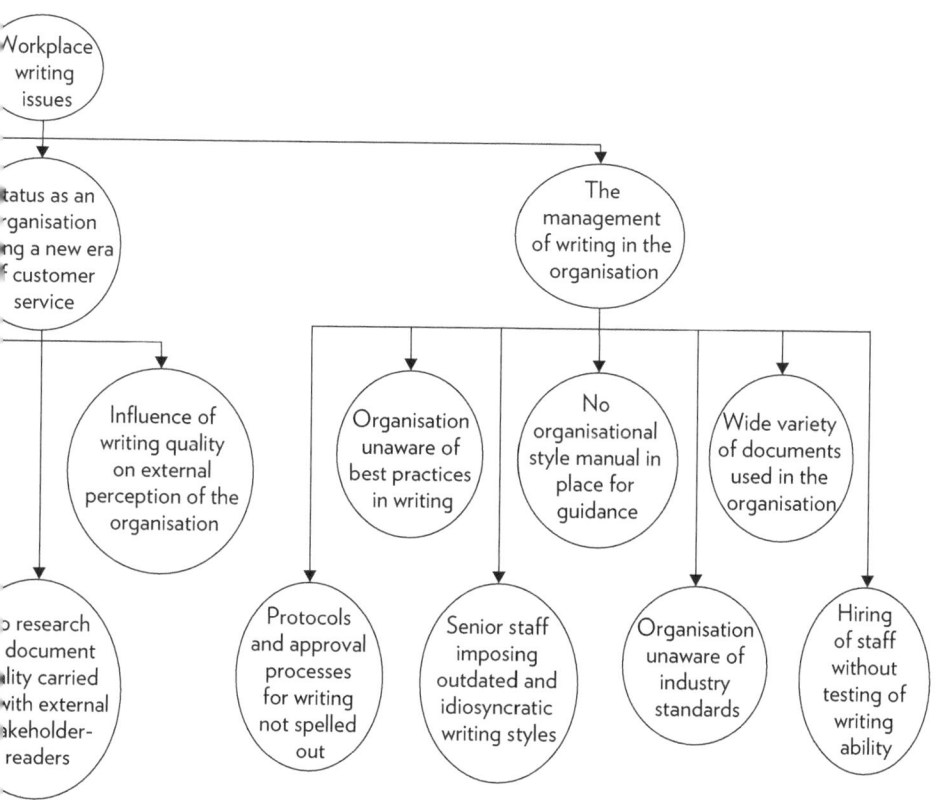

'the wood for the trees' by giving you options to hide or reveal different levels of a hierarchy in order to grasp an overall simplified structure or alternatively examine a detail. Eventually, you might remove some of the provisional headings or numbering, but the logical structure will remain.

Most word-processing programs such as Microsoft Word have an outlining facility that can assign a 'style' to headings and subheadings and manipulate blocks of writing assigned under these headings. In Word, for example, to start an outline file click on the 'View' tab, then select 'Outline' from the 'Document Views' panel, and then use the commands available. As the writing process can be 'organic' as well as

1. Status as an organisation facing a new era of customer service
    1.1. Influence of writing quality on external perception of the organisation
    1.2. No research on document quality carried out with external stakeholder-readers
    1.3. Lack of understanding of how readers access and use documents.
2. The management of writing in the organisation
    2.1. Protocols and approvals processes for writing not spelled out
    2.2. Organisation unaware of best practices in writing
    2.3. Organisation unaware of industry standards
    2.4. Wide variety of documents used in the organisation
    2.5. No organisational style manual in place for guidance
    2.6. Hiring of staff without testing writing ability
    2.7. Senior staff imposing outdated and idiosyncratic writing styles.
3. The writers
    3.1. Good writing expected but inadequate training provided
    3.2. Writing seen as a chore, not an opportunity
    3.3. Impossible deadlines for documents
    3.4. No exemplary documents available on the intranet
    3.5. No templates available on the intranet
    3.6. Feedback on writing not always forthcoming
    3.7. Documents returned covered in red ink with no explanations
    3.8. Relationship between writing skills and career advancement not obvious.

Figure 7.5 A numbered outline to illustrate workplace writing issues

structured, you would probably have other files from which you would import material into this more organised file as you needed it.

However, there are also programs and applications, or 'apps', that specialise in this task to make it simpler and more convenient. While many of these programs, generically called 'outliners', are more geared to creating shopping lists or functioning as personal organisers, some are specifically designed for writers and even for specific types and genres of writing such as the novel and scriptwriting. And some of these even automatically convert data from other forms of idea generation, such as mind mapping, into outlines. These outliners can be very useful in the earlier stages of writing, but often lack desirable bibliographic and formatting capabilities, so you may finally want to transfer the writing back to your usual word-processing program. An exception to this is online collaboration and Web publishing, for which specialised outliners exist.

New outliner programs appear regularly and old programs constantly develop new capabilities, so it is futile to try to cover all of their functionalities. However, I will discuss some notable programs to suggest a range of what is currently available.

Probably the oldest computer application of any kind still in regular use is an outliner for the personal computer (PC) called EccoPro. Now in the public domain, EccoPro was a personal information manager produced by Arabesque Software in 1993 that ceased development in 1997. Despite this, its compatibility with the Windows operating system has been maintained by enthusiasts, and you do not need to use its fairly dated calendar, email, and networking interface to take advantage of its still very convenient outlining capabilities. Easily exporting to and importing from word-processing programs, EccoPro employs what is called a 'single-pane' outliner—meaning that all its contents are in one window and are not stored as separate files, although they may be collapsed and expanded.

In contrast, a two-pane outliner shows a database tree structure in one window and the content of a node in the other. The latter format may be more useful for very large documents where you might like to maintain awareness of the whole structure while working on a detail, or need to navigate quickly to a remote node. However, it is less effective for maintaining connections between adjacent nodes, which is best accomplished if they are seen simultaneously. In EccoPro, nodes can be moved and promoted or demoted with a single mouse or stylus drag, or by using Alt and an arrow key. For both construction and editing of a modestly sized document, a single-pane outliner is ideal.

A commercial single-pane outliner for both Mac and PC widely used in education is Inspiration. Inspiration uses a single-window format not unlike that of EccoPro but with more format alternatives. Unlike other outliners, it enables you to generate and present the same information in multiple ways. You can build up a mind map enlivened with graphic organisers from a library of visual symbols and then, in one keystroke, see how it would look as a sequential text-only outline, or a diagram, or a slide presentation. If you work on the file in any of these formats, all changes are registered in the other views. Thus Inspiration enables you to plan your document using some of the spatial and visual prompts that linear outlining lacks. Inspiration also offers generic templates for various kinds of documents and forms of exposition and argument that can guide you in structuring documents.

A more ambitious commercial multiple-pane outliner for both Mac and Windows is Scrivener. Scrivener is designed as a total research organiser. With Scrivener, you can store and categorise research sources in almost any format and view them alongside your developing document, together with notes and summaries. A file-card metaphor is used to add a sense of spatial organisation to large amounts of data. Card-like rectangles of text can be shuffled and organised onscreen with a mouse. This program is more suited to outlining on a macro scale than on paragraph level. Developed originally for creative writing, it has found wide application in thesis writing and professional preparation of complex documents. However, it has been criticised for its lack of an easy interface with citation software such as EndNote.

Another large document outliner, Outline 4D, which has remained dedicated to creative writing (but may also be used for writing reports and theses with narrative content) uses timelines and visual cues rather than hierarchy to help organise events, characters, objects, and keywords in complex narratives.

Finally, there is the trend for online services to replace onboard software. These come in many forms, and include note-taking programs such as Microsoft's OneNote and Evernote, and also HTML Web-based outliners such as The Outliner of Giants, which comes integrated with Google Docs. These services promise to both organise and store a writer's whole creative or research output, but can be controversial because of privacy and copyright issues.

Outlining on a computer can help you to establish and arrange complex organisational categories and subcategories, but if you're not used to outlining on a computer and you have a deadline, wait until you have time to experiment with the software.

Organising a document

As a writer–designer–editor, draw on your rhetorical repertoire to organise a document.

The rhetorical situation will determine your research. Remember the 5 Ws and an H—what, when, where, who, why, and how.

Understand why you are writing (the purpose of your document), who your readers are, and what they hope to find (rhetoric centres around the beliefs of the audience). Take into account your readers' education, professional experience, familiarity with the subject, and their motivation to receive the information and the urgency with which they need it.

Generate information via research in your organisation's archives and your own files; read newspapers, magazines, journals, and books; consult colleagues; interview experts; surf the internet; search databases; brainstorm; call on your personal experience via internal dialogue; exploit crowdsourcing, for example, asking your Facebook connections for input; and explore your metaknowledge (what you already know).

How do your points relate to each other? Start to categorise your material. What are the most convincing pieces of evidence to back up your points? Using topics such as definition, comparison, cause and effect, past and future can be useful, as can authoritative material from experts. Why have you chosen this particular order?

Organise information using Wurman's categories (see the discussion of the LATCH mnemonic earlier in this chapter) and graphic techniques to show relationships: 'chunk', categorise, and label. Graphic techniques include:

- a flow chart (see Figure 7.1)
- a mind map (concept map; see Figure 7.2)
- a matrix (thinking grid; see Figure 7.3)
- an issue tree (see Figure 7.4)
- a numbered outline (see Figure 7.5).

The Graphic Organizer is a terrific educational site that sets out these and other techniques (see graphic.org).

Write a draft outline from your readers' perspective. If you were the reader, where would you want this document to begin? Create a guided tour, a 'reading path' that your readers can follow to interpret the text as they move through it. (Remember reading theory in Chapter 2.) If you get stuck, don't hesitate to go back and redraft. Value recursivity.

Your structure and content need to be complemented with typography and layout, because design decisions dramatically affect the ease with which a document can be read. In the following section I discuss core principles of document design.

Design considerations

Design to communicate! People look first. They read only when you give them reason to. Design needs to be functional, not decorative. People need to be able to easily find out what they need to do in response to the document. Design is about the interactions between people and the complex patterns of written and graphic information that affect their lives: forms, instructions, webpages, books, signs, diagrams, and so on.

Consider your readers:
- What do they know?
- Why will they read?
- How will they read? For example, will they skim/scan quickly or read deliberately, deeply, and slowly, pencil in hand?
- What depth and breadth of information do they expect?

Develop visual sensibility. Consider how design:
- engenders or diminishes interest (invites or intimidates)
- enhances verbal content
- communicates ethos, logos, and pathos (credibility, authority, and emotional connections).

The three key aspects of design are:
1. the text (words and numbers)
2. the typography and layout
3. the illustrative material (graphs, tables, charts, maps, photographs, and diagrams).

Text

Text includes introductions; advance organisers (titles, headings); lists, numbering; retrievability or access aids (table of contents, index, glossary, tabs and separators in paper documents); summaries; notes and appendices; page numbering; and headers and footers.

Typography and layout

Typography and layout include page size; typeface; upper and lower case; highlighting techniques (bold, italics, colour, different point sizes); type weight (bold or normal); sharpness of type (crisp, well defined); margins; line length (or measure); justification; white space; space between paragraphs; indentation; and leading (space between lines).

A **typeface** comprises a family of fonts, for example, bold, italic, and narrow. A font is a specific member of a typeface family: Times Roman is a typeface; Times Roman Italic is a font within it. The two main groups of typefaces are serif and sans (the French word for without) serif. Serifs are the little 'flicks' on the ends of a letter in serif typefaces such as Times. A school of thought recommends serif typefaces for paper and sans serif for online texts, but studies of typography have not conclusively proven that serif typefaces are more easily read on paper and sans serif typefaces are more easily read online. Sans serif typefaces are used for signage and in texts for children learning to read.

More than 100,000 typefaces exist. Typefaces can be amazingly powerful. In 2008, a typeface, Gotham, was hyperbolically credited with helping Barack Obama win the United States presidential election, because the clean visual signature came to define his campaign.

The following list encapsulates design advice for reader-friendly typography and layout in professional documents.

- Avoid typewriting habits such as underlining and putting two spaces (instead of the recommended one) after a full stop. Underlining isolates and rigidifies words in headings, and chops off descenders (bottoms of letters such as *y* and *g*), as well as being aesthetically displeasing.
- Don't use all capital letters for headings and emphasis. Capital letters form into rectangles that are harder to read than lower-case letters. Also, many readers see ALL CAPS as equivalent to shouting.
- A type size of 10 or 11 points is usually ideal for body text. Use 14 points for headings when the body text is around 11 points.
- Leading (pronounced ledding) is the term for the measurement from baseline to baseline (the invisible line on which most letters sit, and

below which descenders such as the bottom of the letter 'y' hang), in other words, the spacing between lines. If you are using 10 point Times Roman, you would set your text with at least 12 point leading. Every typeface is different, and leading can be adjusted to produce the effect you wish to achieve.
- For academic and workplace documents, justify your text only on the left side of the page (range left or ragged right). Some people argue that fully justified text looks neat, but it creates uneven spaces within lines, called 'rivers of white'. Books are usually fully justified, which creates a block of text in which both sides are even.
- Make sure that you have plenty of white space on your page (some say 50 per cent). Aim to make your page look elegant and welcoming.
- Carefully consider the width of the text, or line length. If your line is too long it is hard for the reader to take in the information at one glance. The line length needs to be considered at the same time as the type size and the margins. When you get the measure to type-size ratio wrong, this results in rivers of white, over-hyphenation, or poor readability.
- Books usually indent paragraphs, and some documentation systems (for example, that of the Modern Language Association) require indentation. Workplace documents are more likely to use an extra line space between paragraphs (called 'interparagraph spacing') instead of indenting. If you do indent the first line of a paragraph, don't do it immediately after a heading.
- Leave more space above a heading than below so that it is visually connected to the related text and set off from the text above.
- Use smart quotation marks (sometimes called 'curly' quotes) rather than straight quote marks. If you cut and paste from different documents, check for the consistency of your quotation marks. Unless you are sending out a media release in which you have a quote, use single quotation marks in the first instance and then double quotation marks for a quote within a quote. (See Chapter 8 for discussion of media releases.)
- Turn off automatic hyphenation and hyphenate manually if you notice that a 'ladder' of hyphens is forming at the end of adjacent lines. If you are using ragged right, you won't need to hyphenate at all.

- Check and adjust your text to eliminate 'widows' and 'orphans'. A page should not begin with the last line of a paragraph (widow). A page should not end with the first line of a new paragraph (orphan). You can select a floating baseline to ensure that this happens automatically.
- Repeat elements such as colour, shape, texture, spatial relationships, and line weight for borders.
- Group related items together.
- Align every element so that it has a visual connection with another element on the page.

Typographic style sheet

Just as writers and editors prepare a style sheet for the text (see Chapter 8), a designer prepares a typographic style sheet. This should cover:
- typefaces and type weight
- capitalisation
- point size and leading
- space above and below a heading
- formatting of line length and margins
- amount of white space
- justification and indentation
- rules, boxes
- colour specifications.

Illustrative material

Illustrative material includes photographs, pictures, illustrations, tables, figures, charts, graphs, and infographics. Use graphic material to complement the text, motivate your readers, clarify and reinforce your explanations, and help long-term recall. Use illustrative material *only* if it is relevant, appropriate, clear, compelling, and well executed.

Make sure that you:
- introduce it before it appears
- give it a label and title
- integrate it seamlessly into your text
- explain it/interpret it in the text
- if appropriate, draw conclusions.

Some people relate to words more than numbers. We might call them 'text or paragraph people', in contrast to those who prefer numbers, whom we might call 'spreadsheet people'. Writers should consider their readers' preferences when deciding how to present information.

Decide which form of graphic illustration will best communicate information to your readers: chart, graph, table, diagram, pictogram (which uses only symbols, instead of words and numbers), photograph, video, map, infographic. The word 'infographic' is a portmanteau word coined from 'information' and 'graphics'. Before the term was invented, the designer Jan V. White called it 'data visualisation'. Infographics are stand-alone visual representations of complex data and information that contain enough textual and visual information to function independently of extra explanatory text. They are not just 'fancy graphics' or decoration; they relate a visual narrative that tells a whole story. There are many sites such as piktochart.com available that you can access to create infographics.

The following list provides key advice for using graphic material:

- Focus the message: how do I make it clear at a glance?
- Use line graphs to show trends and changes over time.
- Use pie charts to show proportions, with four or five segments and figures converted to a percentage.
- Use bar graphs to show discrete units of different but related items.
- Use tables for complex statistical and financial data.
- Round off numbers; include averages.
- Put figures into vertical columns rather than horizontal rows so they are easier to compare.
- Consider using shading for alternate lines and columns.
- Aim for clarity and brevity. Provide brief, clear titles, because readers skim.
- Make text legible for small spaces.

Also, avoid ghastly, gratuitous graphics. Microsoft closed its Clip Art library in 2014. Not before time. Its PowerPoint software is also controversial. Is it appalling or enthralling? Peter Norvig converted the Gettysburg Address into PowerPoint to cleverly illustrate how truly banal PowerPoint can be. See Further Reading for a link to Norvig's presentation and Box 7.1 for questions to ask about graphic material.

> **BOX 7.1 Checklist for evaluating graphic material**
>
> - Does the layout allow for easy comparisons between the data?
> - Have you provided emphasis where necessary?
> - Are table titles, column headings, and row items clear?
> - Do the numbers tally?
> - Are abbreviations used consistently?
> - Is the material positioned correctly, following its in-text reference?

Working with designers

Because information design software has become so accessible with the upsurge of desktop publishing, many people are now using programs such as InDesign that they would once have relied upon graphic designers to handle. In fact, many of the jobs for writers in small organisations now list an ability to use InDesign as a desirable criterion. Large organisations often have a graphic designer on staff; others use freelance graphic designers.

If you need to brief a designer in the workplace, Box 7.2 sets out the key areas you will need to address. There's also a plethora of design sites on the internet that provide useful advice, such as that of The Visual Communication Guy (Curtis Newbold). See the list of design sites in Box 7.3.

It is crucial to have a great relationship with printers and (Web) designers. I edited and published an academic journal, the *Australian Journal of Communication*, from 1988 to 2013, and used the same printing company and the same cover designer for all that time. Having people whom you can rely on to do high-quality work and who are responsive to the inevitable last-minute changes to text can never be underestimated.

The Chicago Manual of Style, which is used extensively in American contexts, and Part 3 of the Australian *Style Manual: For authors, editors and printers* (Snooks & Co., 2002) give extensive guidance on all aspects of designing and illustrating. Box 7.3 lists some design sites that you might like to explore for inspiration and further advice.

BOX 7.2 **Design briefing**

Background and aim
Ask to see the portfolio or work samples of any new designer before you hire them.
   Clarify the history of any publication that you are hiring them to design—i.e., why it is being produced or reproduced.
   How will the results of a design be measured?

Readership
Who are your readers?

Style
Is it to be on paper, online, or both? What kind of 'look' is it to have— e.g., glossy and expensive, or practical and inexpensive? Check whether the publication needs to fit in with an existing 'family' of publications. Get exemplars! What styles *don't* your colleagues and readers like?

Format
Will it be on paper: e.g., A4 double-sided; A4 folded to post; online?

Content
What information will be included? If it is a redesign, what feedback have you collected from managers about changes?

Graphic content
Are any specific photos or graphics proposed? If so, when and how can these be obtained?

Quantity
If on paper, what size is the print run?

Timing
When is it needed by? (Particularly important if it is needed for an event.)

Final approval
Make sure it is clear who will be giving final approval for the publication. Who else will vet it on the way?

Distribution
How is it to be distributed? Who will be responsible for distribution?

Budget
Ensure that there is an agreed budget for the publication. How will 'extras' be costed? Agree in advance on a kill fee (a payment to be made if the project or contract is cancelled for any reason).

BOX 7.3 **Design sites**
The leading American designers are the pioneering Edward Tufte ('the Leonardo da Vinci of data'); Don Norman (of The Design Lab at the University of California, San Diego); Saul Wurman (architect and graphic designer nonpareil); Karen Schriver (information design guru); Alberto Cairo (infographics guru); and Chip Kidd (renowned graphic artist and book-cover designer).

In the UK, a leading information designer is Rob Waller, who runs the Simplification Centre. In Australia, a leading information designer is David Whitbread.

The following sites make useful reading:
aerogrammestudio.com
bigthink.com/ideafeed/
    how-typefaces-and-fonts-affect-your-subconscious
bloomberg.com/politics/
    graphics/2015-hillary-womens-movement-timeline/
compoundchem.com
coolinfographics.com (a blog about infographics)
dailyinfographic.com/guide-to-note-taking-in-class
designtaxi.com/news/379158/Infographic-How-Steve-Jobs-Bill-
    Gates-Successful-Leaders-Deal-With-Stress/
design.tutsplus.com/articles/15-indesign-tutorials-for-magazine-and-
    layout-design--vector-5456
fastcodesign.com/3046365/
    errol-morris-how-typography-shapes-our-perception-of-truth
theguardian.com/membership/2014/sep/10/
    best-infographic-graphic-design
indesignsecrets.com/issues
informationisbeautiful.net/visualizations/
    american-novels-everyone-should-read/
insights.spotify.com/au/2015/07/13/musical-map-of-the-world/
presentationzen.com/presentationzen/2009/08/10-tips-on-how-to-
    think-like-a-designer.html

The Visual Communication Guy has design rules for using text, typography and layout, and illustrative material:
thevisualcommunicationguy.com/2014/07/01/18-rules-for-using-text/
thevisualcommunicationguy.com/2015/05/04/
    the-ultimate-visual-guide-to-citing-sources-in-mla-format/

thevisualcommunicationguy.com/2014/06/24/
  10-crucial-document-design-terms-that-writers-designers-and-
  communicators-need-to-know/
thevisualcommunicationguy.com/2014/07/02/
  would-a-course-syllabus-be-better-as-an-infographic/

The last word

As you will see if you explore items listed in Box 7.3, what would once have been a domain inhabited mainly by graphic designers has now expanded to become one of serious intrinsic interest to writers. Taking an interest in information design that goes beyond learning to structure information in a document, such as I covered in the first part of this chapter, and perhaps learning to use the graphics software available, will expand your repertoire and your options as a writer. No one would dispute that being in command of both your writing and designing is an accomplishment that is both personally rewarding and career enhancing.

Activities

1. Find and analyse samples of good (i.e., simple and transparent) design, and of design that ignores the guidelines.
2. If you are a student writer, or a workplace writer thinking about going back to further study, graphically structure the brainstormed notes below into an outline that you could use for a report to the student services unit at your university on considerations for mature students returning to study. Make sure that you 'chunk' (categorise), arrange, and label (coordinate and subordinate levels) your points.
   - Improve financial situation
   - Fill in the gaps in my education
   - Find a mentor/make human contact with lecturers and make a good impression
   - Be committed
   - Be aware and wary of pitfalls such as underestimating the time commitment required

- Get serious
- Postgraduate standards intimidating/competitive
- Coping with study (again)
- Get organised
- Skill up in word processing, email, and the internet
- Poor choice of course/not knowing the options
- Financial strain
- Long-term commitment (several semesters)
- Fear of failure/fear of not making it
- Get accurate information from proper sources
- Change career to get out of a dead-end job or a quarter-life crisis
- Uncertainty about end job
- Enhance self-esteem
- Extend current work capabilities
- Thirst for new knowledge
- All my children have a degree
- Get guidance when you need it
- Personal fulfilment
- Unrealistic expectations
- Pressure of understanding 'university-level' postgraduate content
- Need developed study skills
- Balancing family, work, social life, free time
- Find out what is expected of you
- Get exemplars of all assignments
- Being 'ghettoised' with other mature-age students
- Lack of support from family
- Meet new people, so have more social options
- Self-development
- Make a contribution to society.

3. Your manager has asked you to prepare a background briefing note that can be used to convince your CEO of the need for policy guidelines that your colleagues can follow when using email and social media. Brainstorm reasons in favour of such a policy and the topics/issues/guidelines that you think should be included in such a policy. Structure your brainstormed information into an outline.

8

How genres and workplace documents work

> The expectations aroused by conventions of various genres ... compel writers of every kind to arrange their work in particular ways.
>
> JACK SELZER

Understanding genre expectations

In classifying writing, we define a genre as a style or category with specific features and purposes that distinguish it from other kinds of writing. The two main genre categories are fiction (e.g., novels, poetry, and plays) and nonfiction (e.g., biography, history, and philosophy, etc.).

The contemporary concept of genre focuses on classifying texts by their purpose—the functions that they perform for their readers. In this chapter I'll cover the genre expectations of function, form, and style in specific workplace documents. The key questions are why someone would need to write a particular document and why anyone would need to read it.

When you are familiar with the conventions of a genre, you can aim to meet your readers' expectations. Many readers of academic and workplace documents react negatively when their genre expectations are not met, particularly in relation to its overall structure; sentence structure;

stylistic features such as language use, tone, and voice; and typography, graphics, and visual layout. Under pressure of a deadline, I once sent off a workplace interim report that was written largely by my research assistant and that deviated from my reader's genre expectations. I was worried that the tone was a little too breezy for the university hierarchy, so I was not too surprised when the report was returned to me with a request to adjust it to a more formal style. It is crucial to respect and adhere to the established conventions of the genre that you're working in; on no account ignore them.

University students who submit an academic assignment such as an essay that doesn't adhere to the conventions of academic style and documentation will generally be penalised, though sometimes they will be given the opportunity to resubmit it. Primary school students in Australia undergoing the annual National Assessment Program—Literacy and Numeracy (NAPLAN) standardised writing test are warned in the marking guide that they will lose marks if they deviate from the required 'generic structure' of the essay, with its introduction, body, and conclusion.

So, as a student or workplace writer, you need to 'crack the code' and conform to the conventions. To repeat my message: You ignore genre conventions at your peril.

Readers of creative writing are less rigid than academic and workplace readers about their genre expectations. They are often more welcoming of documents that subvert genre conventions, though they may not go as far as Lynda Barry, the iconoclastic American professor, author, and graphic artist, who says: 'People think if you're writing a story that you have to follow story structure. It's like thinking the only reason we have teeth is because there are dentists' (Randle, 2015).

Writing in a professional context: workplace genres

Although writing is a mainstream activity in most professions and organisations, and an employee's writing ability is highly likely to be critical to their career path, many writers in organisations do not reflect on the importance of writing in their working lives. This particularly applies to those who are 'writing workers' as opposed to 'working writers' (see Chapter 1).

Writing is not intrinsically interesting to many writing workers, nor is it particularly visible until a document-related crisis occurs. Many organisations don't have a style manual with strictures about style, tone, punctuation, typography, format, etc. This is unfortunate because of the political complexity and sensitivity of different documents that an organisation relies on for its credibility and to protect itself from exposure to risk.

Managers and writers need to be aware of the importance of proper briefing for writing tasks. The brief should take into account and cover the purpose of the document; the primary and other readers of the document; the expertise and experience of the writer; format; and organisational policy and protocols for collaborative writing and checking of documents.

Box 8.1 lists types of workplace documents that I have come across when consulting to organisations about their writing and editing practices and processes. Read through the list and see whether you can think of others. I'm sure there are many. I cover the genre conventions of some key workplace documents in this chapter and academic documents in the next. I hope that you will be able to transfer the elements and functions that I discuss to any other documents that you need to write.

In this chapter I'll cover letters, reports, proposals, job applications, style manuals, instruction manuals, media releases, and speeches. Email messages are covered in Chapter 10, on digital writing.

Letters

On the same day that a large Australian bank posted a loss of millions of dollars, it posted me a letter that was riddled with problems of fact, detail, logic, structure, punctuation, spelling, grammar, and tone. The bank was not amused when, having got in touch with its staff to point out the problems in the letter, I suggested to them that the two events, the huge loss and the poor-quality letter, could be linked.

In the bank's letter of apology to me—which, unsurprisingly, was also embarrassingly flawed—it maintained that the letter I had received was not representative of its usual high-quality correspondence. It assured me that quality control measures were in place and claimed to be puzzled about how correspondence from an untrained, unsupervised new employee had escaped the notice of the managers' 'editorial eye'. I remained unconvinced, as I was now in possession of two flawed documents from the bank.

HOW GENRES AND WORKPLACE DOCUMENTS WORK

BOX 8.1 Workplace documents

announcement
annual report
anthology
apology
bid proposal
blog post
book (many types)
book blurb
book proposal
booklet/flyer
brochure
business plan
call centre script
call for papers
catalogue copy
column
competition rules
complaint letter
contract
cookbook
correction notice
critique
CV (curriculum vitae)
dedication
didactic panels (in galleries and museums)
directions
editorial
email message
encyclopedia entry
epilogue
essay
eulogy
event promotion
fact sheet
family history
feature article
financial statement
foreword and afterword
fundraising request
game rules
how-to instructions
index
interview questions
invoice
label
lecture
legal ruling
letter (many types)
liner notes (music album)
manual
media release
memo
menu
mission statement
new product release
news story
newsletter
obituary
patent application
political satire
PowerPoint presentation
press kit
program notes
prologue
promotion for event
prospectus
protocol
publicity material
quotation
radio commercial
recipe
reference
report (many types)
request for proposal
request for quotation
response to selection criteria
résumé
review
scholarship application
service agreement
slogan
speech
study aid
tender document
test
text message
textbook
toast
training material
translation
TV commercial
tweet
webpage content

A comprehensive checklist for letters is provided in Box 8.2.

I have included a sample cover letter that you might send as part of the job application process later in this chapter.

BOX 8.2 **Letter checklist**

Content and structure
1. Is a letter the best way to communicate in this situation?
2. Does the letter have a subject line and/or reference number?
3. Will the reader be able to act on the letter (if necessary)?
4. If it's a reply to an earlier letter, does it respond appropriately?
5. Does the letter follow a logical sequence?
6. Are the sentences and paragraphs clearly structured?
7. Is there an appropriate salutation and close?
8. Is there a copy notation (if a copy of the letter is being sent to other people)?
9. Is there an 'attachment' note (if the letter has an attachment)?

Style and tone
10. Is the opening friendly and motivating?
11. Is the letter's tone appropriately helpful, positive, sincere, polite, and tactful?
12. Is the letter's style appropriate for the reader?
13. Is the letter clear and direct, with no unnecessary jargon or colloquialisms?
14. If it's a 'form' letter, is it personalised for the reader?
15. Is it non-discriminatory in all respects?

Format and layout
16. Does the letter follow open, full-block format (all text starting on the left margin and minimal punctuation in the salutation and sign-off)?

Mechanics
17. Is the recipient's name and all other details correct?
18. Is the letter error-free?
19. Is there a follow-up date on the letter (if relevant)?
20. If the letter is confidential, is it marked as such?

Reports

Reports are written to report on an activity, program, or project that is taking place (interim) or has taken place (final). The writer's intention is usually:

- to inform—by presenting findings in a way that is clear and easily understood
- to persuade—by supporting conclusions with credible, authoritative evidence
- to achieve change and improvement—by providing recommendations that are valid, worthwhile, constructive, and practical.

Most reports will contain the following sections:
- title
- summary (if the report is longer than five pages; encapsulates entire report)
- foreword/introduction/preface (in annual company reports)
- table of contents (if the report is longer than five pages)
- purpose
- scope
- procedure/method
- findings/decisions/results
- conclusions
- recommendations
- index (for long reports)
- appendices.

An 'advance organiser' can be a useful device at various stages of a report. For example, *This report will cover the following matters*.

Common problems with reports include:
- lack of tailoring for the spectrum of potential readers
- lack of a coherent overall structure
- sloppy, inaccurate, and conflicting data
- inclusion of superseded, irrelevant detail
- complaints with no suggested solutions
- unsupported conclusions
- uninviting format.

Reports should be written in a clear, easily understood style. Language should be straightforward, paragraphs should be short, and sections should be clearly signposted by judicious use of headings. The body of a report must comprehensively discuss its topic, citing reliable and accurate data on which the discussion is based. This does not mean that a report must necessarily be long. Length will be dictated by a report's topic, purpose, and audience. However, any report over five pages in length will require a summary, which should concisely present the report's major findings, conclusions, and recommendations. A summary should be an acceptable substitute for the whole report, and not omit any significant information, because it may be the only part of the report that many of its readers read.

It is especially important that reports be:
- dignified and tasteful in appearance, with clear layout and plenty of white space
- logically organised with headings and subheadings
- divided into coherent sections
- honest, open, and accessible (dealing with both positive and negative information)
- mechanically, grammatically, and typographically correct
- precise and consistent in their use of terms and concepts
- hyperlinked to the company's website, if it has one (as most do).

The Australasian Reporting Awards

In 1950, to improve the standards of financial reporting in Australia, a group of leading businesspeople established the Annual Report Awards. The awards are now known as the Australasian Reporting Awards (ARA). They are run by an independent not-for-profit organisation supported by volunteer professionals from the business community and professional bodies concerned about the quality of financial and business reporting.

Woodside Petroleum Limited received the 2015 Report of the Year Award for listed companies and other commercial organisations. The ARA judges said that Woodside Petroleum, Australia's largest independent oil and gas company, had 'provided a visually attractive report that provides stakeholders with easy-to-read information that clearly describes the organisation's activities and performance. High quality information is provided throughout'.

The Commonwealth Scientific and Industrial Research Organisation (CSIRO) received the 2015 Report of the Year Award for non-commercial (government) organisations. The judges said that the 2015 award-winning report was 'well-presented and easy-to-read and to comprehend despite the wide range of topics it covers. The use of relevant pictures and explanatory captions captures attention and encourages the reader to read the whole story'.

Indeed, the narrative element is being increasingly encouraged in many workplace documents: 'Corporate storytelling can take on many guises as it addresses a company's heritage and tradition, customer services, employee engagement and of course, the thoughts and direction of the company's leadership'. (See 'Once upon a time: Storytelling in corporate reporting', *Communicate* magazine, September 2013.)

Box 8.3 presents the criteria used to judge one of the award categories: online reports. If you keep these criteria in mind as you are writing a report and then use the criteria as a checklist, you will be well on your way to writing a prize-winning report.

BOX 8.3 **ARA criteria for online reports**
- readability
- presentation
- navigation
- printability
- financial information
- branding and linkages.

Proposals

Reports usually follow events. Proposals precede them. As their name suggests, proposals propose something. A proposal is a request for support—usually funding—for work that a proposer wants to do (e.g., an analysis of a problem or the provision of a new service or product).

The proposal must convince the person who receives it—the potential funder or supporter—that the proposed activity will be a good investment; that is, that the activity is worthy of support and will advance the funder's objectives, produce high-quality results, and do all this better than other activities competing for the same funds. To make things even more difficult, the proposal must make these arguments to busy readers trying to divide too few resources among too many applicants.

Proposals may be solicited or unsolicited. To avoid being inundated, and to provide guidelines for reviewers, many organisations have a request for proposal (RFP) template that serves as a guideline for applicants. These are often very specific about word and character count, layout, typeface, etc.

Before writing a proposal, ask yourself and/or your colleagues:
- Is the methodology appropriate, clearly defined, and well thought out?
- Can the results be adequately evaluated?
- Is the proposer qualified to do the activity or work? Are they better qualified than others?
- Will the results of the research (if funded) be disseminated publicly?
- Is the proposed schedule of activity and budget reasonable?

Answers to these questions will depend on the particular guidelines, interests, and standards of specific funders. To be sure that your proposal meets the expectations of a given funder, examine what you can of the organisation, such as its annual report. Communicating with the project officer or manager is advisable because they often play a major role in the decision-making process—screening proposals, selecting reviewers, presenting selected proposals to the final selection committee, etc.

To be successful in this environment, you must quickly and clearly answer the questions a potential funder will bring to any request for support:
- What does the proposer (i.e., you) want to do?
- How much will it cost?
- Is the problem to be solved important or relevant to the funder's interests?
- Will the proposed activity solve or reduce the problem?
- Can the proposed activity be done?
- Will it duplicate work already done by others?

Content
A proposal will usually contain the following sections or slots:

- Summary—a short overview of the problem; its importance, objectives, evaluation, impact, cost; why the proposed activity should be funded or conducted; how it will solve the problem; what benefits the funder or society will receive; why the proposers are qualified.
- Situation/background/problem/need—why the project is important.
- Objectives of the proposed activity.
- Benefits/significance/justification. People don't want to pay to see the wheel reinvented. Do a literature review/survey of previous work in the area.
- Methods/procedures/approach to achieving the stated objectives. This section needs to be realistic; thought and spelled out specifically; and achievable within institutional resources and commitments, proposed staffing, and their qualifications and experience.
- Costs/budget. This needs to be worked out in fine detail and presented meticulously.
- Schedule/timetable—starting date, duration.
- Limitations of the proposed methodology, if there are any.
- Evaluation of results. How will this be carried out? The funder needs to be assured that you know how to prove how useful your work will be.
- Appendices, attachments, and references.

A good proposal should anticipate (and answer) a reader's objections, questions, and reservations. You need to think through what you are proposing to the funder. Instead of believing that your reader will be eager to read your proposal and grateful for your solution to a problem, it's better to presume that the potential funder would find it much more justifiable to choose one of your competitors. Proposals frequently don't win jobs as much as they clinch or lose them.

Prepare a flow chart for the structure of your proposal that follows the steps below. A proposal isn't a collection of discrete elements. It is a highly integrated, coherent argument that happens to be segmented for a reader's convenience. All the steps connect intimately with each other.

1. The funder's background situation/problem.
2. Given that problem, your objectives for solving it.
3. Given those objectives, your methods for achieving them.
4. Given those methods, your qualifications to perform them.

5. Given your methods and qualifications, how much it will cost.
6. Given that cost, what the benefits will be.
7. Given all these considerations, how long it will take.

If you will be chiefly responsible for implementing a proposal, then your credibility is an important factor in persuading readers to respond in the desired way. To convince them that you are a 'person of substance', you should address the following points: qualifications, track record, sound knowledge and deep understanding of your area of proposed investigation, and technical and managerial competence. Remember, there is no substitute for substance.

Style and tone

Proposals are generally significant documents, often dealing with large amounts of money. Therefore, their style and tone should be clear, concise, serious, and considered. However, this does not mean that you should lapse into pomposity or wordiness in an effort to sound 'impressive'. In particular, you should avoid the following: an unprofessional appearance, such as obvious and offensive 'cut-and-paste'; poor logic and organisation; more focus on the writer than on the reader's organisation; fuzzy, overly complex, inadequate, or seemingly irrelevant research; unrealistic promises; unjustified claims; specialised or inaccessible jargon; wordiness; unnecessary repetition; vagueness; and lengthy sentences and paragraphs.

Presentation (on paper and online)

A proposal should be presented in a way that makes it accessible and easy to read. Its design should include plenty of white space to balance its (often lengthy) text, along with appropriate graphics to illustrate the ideas that it's trying to convey. If it's an organisational proposal to an outside body (e.g., a tender document), the presentation of the proposal will convey as much about the credibility and reliability of your organisation as the words it contains. Comply rigidly with the criteria.

Finally, your work is not finished once a proposal is submitted. If it's successful, you can look forward to implementing your ideas. If it's unsuccessful, try to get feedback from those who made the decision.

Job applications

An important set of documents allied to the proposal genre is that needed for the job search.

When you set out to find a job, you'll need to prepare a set of documents consisting of several subgenres: a self-analysis; a working/prototype résumé; a cover/application letter; a response to the selection criteria; and, if you make the short list and get interviewed, a 'thanks for the interview' letter. It could also include a portfolio of your work, such as research assignments or reports. Keep a personal record of interviews and visits to organisations (so you don't forget where you've been), as well as applications for jobs, work experience, scholarships, international exchanges/study abroad, etc.

Self-analysis

Conduct a self-analysis to construct an inventory of your personal traits, training, and experience that is more detailed than your résumé. Use this inventory when you are ready to apply for jobs.

What have you learned from:
- your courses and assignments?
- your internships and work experience?
- your extracurricular activities?
- your most significant academic experience?

Ask yourself:
- What are you good at?
- What's your major weakness?
- What's your ideal job?
- What's important to you in a job?
- What are your professional ambitions?
- Do you have a life outside work? (A panel might ask you that.)

As part of your self-analysis, research information about your desired career, industry, and specific organisations that you'd be interested in working for. Search for and collect job ads—the duty statement, and essential and desirable selection criteria. What opportunities would this position give you? What attracts you about this organisation? Research the organisation:

- its products and services
- its organisational philosophy and objectives (e.g., its mission statement)
- its history
- its size and management structure
- its ownership and links to other companies
- its competitors
- its policies (e.g., access and equity)
- relevant statistics (e.g., market share, sales, profits).

Résumé

Based on the information in your self-analysis, prepare a working/prototype résumé outlining your educational qualifications, skills, work experience, and interests. Make sure that you are able to customise it for different jobs. Cover the areas discussed below.

Personal data: Contact details—name, address, mobile telephone number, and email address.

Educational background and qualifications: Begin with your most recent study and work backwards chronologically. If you have not yet completed your tertiary qualification, note the date on which you expect to complete it. Summarise subjects and results, and indicate that you have attached a copy of your academic records. Summarise your secondary school results if you are still at university and entered university straight from school, if they are impressive, or if they seem particularly relevant.

Work experience/employment history: Begin with your most recent employment and work backwards chronologically. For each position, include the month and year when you began and finished employment, the name and address of your employer, your job title, and a description of your major responsibilities. If you have not held a full-time job, list all part-time jobs, even if they seem irrelevant, because they will demonstrate your work ethic. Include any volunteer or community work that you have done. Volunteer work is looked upon very favourably.

When you are describing your past job responsibilities, ignore my warnings about the thesaurus syndrome in Chapter 3 because they apply primarily to nouns. Use action words like those listed in Box 8.4.

> **BOX 8.4 Action words to describe job responsibilities**
>
> | | | |
> |---|---|---|
> | analysed | headed | published |
> | applied | implemented | raised |
> | conceived | improved | ran |
> | coordinated | installed | recruited |
> | created | introduced | reshaped |
> | delegated | invented | restored |
> | designed | judged | revised |
> | developed | launched | served |
> | directed | managed | shaped |
> | discovered | negotiated | solved |
> | employed | operated | stabilised |
> | established | organised | started |
> | evaluated | originated | steered |
> | governed | planned | supervised |
> | guided | prepared | trained |
> | handled | presented | |

Professional achievements: Include awards, active contributions to professional associations, courses completed, and conferences and seminars attended.

Publications: Include any articles that you have had published and any presentations that you have done.

Career objectives: Perhaps include immediate and long-term goals, including plans for further formal education, but only if appropriate.

Personal interests, achievements, skills: List only those relevant to the position you're applying for (e.g., photography, desktop publishing, performance abilities, travel, sport, and communication, leadership and supervisory skills). Familiarity with design programs, such as InDesign, and a range of social media platforms is a distinct advantage, as is your record of volunteer and/or charity work.

Referees: For each referee, include their name, their job title, the organisation they work for, their telephone number, and their email address. Or you may say 'References available on request', but check the job advertisement, which will usually tell you what the potential employer requires in the way of referees. Americans use the term *reference* for *referee*.

The presentation of your résumé is also critical. If it's on paper, it should be printed on good-quality paper with generous margins and plenty of white space. If you are applying for an entry-level position, it should be no more than two A4 pages. A higher-level position warrants more than two pages. Perhaps four. Your résumé should be neat, legible, and accurate. It should be easy to photocopy for members of the interview panel (i.e., not rigidly bound or enclosed in a plastic folder). Online résumés and connections through social media are now common. Many LinkedIn profiles are splendidly rhetorical. Aim to produce a deftly crafted résumé that adequately reflects all you have to offer to an employer.

Cover letter
A cover letter aims to motivate an employer to read your résumé. It usually follows the format and includes the information shown in Box 8.5.

At this stage, potential employers don't expect you to mention salary, superannuation, holidays, time off, or the shortcomings of your present employment situation.

Response to selection criteria
Most job applications will require responses to selection criteria. It is vital that you address all the selection criteria as fully as you can. Box 8.6 provides an example of a response.

'Thanks for the interview' letter
If you are interviewed for a job and would accept it if it were offered to you, a good strategy is to send a thank-you note or email to the panel after the interview. Box 8.7 shows the body of a sample letter.

Style manuals
I mentioned earlier in this chapter that many organisations don't have a style manual that sets out the requirements for writing that their writers

BOX 8.5 **Sample cover letter (job application)**

Sender's name, address, mobile telephone number, and email address

Date

Recipient's name and address

Opening salutation ('Dear . . .' If possible, find out their name.)

Subject line: (in which you include the reference number for the position)

Introduction: the position for which you wish to be considered, how you learned about the position, evidence that you know something about the organisation, why you want to work for this organisation, your career goals, your availability, your most important qualification for the job, and anything unique about your background that will make you an asset.

Body: a reference to your enclosed résumé (noting that it is enclosed, or amplifying relevant aspects of it, but not simply repeating its contents), a mention of your willingness to supply additional material (e.g., your writing portfolio, final-year project, etc.) or information (e.g., written references), and a polite request for an interview.

Conclusion: an indication of how, where, and when you may be contacted. Use an appropriate tone. Avoid presumptuous and pompous comments such as the following, which I have received:

> I will phone you to find out when you would like to interview me.

> For details of my academic and employment histories, records, and references, please consult my enclosed résumé, which I would like returned to me should and if my application for the position is unsuccessful.

Closing salutation ('Yours sincerely' and your name)

> **BOX 8.6 Sample response to a selection criterion**
>
> **Criterion:** *Highly developed copywriting and editing skills, and demonstrated understanding of content flow issues applied during at least one year's successful writing in the online Web space.*
>
> **Response:** My writing skills became highly developed during my Bachelor of Arts degree in English Literature, and have been further extended by a Graduate Diploma of Arts in Writing, Editing, and Publishing. Wanting to shape my skills for the Web and gain experience in the online environment, this year I built and wrote the content of a website for the *Pacific Journal of Communication*, which I work on as the editorial assistant.
>
> This experience resulted in my becoming co-editor of an email newsletter and supporting website for the Faculty of Arts at the University of Brisbane. Through these Web projects, I have gained the skill and ability to:
> - tailor my writing for the internet
> - write informatively, succinctly, and engagingly
> - maintain coherent and consistent content, style, and tone across a website
> - target webpage content to specific audiences.
>
> My editing skills are excellent, as demonstrated by my work on the *Pacific Journal of Communication*. As editorial assistant, I am responsible for:
> - copyediting papers that are accepted for publication
> - correcting mechanical errors and clarifying expression where necessary
> - ensuring that papers fit the stylistic requirements of the journal.

are expected to adhere to. One way to get to the first stage of designing a style manual is to start with a style sheet.

Creating a style sheet

As a record of editorial decisions that must be applied rigorously and consistently, a style sheet comprises alphabetised or miscellaneous categories relating to issues of spelling, diacritics (the use of accents

> BOX 8.7 **'Thanks for the interview' sample letter**
>
> Dear interview panel [use names of people on the panel]
>
> Thank you for the opportunity to meet with you yesterday. I was impressed by your commitment to the company and its plans and prospects. I hope I was able to convey my enthusiasm to work for your company, which is well placed in such an exciting industry.
>
> I believe my qualifications and experience make me an appropriate candidate for this position. I hope that you think so, too, as I would love to be a part of your team.
>
> Please let me know if there is any further information that I can provide.
>
> Thank you again for considering me for this position.
>
> Yours sincerely
>
> [Your name]

and other marks on particular words), punctuation, numbering, dates, etc. It can also include guidance on formatting and documentation.

Figure 8.1 shows a few boxes of the style sheet that my students and I created and used when we edited the program of the Brisbane International Film Festival for several years.

Creating a style manual
A style manual:
- helps writers to identify their readers (actual and potential)
- provides guidance on the organisation's communication style
- orients new staff by providing information in one accessible document
- ensures systematic consistency by addressing issues of policy, terminology, structure, and format
- specifies critical control points in the publication process

A	B	C	D
A-list Academy Award (not Oscar) artefact arthouse auteur *avant-garde*		*cinéaste* *cinéma vérité* CinemaScope close-up Communism Critics' week	
E	F	G	H
I	J	K	L
M	N	O	P
Q	R	S	T
U	V	W	XYZ

Numbers	Dates and time	Punctuation	References
Spell out up to and including ten	8 March 2016 2 pm	Use curly (smart) quote marks rather than straight (dumb) quotes. Check for consistency, if you have used cut-and-pasted material.	Use single inverted commas for parts of a document and italics for whole documents such as books or reports.
Names	Capitalisation	Headings	Other style points

Figure 8.1 Sample style sheet

- works as a reminder of dubious and/or ambiguous issues
- settles arguments about stylistic preferences fuelled by the idiosyncratic and/or pedantic desires of individual writers
- saves an organisation time and money by making the publication process more efficient and the documents more effective
- enhances an organisation's credibility and brand
- reduces risk.

When constructing a style sheet or manual, refer to:
- existing organisational documents
- published style manuals
- grammar, style, and punctuation handbooks
- usage guides (advice on writing and word choice).

Many style manuals, such as *The Chicago Manual of Style* and those of *The Guardian, The Economist*, the Modern Language Association (*MLA Style Manual and Guide to Scholarly Publishing*), and the American Psychological Association (*Publication Manual of the American Psychological Association*), are online. *The Chicago Manual of Style*, which has a very useful online question-and-answer site, is used extensively by organisations and publishing companies in the United States and elsewhere. It is often used as a backup reference by Australian organisations if issues can't be resolved by reference to the official Australian *Style Manual: For authors, editors and printers* (2002, 6th edition) by Snooks & Co. Most Australian government organisations base their guides on this manual, but its advice is often customised by organisations for their own purposes and then posted on their intranets. Buzzfeed and the CIA have unique style manuals.

Instruction manuals

Saul Wurman reminds us that 'instructions are the most basic thing we communicate. We give and receive them all day, every day, but we seldom think about how to ensure that they are understandable. They can take the form of posters, charts, diagrams, quick-reference cards, manuals, handbooks, even conversation' (1989, p. 30).

He goes on to remind us to take into account the level of understanding of our users, which may not be the same as our own. He also warns us about what he calls the 'disease of familiarity', meaning that we may be too familiar with a subject to be able to put ourselves in the place of a neophyte user. What may seem redundant or irrelevant to us as writers may not be obvious to them.

Documentation instructions are often written retrospectively, whereas they should be written when the product is evolving and the steps should be tested with people who are unfamiliar with the process so that the instructions can be adjusted, because it's impossible for those writing the instructions to remember what it was like 'not to know'.

Instruction manuals are increasingly being placed online, or have minimal instructions on paper (often with no words!) that direct users to online help. The key principles to keep in mind when preparing to write instructions are ordering information to parallel the steps a user would take in following the instructions, using words as economically and clearly as possible, using illustrative material, and providing trouble-shooting steps for users who get into difficulties.

We should put checkpoints into place to give our readers a sense of what they can expect at any stage of the process, so that they know when they have gone too far or taken a wrong turn. Online forums for user help are often the port of call after users fail to get the help they need from companies' online help sites. These have the advantage of offering advice that comes from other users, which is also often reassuring.

Writers should keep in mind that people usually prefer to learn about a product by trial and error, consulting a manual as a last-ditch alternative, after exhausting all other avenues—including human help. The strategy that people usually follow is 'When all else fails, read the manual'. Then: 'When that doesn't work, do what it says'. I used my portable sewing machine for about twenty years before I realised that I had been issued with a manual for a different model.

There's an amusing discussion of the term 'manual' by J.A. Cuddon in *A Dictionary of Literary Terms*, where he mentions the *British Railways Handbook*, which catered for 'every conceivable contingency in a railwayman's life': 'This is a masterpiece in its way because of its opaque, convoluted, and, at times, mandarin prose, which might have been written by Henry James while under hypnosis'.

My cousin in California once owned a vintage Packard car. Under the heading in the manual 'General Operations, How to start the car', it says: 'First take a position behind the steering wheel'. This is the kind of basic instruction that would be helpful for many people.

Box 8.8 provides a list of aspects to consider when writing instructions.

> BOX 8.8 **Plan sheet for giving instructions**
>
> **Analysis of situation requiring instructions**
> What is the subject or process to be explained?
> For whom are the instructions intended?
> How will the instructions be used?
> In what form will the instructions be given?
>
> **Significance**
> The operation is important or useful because . . . (by whom, when, where, and why this operation is carried out)
>
> **Equipment and materials**
> For these instructions to be carried out, the following equipment and materials are necessary:
>
> **Terms**
> I may need to identify or explain these words or terms:
>
> **Steps**
> The major steps are these: (list as imperative verbs, such as *turn on*)
>
> **Precautions (troubleshooting)**
> I may want to emphasise these crucial steps or these possible difficulties or these places where errors are likely to occur:
>
> **Visuals**
> To make my instructions clearer, I may want to use illustrations such as diagrams and photos.

Media releases

When you decide that a media release sent to a journalist may help you to get free publicity for a product or cause, you first need to find an angle or 'hook'.

Ask yourself: who is my main audience? Once you have decided this, consider potential media that you can best use to reach that audience: newspapers, radio, TV, or social media? Local, statewide, national, or international? Rural or metropolitan? What message am I trying to get across? What action do I hope will follow? Pick the angle that will appeal most to your audience and best fit your goal.

You will need to tailor different releases on the same topic for different publications and audiences.

Tips on quotations
- Use quotes to add authority to your message.
- Quotes can be powerful persuaders, but make sure that you clearly attribute every quote (i.e., identify who said it).
- Choose verbatim (in their exact words) quotes from people who are credible and appropriate.
- Make sure you have permission to quote them.
- Make sure the quote adds something to the release; don't just repeat information.
- 'Set up' the quote in the previous paragraph (i.e., prepare the reader for what's about to come). See Box 8.9 below.

Follow the conventions for punctuating quotes in news and feature writing:
- use double quotation marks, because newspapers and magazines follow that convention
- insert quotation marks at the start of a direct quote
- don't close them at the end of the paragraph if the quote continues in the next paragraph
- but do open them again at the start of the new paragraph.

One of the easiest ways to become familiar with the placement of quotation marks and commas in news and feature writing is to use a newspaper or magazine as a model and copy its style.

Box 8.9 shows part of the media release that was sent out by the University of Queensland to publicise the launch of WRITE101x, English Grammar and Style, the MOOC (massive open online course) that I developed and ran in 2014 and which attracted 70,000 students. The

2015 run attracted 103,000 students. By 2016, on its third run, it had attracted more than 200,000 students. This media release was very successful; it led to several national and international newspaper and magazine articles and several interviews with me, thereby achieving the goal of FREE extensive media exposure for the university.

BOX 8.9 **Sample media release**

Massive enrolment shows the clamour for grammar
More than 40,000 students from around the world began a grammar course this week at the University of Queensland.

The free, online UQx subject, WRITE101x – English Grammar and Style, has been developed by Associate Professor Roslyn Petelin, from the School of English, Media Studies, and Art History.

"Students range in age from 11 to more than 80, and they are from Paris, France, to Paris, Texas, from Argentina to Venezuela, and from New York to Noosa," Dr Petelin said.

"Since grammar disappeared from primary-school classrooms in the late 1950s, generations of students have been deprived of the utilitarian and recreational pleasure of understanding just how words work to create grammatically correct sentences.

"Clearly, there is a clamour for grammar."

In developing the course, Dr Petelin was supported by "a crack team of young grammar-loving students" who present many of the course videos.

In developing the course, she interviewed world-leading grammarians Professor David Crystal and Professor Geoff Pullum, who has provocatively claimed that "public discussion of grammar is in roughly the same state that public understanding of aeronautical engineering would be if educated adults believed that airplane wings flapped and had feathers".

Dr Petelin also convenes UQ's postgraduate Master of Arts (Writing, Editing and Publishing) Program.

Media: Carolyn Varley +61 7 3365 1120

Speeches

Speeches are written and presented to inform, persuade, motivate, inspire, entertain, and influence.

Speeches are delivered in the workplace at elections, inaugurations, resignations, and openings of new buildings. They are usually delivered to publicise an idea, an issue, or a policy. Speeches are delivered in universities at commencement or orientation and on graduation, by eminent citizens, vice-chancellors, and students, among others.

Good speeches are provocative and memorable. They often have a life way beyond their delivery. One challenging piece of advice that is often given to speechwriters is to try to encapsulate the message so that it will fit onto a bumper sticker.

The late Steve Jobs gave a commencement speech at Stanford University in 2005 that is still talked about; J.K. Rowling gave one at Harvard University in 2008; Bill Gates has given several speeches at Stanford University and Harvard University. The late David Foster Wallace gave a memorable one in 2005 at Kenyon College, Ohio, that aroused widespread interest and is often referred to. There are many, many speeches on YouTube that are inspirational and worth watching. There was one notorious commencement address apparently by Kurt Vonnegut at Massachusetts Institute of Technology in 1997 that was circulated so widely over the internet that his wife called to congratulate him on his wit and eloquence. It turned out that he hadn't delivered the speech. It was a hoax.

When the high-profile environmentalist Paul Hawken was invited to give a commencement speech at the University of Portland in 2009, he was asked to give 'a simple short talk that is direct, naked, taut, honest, passionate, lean, shivering, startling, and graceful'. Read it online to see whether he managed to fulfil the request.

What are the characteristics of a good speech?
- It is interesting enough to attract attention in advance publicity.
- It suits the presentation style and personality of the speaker.
- It has a coherent structure, with an introduction that grabs the audience's attention by establishing or reinforcing the credibility of the speaker and a close that stimulates action and conveys a sense of finality.

- It should not sound like an 'essay up on its hind legs' (William Norwood Brigance).
- It has simple, declarative, active-voice sentences featuring parallelism and repetition.
- It exhibits flair, imagination, and authority.

Style

Speeches are written in oral style, that is, 'talking words' appropriate for speaking in public. A speech should be written in an informal style, but not so informal that the audience is distracted by its style and doesn't focus on the message.

Oral style is characterised by:

- simple, precise, vivid diction; repetition (because listeners cannot rehear)
- clear, punchy copy, but not as concise as other written documents (again because listeners cannot rehear)
- pseudo-quantitative generalisation (*many, a lot*)
- humour (wit, not jokes), to relax the audience and humanise the speaker
- a conversational flavour (*it seems as though, it appears*)
- imagery, expressed in figurative language (similes, metaphors, analogies; see Chapter 3)
- self-references to the speaker, the audience, and the situation, but with careful consideration about the amount of self-disclosure
- an absence of clichés, slang, pompous words, and tongue-twisters.

Many high-profile speechwriters have worked closely with particular politicians, for example, Graham Freudenberg with Prime Minister Gough Whitlam and Don Watson with Prime Minister Paul Keating. Freudenberg is quoted by Margaret Simons (2003) as saying 'a speech has less to do with words than commitment to a cause'. Watson echoes him: 'Words and ideas are inseparable and you will never get good speeches if you demand that writers deal only with words. . . . Outrageous as it may seem to modern political geniuses, writing a speech is not the equivalent of cake decoration. You actually have to be in on the cake itself. That is why politicians will often write better speeches for themselves than their staff will be able to come up with' (Simons, 2003).

Jon Favreau, who was President Obama's speechwriter for eight years from 2005 to 2013, gave a talk at Duke University in 2015 in which he presented five major lessons he learned during his time working with the president. Here are his tips:

1. The story is more important than the words: avoid chasing catchy slogans in favour of focusing on the overall argument.
2. The importance of humour: take your job seriously, but not yourself.
3. Talk like 'a normal human being': leave out shorthand and jargon to be accessible.
4. There is a need for honesty and authenticity: be personal and be courageous.
5. Maintain idealism: cynicism and hope are both choices, so choose hope. (Scott, 2015)

I have reproduced in full in the activities section at the end of this chapter a valedictory speech given at a graduation ceremony at the University of Queensland by a student, Deânne Sheldon-Collins, so that you can analyse it using the principles of speechwriting outlined in this section.

The last word

You may find yourself writing across a range of documents in the workplace. Some writing workers specialise in producing one kind of document, such as writing decision letters in response to requests under Right to Information Acts. Others write a wide variety of documents. Some organisations hire writers who specialise in public relations. Increasingly, writers are being hired to handle an organisation's social-media presence, an initiative that I'll cover extensively in Chapter 10. The key to successful writing in the workplace is to consider your reader, conform to genre conventions, and consider the consequences of not adhering to those principles.

Activities

1. Interview a workplace writer to obtain the material you'd need if you were to write an article on 'A day in the life of a workplace writer'. You

can choose a working writer or a writing worker. Their observations will reflect their background. Write the article and try to get it published.

2. Write an unsolicited proposal to a company to convince them to hire you as a freelance technical writer/editor.
3. Write a letter to a company complaining about a product or a service that you are dissatisfied with. Your best chance of getting a satisfactory reply will depend on what you want (an apology, replacement of a product, compensation) and the tone that you use in your letter to the company. Aim, to communicate, in the 'nicest possible way', what you want from them.
4. Write a set of instructions for new students about how to get the most out of university life.
5. If you are setting out on a job hunt, write a letter to a former lecturer or manager who is familiar with you and your work, asking them whether they are prepared to act as your referee in your search. You can also ask them if they are prepared to act as a referee for any subsequent jobs that you may apply for. Promise to send them the job specification and the application for each job that you plan to apply for.
6. Analyse the part of the media release in Box 8.9 above and ascertain whether it follows the advice given in this chapter on media releases. Why was it so successful?
7. Analyse the following student speech to see whether it fulfils the criteria for speeches given in this chapter.

> Chancellor, Vice-Chancellor, members of Senate, academic staff of the university, distinguished guests, fellow graduates, ladies and gentlemen, good afternoon.
>
> I had not been an Arts student for long before I became sick of a certain word: 'and'. More specifically, I became sick of hearing this word phrased as a question, the inevitable question that came whenever I told someone what I was studying. 'What's your program?' 'I'm studying to become a Bachelor of Arts'. '. . . And?'
>
> It seemed that Arts by itself was a rare thing. People did not study Arts simply to obtain a BA. They studied Arts to 'get their foot in the door', to combine it with another degree, to use it as a

starting point for many years' more study. Apparently, Arts could only be justified in conjunction with something else.

This viewpoint didn't worry me for long, however. Exploring courses across a range of subjects, I came to a realisation: that Arts was, indeed, the broad program people said it was—but that this broadness was its strength, rather than its weakness.

I *have* found Arts to be foundational. I agree that it is an excellent starting point for further study, but I also think that it is an excellent starting point for *anything*, whether you intend to build on it with another degree or not. My courses taught factual knowledge, but also new ways to think. I've learned how to approach tasks in different ways, to critically interact with information I'm given, and to question more deeply than I did before. I've even learned how to better manage my time: these days, procrastination means starting an assignment two weeks before it's due, rather than two days, which I consider definite progress. However much I may continue to build on this basis, Arts provided the necessary foundation.

By exploring the many options offered, I was able to find my way to areas that truly interested me. Studying what interested me meant studying what I loved; studying what I loved meant studying with a passion; studying with a passion meant I was motivated to work and to strive for my best. The range of possibilities Arts offers has encouraged me to engage with my courses—to make connections between seemingly disparate areas of study. For example, Writing, Art History, Literature, and Classics examined many of the same critics from different perspectives. Art studied in Classics influenced movements studied in Art History. Writers studied in Classics influenced texts studied in Literature. Literature reflected History and History informed Literature. These are just a few examples of the many ways an understanding of one topic often proved to enhance an understanding of others. And this is why I assert that the broadness of Arts is its strength, and not its weakness.

This has been my personal experience of the last three years, but I know that many others have thrived on the chance to explore diverse areas of study, just as I have, finding the links and the divergences between them, just as I have. Everybody finds their way differently, but, however unique the experiences that have brought us here, today we've come together to the same point, which I hope you all find as satisfying as I do. Congratulations to all my fellow graduates. I don't need to tell you how hard you've worked to reach this point, and that you deserve what you receive today.

What now? Perhaps you intend to continue your studies. Perhaps you intend to enter a particular career. Perhaps you intend to go home, curl up with your degree, feel very self-satisfied, and vow never to risk academia again. Or perhaps you have no idea what you want to do. Wherever you go from this point, I wish you the best of luck. I'm certain your degree will serve you well, and I hope you enjoyed obtaining it as much as I did.

I also hope you've been as fortunate in your teachers as I have. Even studying subjects I was passionate about would not have been enough to motivate me if I had not had excellent lecturers and tutors working to convey their own passions for what they taught, to encourage students to think as well as to learn, and to make their classes as useful and interesting as they could. For myself, and on behalf of my fellow graduates, I would like to extend a sincere thank-you to the staff of this university.

Thank you also to the friends and families who have seen us this far. Your support has been invaluable, even if you did occasionally ask '. . . And?' Thank you.

Deânne Sheldon-Collins,
valedictory address to a graduation ceremony at
The University of Queensland, 2010

9

How genres and academic writing work

> Every time a student sits down to write for us, [the student] has to invent the university for the occasion—invent the university, that is, or a branch of it, like history or anthropology or economics or English. The student has to learn to speak our language, to speak as we do, to try on the peculiar ways of knowing, selecting, evaluating, reporting, concluding, and arguing that define the discourse of our community . . . to write, for example, as a literary critic one day and as an experimental psychologist the next.
>
> DAVID BARTHOLOMAE

Research-based writing: How academic writing works

Academic documents are researched, written, and published to increase the base of scholarly knowledge. The main genres that academics rely on to do this are the annotated bibliography, the literature review, and the research paper. These documents are ubiquitous in the university; they are also central to many government and industry workplaces. Reports requiring academic research are common in the professional workplace, as are research-based articles for trade magazines and websites.

An **annotated bibliography** is a list of documents such as books, papers, and articles (in hard copy and online) that includes a description of each document's content and comments on its value. A **literature**

review is an overview of what scholars have written about a specific topic, and when and where they have published their contribution to knowledge about the topic. A literature review identifies and discusses the concepts, issues, theories, and research related to a particular topic or subject area. A **research paper** takes content from the sources uncovered in a literature review and moves on from them to make an argument. As Jennie Nelson states: 'It is not a report of facts, but a careful marshalling of the judgments, opinions, and ideas of others to support your own position' (1990, p. 383).

In this chapter, I'll cover these genres and suggest strategies that will enhance your writing in an academic context. These strategies are also valuable when you write research-based workplace documents. The need for you to reliably produce high-quality writing in the course of your tertiary education (and in your profession after graduation) is undeniable. Comments by employers and tertiary teachers consistently highlight the need for students and graduates to be confident, competent, and rhetorically sophisticated writers. Unfortunately, many students lack the confidence and motivation to write, and few institutions have the mechanisms in place that help students to enhance their writing skills.

As a student at a tertiary institution, you may need to write a far wider variety of documents than you expected to when you began your course. Box 9.1 presents a list of the extraordinarily diverse range of written assignments being set in different disciplines in one university. As you can see from the list, many of the written assignments set for tertiary students are designed to mirror the writing tasks expected of professionals in the workplace. I discussed the most common of these organisational workplace documents, including reports and proposals, in Chapter 8, and I cover web content and blog posts in Chapter 10.

University students are expected to produce well-written and cogently argued writing as part of their studies. Students of every discipline are expected to complete some written assessment, and many of the subjects that require extensive writing are in disciplines not typically thought of by students as writing-intensive, for example, dance, economics, engineering, information technology, and mathematics. Furthermore, lecturers and tutors in many disciplines specify that written work must be clear, well structured, and mechanically correct, while, in advanced

> **BOX 9.1 University documents**
>
> | | |
> |---|---|
> | advertisement copy | media release |
> | annotated bibliography | news and feature article |
> | blog post | newsletter |
> | case study | public relations campaign |
> | catalogue copy | policy statement |
> | curriculum materials | proposal |
> | essay | report |
> | exam | research paper |
> | journal | résumé |
> | learning contract | review of arts events |
> | legal brief and opinion | script (for a film or a play) |
> | letter | seminar presentation |
> | literature review | short story |
> | log book | speech |
> | manual | training program |
> | mathematical argument | web content |

subjects, students are often required to produce writing 'of a professional standard' or 'fit for publication'. Your ability to write efficiently and effectively will be crucial to your academic success, regardless of the course in which you are enrolled.

Academic research

Academic research is a systematic process of investigation; data gathering, interpretation, and analysis; problem-solving; and argument. The English word *research* derives its current meaning from the French word *chercher* ('to look for') and from the Latin word *circare* ('to circle around', 'to explore'). Lunsford and Connors (1989) point out that 'much, if not most, work relies on research: we find something out, and then we report on it' (p. 515). They argue that students already know how to do research because they know how to combine experience, observation, and new information whenever they try to solve a problem.

Academic writing—sometimes called analytic writing—more or less equates with 'writing from sources'. These may be secondary sources (such as books and journal articles) or primary sources (such as interviews, surveys, or experiments that you conduct, or first-hand accounts by you and others). Selecting and using such sources appropriately is critical to successful academic writing. As Brodkey (1990) notes, 'learning to read and write academic prose is a matter of learning conventions such as whom to cite and when to do so, for these conventions are part of the cultural repertoire of all academia' (p. 23).

To be a successful academic writer, you must learn to:
- take an interest in topics that lend themselves to analysis
- differentiate legitimate academic sources from 'popular' sources
- analyse, synthesise, and integrate ideas gained from sources
- develop your own ideas, and extend, critique, and challenge (not just summarise) those put forward by others
- develop and support a thesis statement (an assertion about your topic)
- use expert opinion and factual detail to support your argument
- write documents according to an approved academic format
- use a style appropriate to scholarly writing
- assume responsibility for your own scholarly rigour
- establish your credibility through the authenticity, accuracy, and precision of your material.

In short, you will be expected to think and write like an academic or scholar, in the field in which you are studying. Even though many of you may not intend to take up a career as an academic, the skills (if not the exact format) you learn for academic writing can be used in other documents and in your professional life. The ability to research, write, and argue your point of view, using credible and appropriate sources, will always stand you in good stead. Furthermore, increasing numbers of students and professionals are completing double degrees, multiple degrees, and higher degrees. This has a twofold effect: first, you may find yourself writing academic assignments for a much longer period than you intended when you first entered university; and second, in a workforce where more and more professionals have tertiary qualifications, competence in academic writing will enhance your ability to communicate. This will, in turn, increase your promotional opportunities.

What is academic writing?

Peter Elbow defines academic writing as 'the discourse that academics use when they publish for other academics' (1991, p. 135). In other words, it is the kind of writing done by 'career' or 'professional' scholars who teach and research in institutions of higher education. Academics publish this writing in scholarly journals, books, and collections of papers delivered at academic conferences. Academic writing is characterised by particular conventions and jargon that are usually quite specific to the discipline or field in which the writer works.

Contrary to popular opinion, jargon is not necessarily a bad thing. It can be an efficient and effective way of communicating with colleagues or specialists in a particular field. However, jargon used unnecessarily or in an inappropriate context can obscure your message and alienate your readers. Academic jargon used in this way is often the butt of criticism in the popular press, because journalists and the general public see its use as exclusionary and elitist. The sociologist C. Wright Mills agrees that this can be a problem. In his book *The Sociological Imagination* (1977), he shows what can happen when writers get carried away with academic jargon. First, he makes a point in fairly straightforward language:

> The most economical way to state a problem is in such a way as to solve as much of it as possible by reasoning alone. By reasoning we try (1) to isolate each question of fact that remains; (2) to ask these questions of fact in such ways that the answers promise to help us solve further problems by further reasoning. (p. 226)

Then he 'translates' it into the kind of pretentious jargon that he says many academics believe they need to use to impress upon their readers that what they are saying is very important:

> Problematic situations have to be formulated with due attention to their theoretical and conceptual implications, and also to appropriate paradigms of empirical research and suitable models of verification ... The theoretical and conceptual implications of problematic situations should first be fully explored. To do this requires the social scientist to

specify each such implication and consider it in relation to every one, but also in such a way that it fits the paradigms of empirical research and the models of verification. (pp. 226-7)

These two passages highlight the confusion in some people's minds about what constitutes 'academic' writing; many would think that the second version is truly 'academic', purely because it is so densely written and difficult to understand. This is not the case. The first version—which, I'm sure you'll agree, is more 'reader-friendly'—exemplifies good, clear, well-reasoned academic writing. The wordiness and jargon of the second version is what gives academic writing a bad name, and is not the style that academics who are considerate of their readers would recommend.

But academic writing is not just the province of academics. It is also the kind of writing that students are expected to produce in all their courses at institutions of higher education. In this context, it serves a number of functions. First, it allows teachers to assess how well students have grasped the content of their courses. As Elbow says, having taught their material, teachers expect students to 'serve it back to them'. This is variously referred to as 'knowledge telling' (Bartholomae, 1985, p. 144) and 'informational writing for the teacher-as-examiner' (McCarthy, 1987, p. 243). It boils down to regurgitation and, on its own, is not an activity that most good teachers advocate.

Instead, good teachers generally expect students to develop and argue their own ideas, using source materials to stimulate and support their thinking. As Charles Bazerman (1989) advises:

> Using everything you have learned about the subject, you must put the information and ideas together in a new way. In this new statement your own ideas and interpretations will dominate. The source materials will only serve to support your ideas or provide points of discussion to allow you to develop your ideas further. (p. 13)

This kind of academic writing is an opportunity for students to produce original work, and enables teachers to assess not only familiarity with course material, but also students' ability to explore, critique, and extend that material.

Most teachers will also assess how competently you apply the conventions of an academic writing style. Learning these conventions is neither a quick nor an easy process. You need to understand the broad conventions of the genre, and those of the particular discipline in which you are studying. This can take a long time because, as Lester Faigley and Kristine Hansen (1985) point out, you 'need to know how that discipline creates and transmits knowledge' (p. 148). You also need to know how new knowledge becomes accepted in different disciplines. Furthermore, as Bartholomae says in the epigraph at the beginning of this chapter, once you have acquired this understanding, you must invoke it each time you write (1985, pp. 134–5).

Becoming skilled in the intellectual and stylistic practices of academic writing will give you a significant advantage. Students who are effective academic writers have a great deal of power over their educational careers, while students who aren't encouraged to master its conventions are being short-changed. As Bartholomae incisively puts it, 'the student has to appropriate (or be appropriated by) a specialized discourse' (1985, p. 135). Furthermore, the processes of critical reasoning encouraged by good academic writing will always be useful to you, especially in the workplace.

Critical reasoning

In surveys of the skills employers look for in graduates, a key desire is for employees with critical-thinking and problem-solving skills. Glen Lewis and Christina Slade (1994) describe critical-thinking skills as those involved in connecting and organising ideas. They distinguish three types: analysis, inference, and evaluation.

Analysis involves:
- identifying what is being said
- distinguishing what is relevant from what is not
- seeing connections between different strands of thought
- recognising vagueness and ambiguity, then clarifying terms if necessary
- identifying members of a class, in terms of likenesses
- identifying counterinstances as different in some respect
- identifying analogies.

Inference involves:
- drawing out the consequences of what is said
- identifying underlying assumptions
- generalising from particular instances, that is, abstracting
- applying analogies to reach new conclusions
- recognising cause–effect relationships.

Evaluation involves:
- giving reasons for beliefs and decisions and then choosing how to act
- criticising ideas constructively
- modifying ideas in response to criticism. (p. 77)

You will have the opportunity to develop all of these skills when you engage in the process of structuring an argument in academic writing.

For 2000 years after Aristotle and well into the twentieth century, many academics claimed that formal logic is the best basis for teaching and analysing argument and reasoning. Derived from mathematics, formal logic is based on proofs that can be expressed through formulae. The classical syllogism, revered as the cornerstone of all argument, is expressed in Figure 9.1.

Major premise: All people are mortal.
Minor premise: Socrates is a person.
Conclusion: Therefore, Socrates is mortal.

Figure 9.1 The classical syllogism

Then, in the late 1950s, philosopher Stephen Toulmin argued that the mathematical basis of such formal syllogistic logic was too static to be applied to the assessment of rational argument used by 'actual' people in the real world. Instead, he developed a system of 'practical' argument, in which claims are justified and supported by data. In *An Introduction to Reasoning*, Toulmin et al. (1984) define argumentation as 'the whole activity of making claims, challenging them, backing them up by producing reasons, criticizing those reasons, rebutting those criticisms, and so on' (p. 13).

Toulmin describes his system of practical argument (which, after he had constructed it, he noticed was similar to legal argument) as a movement from accepted data (grounds), through a warrant (a licence to make an inference, authority to move forward from grounds), to a claim (conclusion). A rebuttal contains reasons for not moving from a warrant to a claim. Sometimes, the claim needs to be qualified (Toulmin, 1958).

Toulmin's system of analysis can be applied to any argument that you encounter in the literature of your field. To apply it, use the following heuristic:

- What is the claim being made?
- What grounds support the claim?
- What underlying assumptions support the grounds?
- What backup evidence is there to add further support?
- What refutations can be made against the claim?
- In what way(s) is the claim qualified?

When you have written a research paper, use Toulmin's heuristic to check the validity of your argument.

Getting started on research

When you embark on research, it is worth bearing in mind the heuristic based on Rudyard Kipling's poem that I quoted in Chapter 1. Kipling's prompts are the ones that every researcher should ask themselves: what? when? where? who? why? how? These questions are valuable when you are searching for information, as shown in Figure 9.2. They can also help you to find and refine your research question, as discussed below.

> What is the key issue?
> Why is it significant?
> Who are the key researchers? theorists? scholars?
> How do you find out about your topic?
> Where do you look?
> When was the material published?

Figure 9.2 A heuristic for research

Choosing a topic and research question

A topic is a broad area or issue of interest. For example, 'non-discriminatory language' is a much-discussed topic in the communication field. A research question is a specific question about a topic that you set out to answer in a piece of academic writing. For every topic, there are many research questions that could be asked. For example, possible research questions about the topic 'non-discriminatory language' include:

- Why is non-discriminatory language desirable/necessary?
- For how long and in what contexts has non-discriminatory language been practised?
- What recent developments have occurred in the practice of non-discriminatory language?
- Does non-discriminatory language affect reader comprehension?
- How do writers go about following guidelines for non-discriminatory language?
- Do your textbooks follow guidelines for non-discriminatory language?

Research questions set by teachers are often framed not as questions but as directives, for example:

- Describe the origins and applications of non-discriminatory language in journalistic writing.
- Discuss non-discriminatory language as a function of the 'political correctness' movement.
- Research the acceptance or otherwise of the singular 'they' by writing authorities in Australia, the United Kingdom, North America, and South-East Asia.

Analyse the directive to find its implicit question or questions.

If you are required to write on a set question, the first hard decision has been made for you. Often, however, you will be asked to develop your own research question. In this situation, I suggest that you choose one that interests and motivates you, either from your major area of study, or from your personal or professional interests.

If you are required to formulate your own research question, it is unlikely that you will be able to do so immediately. Instead, you will need to become familiar with a topic, and then use your understanding of the topic to formulate an interesting and manageable research question. You may have to do preliminary library research to get inspired or to gain confidence that there's enough material on your chosen topic. A good strategy is to peruse theme issues of journals, which usually cover the current thinking on a particular topic. It will also be useful to speak to an expert, or read their work, to get an idea of the key issues and writers in a field. Experts include your teachers, other scholars and researchers, practitioners, and librarians. You should also think about the information you have already received. Your teacher may have given you a great deal of advance assistance by providing suggested questions, examples of questions that have been dealt with by previous students, sample papers done by such students, or a list of relevant sources.

You will also find relevant articles in newspapers, magazines, and popular journals, in hard copy and online, but make sure that you balance these with material from 'scholarly' sources. Wikipedia can get you off to a good start in your research. Journalist Elizabeth Farrelly (2015) claims that 'we all use Wikipedia. It's hard to avoid. On just about any Google search, Wiki tops the list. Because it's also astoundingly comprehensive, intelligible and reliable, it has become [the] ubiquitous go-to start point'.

However, as Wikipedia says on its own site:

> not everything in Wikipedia is accurate, comprehensive, or unbiased. Many of the general rules of thumb for conducting research apply to Wikipedia, including:
> - Always be wary of any one single source (in any medium . . .), or of multiple works that derive from a single source.
> - Where articles have references to single sources (whether online or not) read the references and check whether they really do support what the article says.

Understanding the field

Developing a thorough understanding of the literature of any field takes time and effort. To do so, you must become part of a previously unfamiliar sphere. Kenneth Burke, a prominent American rhetorical scholar, likens this process to being a latecomer to a conversation:

> Imagine that you enter a parlor. You come late. When you arrive, others have long preceded you and they are engaged in a heated discussion, a discussion too heated for them to pause and tell you exactly what it is about. In fact, the discussion had already begun long before any of them got there, so that no one present is qualified to retrace for you all of the steps that had gone before. You listen for a while, until you decide that you have caught the tenor of the argument; then you put in your oar. (1941, pp. 110–11)

The best way to 'enter the parlor' and start to become familiar with the seminal and current literature in a field is to read widely. This will increase your ability and your confidence to distinguish the important from the peripheral and the ephemeral.

Linking sources

As you do your research and become familiar with the literature, you will see who the seminal and key scholars are, because they will be cited by many other scholars. One source will lead you to another—what is called the 'snowball effect'. You will also see issues or debates recurring in a number of articles. Failure to cite important scholars, issues, and debates is likely to damage your credibility with readers. For instance, if you write a paper on critical pedagogy and don't cite Paulo Freire (a seminal writer on the topic) and his key followers—Ira Shor, Stanley Aronowitz, and Henry Giroux—or mention the pedagogy of oppressed groups (a major issue in this field), an informed reader (such as your teacher) will infer that you have done very little reading on your selected topic or that you have been unable to identify the leading scholars on the topic.

As you work your way through library material, look for a pattern of connections among the various sources. Develop an overall assertion about how the various sources relate to one another. Try to establish the current consensus of experts on the topic. You should also notice any contrary arguments, because you will usually be expected to present both sides of an issue. Many academic journals have a 'Forum' section where readers respond to articles published in earlier issues. A section such as this highlights controversies in specific areas, and can be a shortcut for you into both sides of an argument.

Evaluating sources

Having located sources that you think may be useful, you must evaluate whether or not they are worth using in your research. Before you take notes or start photocopying, assess how relevant, authoritative, and up to date each source is. Be selective: use only those sources that are relevant to your research question, that say something significant on the topic, and (unless they are key or seminal works in the field) that have been written in the past ten years.

Remember, the fact that a book or article has been published is no guarantee that it is of high quality. An enormous amount of material gets published, and not all of it is good. (That's one of the reasons why it's important to become familiar with the respected scholars in your field.)

Rebecca Rubin et al. (2016) suggest ways of judging the quality of books that you read in your research. I have adapted their discussion to produce the following checklist. You might also like to return to the book reviewing advice at the end of Chapter 2:

- Read the preface and/or introduction to establish why the work was written (e.g., to inform, interpret, explain, or share new discoveries).
- Check the intended level of readership to determine the book's appropriateness for your purposes.
- Determine how recent the material is.
- Examine the book's methodology and data for appropriateness and scholarship. Unless you are already an expert on the topic, try to find reviews of the book. Book reviews may be of uneven quality as well, so be wary of this. Books that win awards are usually of a very high quality.
- Check the author's background and qualifications to establish their expertise.
- Note whether the book has been published by a reputable publisher or self-published.
- Check the end of the book for an index. A book without an index will be much less useful than an indexed book.
- Check that generalisations are supported by data and examples.

Most of the above points apply particularly to books, but you can adapt them when you evaluate articles in journals, on paper or online.

Recording information from sources

Once you've decided that a source is worth using, be meticulous in recording information from it. You can use index cards for each source, as they are very easy to shuffle around when you are arranging your information into a sequence. However, writers are increasingly using bibliographic utilities such as EndNote. These are useful because, once you have keyed in your information, you can automatically generate a reference in whatever documentation system you require. Many word-processing programs have bibliographic utilities.

Make a note of all the information required to document a particular source.

For books, record the following information:
- call number
- author(s)
- editor(s), if applicable
- publication date
- title of essay or chapter (if relevant)
- title of book
- edition
- volume number, if applicable
- place of publication
- publisher
- page numbers of essay/chapter (if relevant).

For journal articles, record the following information:
- call number
- author(s), first three then et al. ('and all the others')
- title of article
- name of journal/magazine
- issue and volume number, if applicable
- page numbers
- digital object identifier, or DOI (the unique alphanumeric string assigned by the international DOI Foundation to identify content and provide a persistent link to an article published in print or electronically).

Also indicate whether your note is a summary or quoted verbatim (word for word), and note the page number of any quoted material. As a rule, summarise material in your own words, quoting verbatim only when a passage makes a point in a more compelling or authoritative way than you could. When you quote verbatim, make sure that you copy everything you need exactly as it is in the original—right down to the exact spelling, punctuation, and conventions such as italics.

Try to construct your argument as you go, and use your argument to help you select useful sources and sections. Without some sense of which points you want to cover, and what you would like to say about them, it is very tempting to simply generate note after note of excerpts and summaries from articles and books. This can result in your amassing a mountain of notes that overwhelms you, to the extent that it's almost impossible to select, sequence, and synthesise all your material. Ideally, the research process should allow you to become progressively more selective: the more you read and think, the more clearly you should know what you do and don't want to record.

Incorporating source materials

An essential feature of writing from sources is citing your sources. There are several reasons for doing so. Primarily, you do it to:
- add authority to a point, statement, or argument
- show the sources of your evidence and opinions
- permit your reader to identify and locate your sources to pursue their own research
- fulfil your moral obligation to give credit.

The material that you should acknowledge using documentation includes:
- direct quotations
- controversial opinions or data that an informed reader might challenge
- ideas or data that you have obtained from another source
- references to additional material that your reader may wish to examine
- definitions of terms (but it's better to give these in your own words).

You can incorporate material from sources such as books, journals, and magazines by quoting verbatim, summarising, or paraphrasing. Each of these processes necessitates citing a source. It is vital that you do this accurately and completely. As the *Publication Manual of the American Psychological Association* (2009) reminds its readers, an inaccurate or incomplete reference 'will stand in print as an annoyance to future investigators and a monument to the writer's carelessness' (p. 175).

Quoting verbatim

The advantage of a verbatim (direct) quote is that you use the author's exact words. You should use a direct quote when it illustrates a point more compellingly and authoritatively than you can through a summary or paraphrase; you want to share it with the reader before analysing or critiquing it.

When you quote verbatim, remember to be meticulous. Accuracy is essential. If there is an error in the original, include it. If you want your reader to know that you recognise the error, place '[*sic*]' immediately after the error.

If you decide to omit material within a quote because the quote is too long or because some material is irrelevant, use an ellipsis (three spaced full stops) to indicate the omission. There is generally no need to use ellipses at the beginning or end of a quote, because it is usually obvious that you are only quoting part of what the original author wrote.

Sometimes, when you want to make a quote flow smoothly with your prose, when you leave material out of a quote, or when you want to explain something that is unclear, you will need to insert an explanatory word or two in the quote. This is called an interpolation, and should be placed in square brackets.

Be careful to make sure that if you omit or insert material, you don't distort the writer's intended meaning. Of course, as I noted in Chapter 2, contemporary reading theory asserts that readers cannot know an author's exact intention in writing particular words, but you must avoid making significant changes to the words, or taking them dramatically out of context, or you will be misquoting. As you look through the journals in your field, you will find plenty of examples of letters to editors from indignant scholars who accuse others of 'deliberately misquoting' them.

Also be careful not to directly quote too much, or the voices of the original authors whom you quote will dominate your work. Never extend a quote more than you need to. Direct quotes should play a secondary role to your own words. Some guides suggest that your work should include no more than 10 to 15 per cent of directly quoted material. Direct quotes are usually not included in a word count of your paper, but check with your teacher on this point.

You can integrate quotes of fewer than 40 words, or four lines, into your text. Use single quotation marks to do this. For quotes longer than 40 words or four lines, indent the quote, single-space it, and don't use quotation marks around it. The visual message of the indented block of print makes quotation marks unnecessary.

Summarising

A summary is a significantly shortened version of an original text, capturing the essence of that text. To summarise, you should delete the less important information and not add any ideas of your own. A summary needs to be concise and focused. Often in academic writing you will be expected to provide a summary of someone else's work. If you use any of their exact phrases or sentences, make sure that you put those words into quotation marks. Even if you don't quote verbatim, identify the original sources of your summary.

You will notice that many academic journals accompany papers with a summary (called an abstract). Usually, this abstract appears just before the article. Abstracts can also be collected into a group and placed at the beginning or end of a journal. Abstracting services publish selections of these abstracts. This can be another source of material for you to explore when you are surveying the literature of your field.

Paraphrasing

A paraphrase is a restatement, in your own words, of someone else's material. It states fully and clearly the meaning of another piece of writing. Because it usually requires explanation, it may be even longer than the original. However, it should not include your personal comment or elaboration. When you paraphrase, you retain control of the voice of the writing, but you must still acknowledge your source.

Remember, to summarise is to cut down to the essence, while to paraphrase is to restate.

Avoiding plagiarism

When you copy a quotation or paraphrase an author, you add authority to your own voice and views, but you must give credit to your source, or you will be accused of plagiarism. Plagiarism occurs when you use someone else's material in your work and do not acknowledge the original author's contribution. It is a serious breach of academic ethics, with severe consequences, particularly for students (e.g., zero marks for an assignment, failure in a course or subject, and possible suspension from the university). Furthermore, authors' words are their property, and are protected by law.

Using documentation styles

It is essential when documenting to use the appropriate system for a particular academic situation, and to be accurate, comprehensive, and consistent. Use whichever system your teacher requires, and follow it without deviation.

There are three main systems of documentation, with many variations within them:
1. the author–date system
2. the author–short-title system
3. the numbered notes system.

Within the author–date system, there are two main variations: the American Psychological Association (APA) system and the Harvard system. (Note that Harvard is just one variation of the author–date system, although some guides equate the author–date system with the Harvard style. There is no authoritative manual of the Harvard system. The Australian Government Publishing Service's *Style Manual: For authors, editors and printers* (6th edition) has a short explanation of author–date style.)

The APA system is the most widely used documentation style in the social sciences, and is also used in sciences such as agriculture, botany, and astronomy. I have used the APA system, with slight variations to conform to the publisher's 'house' style, to document my sources in this book. The Harvard system is widely used in law, the sciences, and cultural studies.

Language and literature scholars generally use the author–short-title system developed by the Modern Language Association (MLA). In 2016, the MLA released a new set of guidelines that writers will be able to apply to any type of source. See style.mla.org for details of the 8th edition.

Finally, the numbered notes system is used in the creative arts and, in a slightly different form, in sciences such as chemistry, mathematics, and medicine. It is sometimes referred to as the Oxford system.

If you cannot find guidance elsewhere, you may wish to look in scholarly journals from the field in which you are writing, because many of them include guides setting out stylistic conventions that editors have developed for potential contributors. If you submit any of your work to a scholarly journal, be sure to document it in the way the editor requires. Editors may give short shrift to papers whose authors have not bothered to adhere to the requested style.

Where to document sources

When writing a paper, you must document your sources in two places: in the paper itself, indicating which pieces of information you have drawn from others' work, and at the end of the paper, where you list the full details of the works you have cited, and sometimes those of other works relevant to your topic.

In-text citations are incorporated in different ways, depending on the system you are using. This book's in-text citations use the APA style. If you are using MLA style or numbered notes, you will need to follow the protocols for them. The lists that appear at the ends of papers may also take different forms, and are variously called a:

- bibliography
- references list
- works-cited list
- notes list.

A bibliography is a list of sources compiled on a specific topic. Bibliographies may include sources in addition to those actually cited: sources you have read but not cited, or sources you have not read but which are relevant. However, a references, works-cited, or notes list includes only those works that you have actually cited, either verbatim or in summarised or paraphrased form.

Annotated bibliography

Writing an annotated bibliography is an efficient way to immerse yourself in a particular discipline. As the name suggests, an annotated bibliography is a list of sources that relate to a particular topic, along with notes briefly describing and/or evaluating each source in the list. Annotated bibliographies can be found at the end of some books, in journals (either as articles in their own right or at the ends of other articles), or as separate volumes.

Box 9.2 shows two entries from an annotated bibliography written by a student, Kirstie Asmussen, on the study and criticism of classical music.

BOX 9.2 **Sample annotated bibliography (extract)**

Alex Ross (2010). *Listen to This*. London: Fourth Estate.
For writers in search of a book on which to model their own music criticism and commentary, *Listen to This* is an exemplary choice. Ross subscribes to the notion that a music critic should take a wide view of the world, and music be approached 'not as a self-sufficient sphere but as a way of knowing the world'. The book is organised thematically, rather than chronologically, placing the likes of Bob Dylan next to Johannes Brahms. In doing so, Ross draws links between the experiences of composers divided by centuries, yet explains that the reception of any composer is affected by comparable circumstances and recurring societal trends.

Matthew Riley (ed.) (2010). *British Music and Modernism, 1895–1960*. Farnham: Ashgate.
There has been a sharp rise in the level of interest surrounding British music of late, which has resulted in the creation of myths about its long-term reception. *British Music and Modernism, 1895–1960* is commendable for explaining varying considerations of all forms of classical music. Riley acknowledges competing definitions, ideologies, and arguments, and allows them to be presented without imposing any form of pointless consistency. All of the chapters address an element of British classical music in a way that clearly demonstrates how modern-day researchers and critics may reconsider 'established' schools of thought. Furthermore, the book demonstrates how 'standardised' hypotheses and opinions of classical music may be continually challenged and cultivated.

Kirstie Asmussen, 2015

The literature review and the research paper

Up to this point in the chapter, I've talked about researching, recording, and attributing sources. But sources have to be incorporated into a document that expresses your ideas. Therefore, this section gives strategies for planning, drafting, and revising a literature review and research paper. In general, the strategies for writing a literature review are similar to those used in writing a research paper, so, for most of this section, I use the generic term 'paper' to refer to both kinds of document.

When you set out to conduct a literature review you will need to find out who has said what about your topic, and when and where they have published their findings. Your research paper will consist of an application of the material in your literature review to a specific example of a text or a practice. For example, if you research the conventions of advertising copywriting in your literature review, in your research paper you could analyse several advertisements and discuss whether they embody the principles and practices advocated in the literature. If you research the principles of 'plain language' in your literature review, in your research paper you could analyse some documents that claim to be in plain language to see how closely they adhere to the principles.

Before you commit yourself to a topic, do a preliminary check on published materials that will provide you with the content of your literature review. If you have prepared an annotated bibliography on the topic of your research paper, you will already have a good understanding of relevant sources. When you have decided on a topic that interests you, try to limit the research question to what you think you can cover in the number of words stipulated in the assignment brief. For example, although the evolution of video games might be a topic that interests you, you cannot cover the entire topic in your research paper because the scope is too wide. A more realistic research question would be 'How have video games changed over the past five years?' or 'To what extent has "gamification" been introduced into tertiary education?' It will be important to specify in your research question the place and/or time on which you are focusing. Your research question must identify clear boundaries, so that you can limit it to a manageable scope.

In planning for a literature review and research paper, use the headings in the sample in Figure 9.3 to help you to focus on the significance and key issues of your topic.

> **Topic:** Collaborative writing: How workplace writers collaborate
> **Significance:** Collaborative writing is common in the business world, but few writers seem prepared to meet its demands.
> **Key researchers:** G. Cross, A. Lunsford & L. Ede, M. Lay, J. Trimbur, W. Karis, J. Forman, K. Le Fevre, K. Bruffee, R. Burnett.
> **Key issues:**
> 1. The definition is elusive.
> 2. Collaboration is not readily accepted in the academic arena, where one writer–one text is perceived as superior scholarship, but it is common in the workplace.
> 3. Several different models of collaboration are practised.
> 4. Conflict in collaboration. Horror stories of collaboration are ubiquitous—group dynamics.
> 5. The difficulty of documenting research on the topic.
>
> **Application:** How people in organisations can work together to produce documents collaboratively.

Figure 9.3 Plan for a research paper

For each paper you write, the point will come when you feel that you have done enough research and it is time to start writing. When you reach this point, spread out all the cards or notes that you have gathered. Read through all of them in a single pass, identifying key issues relating to your research question.

As you go through your cards or notes, you may wish to separately jot down broad headings that expand on the headings on your main card describing the issues you have uncovered. This is particularly useful if you have a large number of notes, or if you've been researching over a long period (and may have forgotten some of what you looked at early on).

If, at this stage, you feel that there is something significant that you don't understand, or that you want more information about, you may decide to do further research. Writing is not the only stage that is recursive; research can be as well, and going back to your sources at this stage may evoke new ideas for you. However, be realistic about the time you have to devote to any one paper, and its value relative to other pieces of work, and don't research excessively. Students often 'over-research' and run out of time to write and refine.

Choosing the issues to discuss

Once you're familiar with the key issues relating to your research question, decide which ones to discuss in your paper. Just as one topic can generate many research questions, one research question can generate many issues, and you must choose among them. While decisions like this aren't set in stone and can be modified later, you will find the writing process much easier if you set some boundaries early on.

If you've been given a specific research question to address, read it carefully, and think about exactly what it is you've been asked to do. Look for key words in your question. Then consider the issues you've identified, and ask yourself the following questions:

- Which issues clearly relate to the research question? (You'd be surprised how many 'key issues' turn out to be tangential to the research question.)
- Which issues seem most important (to the field, to your teacher, to you)?
- Which issues are closely related and can be addressed together without a lot of difficulty?
- Which issues can be addressed adequately in the number of words set for the paper?
- Which issues would you like to write about?
- Which issues are interesting but don't fit and would be better left for another time?

Answering these questions will help you to decide exactly what issues you will talk about in your paper. It will also help you to decide what issues you won't discuss, which is just as important, and much harder to do. It can be agonising not to use all of the material that you have so carefully researched, but this is essential if you are to produce concise, compelling writing. Most experienced academic writers use only a portion of the research material that they unearth.

Developing a research thesis

At this point you should also try to develop your research thesis. A research thesis is the answer to your research question, and is what your paper sets out to prove. It is your opinion about your question, not just a regurgitation of what everyone else has said. If you don't develop a research thesis, it is easy to fall into the trap of simply collecting various sources and summarising them, thereby putting the responsibility onto your reader to make connections and judgements. In proposing a research thesis, you are forced to make the connections and judgements that are part of the writer's job. The harder you—the writer—work, the less work your reader has to do, and the more they will enjoy and be convinced by your paper.

Sometimes you will already have developed a research thesis by this stage of the process, especially if you have chosen your question carefully and begun to develop your argument while you are researching, as I advocated earlier. If you haven't, now is the time to do so. As always, your views may change once you start to write, but it is highly desirable to begin with a thesis, so that there is a 'point' or 'goal' to your writing.

In a literature review, you're expected to synthesise what different writers have said about your topic; that is, identify the major theorists and theories, analyse the relationships between them, and draw some conclusions about what has been said. It is particularly important that you note points on which different writers agree or disagree. Therefore, in a literature review, your thesis will relate to your review and analysis of the relevant literature. In a research paper, you're expected to move on from the findings of your literature review to develop a more substantial thesis, which should relate to the subject matter itself, and not just to what other people have said about it.

Structuring the issues

Once you know what you're going to write about, consider how you will write about it; that is, plan (at least tentatively) a structure for your paper. Your structure and sequence must be planned so that they allow you to convey your thesis and supporting arguments effectively.

Using a structuring device such as those offered by Wurman and Selzer in Chapter 7, or any other device you know, take the issues you have chosen and try to structure them into an arrangement that you can use as a plan or map for your paper. If you have the time, try more than one arrangement. There are many ways of structuring any set of issues using words and/or graphics, and experimenting may reveal effective or innovative structures that you will not otherwise discover.

Again, the plan you develop at this stage can be modified later on, but having a plan of some kind will make writing your paper quicker, easier, and more focused.

Drafting, incubating, and revising

Now you must actually sit down and write the first draft of your paper, documenting your sources accurately and fully as you write. As an introduction, force yourself to write a sentence that sums up the major thrust of your paper. For example, you might write: 'In this literature review, I survey the literature on the worldwide uptake of plain English since the 1970s'. You might then introduce your research paper with the following: 'In this paper, I address the research question of the impact of plain-language initiatives in Australia since the 1970s'.

As you write, you may wish to alter your plan to accommodate new thoughts or better ways of organising your material. Try not to be too judgemental in this first draft; it's better to have something 'imperfect' on paper to work with than to sit and wait for the 'perfect' words to come. They rarely will. Also, as I emphasise in Chapter 11, never underestimate the impact that reviewing a draft can have on the production of more text.

When your first draft is finished, set it aside and let it 'incubate' for as long as possible (at least overnight, but a week is better). Then reread your work and revise ('re-see') it, looking primarily for flaws of argument or structure, and potential improvements. Check that all your points are adequately supported by evidence, and that all your material contributes to the points you are trying to express. When you identify areas for change, edit, rewrite, and reorganise your material until you are satisfied with it.

As you are revising your work, you may also notice stylistic or mechanical problems (e.g., awkward phrases, punctuation or spelling errors, typographical mistakes). It may be appropriate to fix some of these while revising early drafts. Be careful, however, not to spend too much time on these 'micro-level' corrections; it's better to save them for later when you're closer to a final draft. Otherwise, you may spend time perfecting a paragraph or section that you ultimately discard because of a 'macro-level' decision about argument or structure.

Using an editing checklist helps to systematise the revision process, and makes it more efficient. The editing checklist at the end of this chapter includes a wide range of criteria that you may wish to check at different points in the writing, revising, and proofreading process. In early drafts, for example, you may wish to apply the criteria under 'Content' and 'Structure', while in later drafts you might concentrate more on those under 'Mechanics', 'Style', and 'Presentation'. However, it is worth bearing all of the criteria in mind whenever possible.

Preparing a summary
Many teachers will ask you to prepare a summary that will appear at the beginning of your paper. If you are required to write a summary, write it last, when you are satisfied that you have produced a final version of your work. Write one to two paragraphs encapsulating the gist of your paper. Include your research question, your research thesis, your key theorists and theories, and any analysis, argument, and conclusions. Your summary should serve as an acceptable substitute for your whole paper.

Proofreading and polishing
When you have completed what you think is your final draft, proofread your paper to eliminate any grammatical, spelling, and typographical errors. It's often a good idea to also get someone else (whose abilities you trust!) to proofread your work. Correct any errors you find, being careful not to introduce any new ones. (See Chapter 11.)

Style in academic writing
Academic writing is generally written in a formal style, often in the third person, although first person is becoming widely acceptable. Academic writing is not usually characterised by the descriptive style found in much creative writing and journalistic writing. Nor does it generally adopt a narrative form.

Pitfalls to avoid include:
- emphatic words such as *absolutely, certainly, definitely, drastically, extremely*, in sentences such as *Cross expresses his view in a drastically different manner*
- weasel words and phrases such as *basically, in fact, in respect of the fact that, with regard to*

- apologetic equivocation, such as *In discussing the points raised, I have neglected to mention others*, or *I have not mentioned many other writers due to an obvious limit in the length of this paper*
- assumed familiarity with a writer's intention, such as *Saussure then decided to organise the synchronic*
- awkward, vague generalities, such as *I have included definitions that have been given in the work of many writers.*

Wherever possible, use the active rather than passive voice in your academic writing. Also try to avoid nominalisations, as discussed in Chapter 4. This involves using 'strong' verbs (rather than 'heavy' nouns) to give your writing a direct, dynamic feel. See examples in Box 9.3.

You will note that all of the verbs listed in Box 9.3 are in the present tense. It is a convention of academic writing style to use the present tense to describe statements with continuing applicability. This is called the 'historic' or 'universal' present tense. For example, you should say 'Faigley and Hansen *state* that . . .', not 'Faigley and Hansen *stated* that . . .'.

BOX 9.3 **'Active' verbs in the 'historic present' (singular)**

argues	maintains
assumes	notes
believes	observes
concludes	outlines
contends	presents
declares	proposes
defines	provides
describes	questions
develops	reasons
discusses	replies
explains	reports
extends	shows
finds	suggests
identifies	thinks
investigates	views

Here is some further guidance on academic style:
- Present your ideas and findings directly, in a clear, economical, interesting, and compelling manner.
- Avoid shifting tense, stance, and tone.
- Use signposts such as headings and transitional words to lead the reader through your text.
- Make sure that your paragraphs are unified and cohesive.
- Use parallel structure for coordinate elements.
- Aim for variety in sentence length and structure.
- Avoid nominalisations and noun strings (see Chapter 4) and thesaurus syndrome (see Chapter 3).
- Avoid colloquial expressions, irreverence, and sarcasm.
- Make sure that your pronouns clearly refer to specific nouns.
- Limit the use of words such as *as*, *since*, and *while* to their temporal meanings. If you mean *because*, use it rather than *as*.
- Avoid the editorial, pre-emptive 'we', sometimes called the 'royal' *we*.

Changes in academic style

Elbow (1991) identifies changes that he has seen in the central intellectual practices and style of academic discourse in the field of English. I have noticed similar developments in the field of communication studies and related areas. They are:
- greater acceptance of a less formal style and a more personal voice
- questioning by feminists and other theorists of linear, hierarchical, deductive models of structure and a growing trend to recognise narrative structure
- the blurring of genres (an impressive example being Susan Leonardi's 1989 article in *Publications of the Modern Language Association*, entitled 'Recipes for reading: Summer pasta, lobster à la Riseholme, and Key Lime pie', in which she mixes recipes with literary theory).

Presentation of academic documents

Presentation is important in academic writing. Although your assignments may be read by one person only, that person (your teacher) will be highly discriminating. Furthermore, while you are not writing for the workplace (with its expectations of professional presentation), your teachers will likely use professional standards of presentation as one of their assessment criteria (follow the guidelines below and use the checklist in Box 9.4 below). As a bonus, you may be able to include a high-quality paper that you have written as a student when you assemble a portfolio for a job application. Therefore, as always, you should take care with the way you present your work. It will affect how, and how well, your message is conveyed.

Check whether your reader wants you to bind your paper (some will prefer you to simply staple your pages in the top left-hand corner). If you are required to bind your work, use a plastic comb-binder or something similar. Do not use vinyl folders with plastic sleeves for each page; they make it difficult for your reader to write comments on your work. Make sure that any binding you use allows your reader to open your paper out flat.

Find out how your readers want you to set out your work, and follow their instructions.

Increasingly, universities are requesting that students submit their written assignments electronically, for reasons including the desire to be able to mark assignments online to save paper, and to detect plagiarism. You may be asked to submit your paper in Portable Document Format (PDF), but you still need to adhere to professional presentation style.

The last word

I cannot recommend highly enough a brilliant book on academic writing, *They Say/I Say: The moves that matter in academic writing*, by Gerald Graff and Cathy Birkenstein (2010), which has been adopted by more than 1500 universities and colleges in the USA. The authors analyse the structure of effective academic argument by using the 'they say/I say' template of their book's title. Their central point is that 'effective persuasive writers do more than make well-supported claims ("I say"); they also map those claims relative to the claims of others ("they say")' (p. xix).

To consolidate the points in this chapter, Box 9.4 provides a checklist of assessment criteria for academic writing. Use this as a quality-control heuristic to enhance your final document.

BOX 9.4 **Assessment criteria for academic writing**

Content
1. Identifies a significant key issue to review.
2. Discusses the key theories and scholars in the area.
3. Substantiates by reference to appropriate and authoritative sources.
4. Analyses and synthesises sources.
5. Substantially covers the key questions on the issue.
6. Substantiates by sound argument and evidence.
7. Avoids excessive reliance on opinion and generalisation.
8. Identifies dissenting scholars and theories, where appropriate.
9. Includes no irrelevant content.
10. Does not introduce new material in the conclusion.

Structure
1. Clarifies hierarchical relationships.
2. Effectively sequences ideas.
3. Relates and integrates ideas by transitions.
4. Smoothly integrates and introduces quotes.
5. Draws conclusions from preceding argument.

Style
1. Uses the most appropriate words and expressions.
2. Avoids contractions, colloquialisms, and abbreviations.
3. Avoids inappropriate jargon.
4. Explains and illustrates vague and complex concepts.
5. Conveys ideas concisely, directly, and concretely.
6. Uses vigorous prose containing a high ratio of positive, active verbs.
7. Uses clear and logical sentence construction.
8. Avoids sentence fragments.
9. Uses fully developed paragraphs with appropriate transitions.
10. Uses a rich and varied vocabulary—avoids clichés.
11. Avoids overreliance on the first person.
12. Avoids expressions in the second person (you).
13. Uses the 'historic present' to refer to source materials.

Mechanics
1. Correct word usage.
2. Correct spelling.
3. Correct grammar.
4. Correct punctuation.
5. Correct, consistent, and thorough documentation.

Presentation (if submitting hard copy)
1. Appropriate cover and binding.
2. Title page information complete with your name, title of your work, your tutor's name, and any other details required.
3. Good-quality white A4 paper.
4. Aesthetically pleasing layout, following the advice on document design in Chapter 7.
5. Consistent use of white space.
6. Margins—approximately 4 cm on left-hand side and 2 cm on other sides.
7. Double-spaced text, with quotes of more than three lines indented and single spaced. References also single spaced.
8. Summary—encapsulates the whole paper—about 5 per cent of the length of the paper.
9. Consistent use and presentation of headings (if headings are used).
10. Adequately proofread—no mechanical errors.

Activities

1. Select one of each of the following:
    - a feature article from a newspaper
    - an advertisement (with a reasonable amount of text) from a magazine
    - an article from an academic journal (or one of your own successful pieces of academic writing).

    It is useful if your three pieces relate to a similar topic, but this is not essential. Read the text of each, and compile a matrix (see Figure 7.3

in Chapter 7) to demonstrate the similarities and differences between academic and non-academic writing in relation to:
- intended readers
- purpose of the piece of writing
- title (evocative? dramatic? descriptive?)
- necessity for readers to have prior knowledge of the topic
- paragraph structure
- use of headings
- methods of proof and reasoning
- connections among ideas
- documentation (if used, which style?)
- sentence structure
- use of active and passive voice
- stance (first, second, or third person)
- word choice and use of jargon
- presence of humour and/or irony
- visual layout.

Use your matrix to write three fully developed, coherent paragraphs that contrast the readerships, structures, and styles of academic and non-academic (popular) writing.

2. Compile a list of key journals in your field.

3. Prepare an index card for a written assignment that you have to submit at a later date. On the card, list:
   a) your research question
   b) why you chose it
   c) the names of five key researchers in this area
   d) five key issues you've come across in your research on the topic
   e) why, in the light of your research, you think your chosen topic is significant
   f) your thesis statement.

4. As an entry in your journal, free-write on what you believe you need to know to write effectively in your discipline.

10

How digital writing works

> We're in the midst of a literacy revolution the likes of which we have not seen since Greek civilization.
>
> ANDREA LUNSFORD

The inexorable rise of digital media

Contemporary writing is changing textually, spatially, temporally, and relationally.

Textually, it is changing through much greater emphasis on design and multimedia with still and video images via Flickr, Instagram, YouTube, Vimeo, and many others.

Spatially, it is changing as people rely on their mobile phones and tablets, rather than on fixed, desktop computers to communicate globally.

Temporally, it is changing as people respond, often 24/7, across international time zones to messages.

Relationally, it is changing with greatly increased interaction between writers and readers as writers aim for meaningful connection through social media in our participatory culture, in which individuals can use digital, networked, and mobile technologies to post content on the internet (Jenkins, Ito, and boyd, 2016).

In this chapter, I'll cover the conventions of digital writing.

Digital writing currently takes many forms—an email message, a blog post, a text message, a tweet, a Facebook status update, a comment on a post on a website, a response to an article on a website or blog, a story uploaded to an online zine, a self-published novel, a book review on Goodreads, and so on.

The so-called 'knowledge' or 'information economy' that has arisen over the past 40 or so years has seen ideas, data, information, knowledge, news—mainly based in written text—gain in economic and social power and consequence. A further development in the first decade of the 21st century was the rise of online self-presentation and interaction (Brandt, 2015) that has been labelled as 'social media'. There's no consensus about what constitutes social media. Some people believe that it refers only to platforms such as Facebook, Twitter, and YouTube, etc., while others extend the term to include websites, blogging, and texting.

While debate exists about the origin of the term 'social media', the entrepreneur Tina Sharkey is generally acknowledged to have been one of the first to use it; in 1994, she applied it to the newly emerging social forms of participatory online media (Bercovici, 2010). Social media are not media in the traditional 'old-media' sense of mass-printed newspapers and magazines and broadcast television and radio. The uptake of social media has changed the way we communicate. In 1980, futurist Alvin Toffler coined the term 'prosumer' when he predicted that the role of producers (of media) and consumers of their products would begin to merge. Toffler was right.

Social media function through platforms, applications, channels, networks, and tools on the internet to facilitate user-generated content and interaction.

The technology boom fuelled by the rise of the internet has led to an explosion of writing worldwide. Writing has become a mass daily experience, with everyone writing more than they ever did (Pullum, 2014; Yagoda, 2013). Writing in social media relies on mobile and web-based technologies to support communal, participative, connected input and interaction. In 21st-century social spaces and workplaces, words matter more than ever.

Ben Yagoda quotes technology journalist Clive Thompson as saying that 'before the Internet came along, most people rarely wrote anything at all for pleasure or intellectual satisfaction after graduating from high school or college', but 'we are now in a global culture of avid writers'. Thompson cites several studies finding that 'when it comes from analytic or critical thought, the effort of communicating to someone else forces you to think more precisely, make deeper connections, and learn more' (Yagoda, 2013).

Across the world, more than 50 social-media platforms have in excess of one million users each. Facebook, 'the website that changed the world' (Brandt, 2015, p. 114), is on course to have a larger digital flock than the population of any country. In an article in *The Guardian* in 2015, 'Seven Ways Facebook has changed the World', Jessica Elgot reported that Facebook had one billion users a day. She quoted founder Mark Zuckerberg as saying that on a single day, 24 August 2015, a seventh of the people in the world used Facebook. However, it has been widely reported that many millennials (those born since 1990) seek newer social media platforms such as Snapchat and don't necessarily want to use Facebook, particularly if their parents use it.

The early years

I first encountered computer-mediated writing in 1985, when the journalism professor I taught with persuaded our budget committee to invest in a computer lab in which to teach writing to our journalism students. Instantly impressed by the distinct advantages offered by word processing for composing and revising text, I started to research the potential of computers to enhance the quality of our students' writing. At that time, personal computers (PCs) were prohibitively expensive. I recall that the PC I bought in 1985 cost $5000—what John McPhee, alluding to the ease of editing by cutting and pasting with word-processing software, would describe as a '$5000 pair of scissors' (McPhee, 2013a).

In a later stage of my research, on which I based my PhD thesis, 'Computers and Composing: From the academy to the workplace', I interviewed some of my public relations graduates after they had moved into writing positions in the workplace. They had written on a computer during the three years of their degree and had expected to take advantage of this skill in their first job. To their dismay, they discovered that typing pools were merely being replaced by word-processing pools whose staff they were required to use to prepare their dictated documents. As highly qualified entry-level employees, they were informed that they were not expected to do their own 'keyboarding'. One graduate said that she felt as if her 'hands had been cut off'. She had enjoyed the benefits of writing on a computer for three years, only to find that her workplace lagged behind the academy in understanding the benefits for writers who did their own word processing.

I started using email seriously in 1995, way behind Queen Elizabeth II, who sent her first email message in 1976 while visiting the scientific research hub of the UK Ministry of Defence. However, I was way ahead of the head of the Australian Royal Commission into Trade Union Governance and Corruption, Dyson Heydon, former justice of the High Court of Australia, who, it was revealed in September 2015, did not own a computer and could not use email. (See Anthony Colangelo's (2015) highly amusing article in *The New Daily* introducing Dyson Heydon to the glories of email.)

The intervening thirty years, which have taken us well into the 21st century, have witnessed the growth of a very different writing landscape from that of 1985 with the rise and rise of digital modes.

In the next section, I'll cover email in the workplace, then move on to websites, blogging, and other social media applications.

Email: insistent and indelible

In Chapter 8, I covered several key workplace documents, but not the use of email. If you rely on email in your workplace, which most organisations do, I'm sure you'll agree that email communication dominates the workplace. However, many organisations are realising that there are other more efficient ways to communicate internally, so they are moving to programs such as Slack, a 'real-time' messaging program. Its website boasts of having NASA's Jet Propulsion Laboratory as 'one of its tens of thousands of teams around the world'. The Slack website states that Slack is not designed to eliminate email completely and that email remains ubiquitous and is quite useful for getting updates from pretty much every service on the internet. Slack has a feature that allows email to be redirected into Slack channels.

Even though most of us use email every day, the following advice is a useful reminder of its potential pitfalls. An email message is very different from a face-to-face conversation because there are no non-verbal cues such as vocal tone, facial expression, eye contact, and body language.

When writing emails, you need to be constantly sensitive to potential misunderstanding, and conscious of your readers' expectations of email communication in the context of their relationship with you. Always conform to the conventions of email and be aware of its constraints.

What follows is advice about using email to maximise your chances of getting the response that you need. Consider the purpose, content, style, structure, and format of your emails.

Purpose
- Ensure that email is the most appropriate medium for your intended message. Do not be an email junkie. Talk to your colleagues. Have a conversation, a discussion. Some managers insist that their staff email them only when they are unavailable to talk. After a conversation, a follow-up email can summarise for the record.
- Use email to send information to people who ask for or need specific information. Use cc (carbon copy—a leftover from typing) judiciously. Use bcc (blind carbon copy) when emailing a group of people to avoid sending a page of addresses and/or revealing your address book. Don't use bcc for political reasons, such as slyly copying in your boss on a message about a colleague that shows the colleague in a bad light. If you do this, you'll gain a reputation with your boss and colleagues for underhandedness.
- Many readers delete 'copy all'/mass/broadcast messages as a matter of course, so avoid sending mass emails whenever possible and avoid sending an email to people who don't need to receive that specific message.

Content
- Manage your priorities and your recipient's expectations. Gauge whether your recipient is expecting an instant response. Build positive relationships with those with whom you are in contact via email by respecting 'netiquette' (a portmanteau word formed from *network* and *etiquette*). Check the email etiquette and protocols that your workplace has established.
- Never put anything in an email that you wouldn't want on the staffroom noticeboard. Never use email to communicate sensitive, emotional, or critical messages. Email is not private. Email cannot be deleted.

Email is forever. If you have a finger that's quick on the trigger, work offline or save your message in draft form to read and rework later on. Or, put in the recipient's address last. Be cautious and thoughtful. Constantly conduct professional self-scrutiny. Do you really, really, really want to send this? Be aware of email's disinhibition effect.

- Read the email that you are responding to more than once to ensure that you are not assuming anything. Also ensure that you answer all the questions that you have been asked, or tell your reader that you'll find out the answers and get back to them ASAP.
- Always reply to an email, even if it's just to say: 'Got your message. Will answer soon'. An unanswered email might unintentionally say no or yes. You cannot *not* communicate.
- Respect confidentiality. If you forward an email, do you need to get the original author's permission? Does the author intend their message to be broadcast? If you are in doubt, check with the original writer. Always check the previous email string when forwarding an email to ensure that there's no potential for embarrassment.
- If you need a response to an email in writing, say so: 'Please review and approve by 10 April'. Don't assume that your email has or has not been received just because you haven't had a reply. You can set up a receipt-of-message function, but that has annoyance potential for many people.
- Avoid the 'long goodbye', in which you thank your reader for an email that they have sent you and they thank you for your thank-you and so on and so on. If you don't need a response, you can say: 'No reply needed'.

Style

- Use Standard English, correct and helpful punctuation, and conventional formatting.
- Always proofread and spell check your messages, though remember that the latter won't catch typos such as *from* for *form* or confusable words such as *affect/effect*, *cue/queue*, *discreet/discrete*, *lead/led*, *principal/principle*, and dozens more (see Box 3.2 in Chapter 3).
- Make your message positive, polite, concise, complete, and to the point, with correct and current information. Concise can sometimes be interpreted as abrupt or even rude, particularly when you are

responding to a detailed message outlining important issues, so be careful to give answers that give proper weight to the original message.
- The appropriate tone is crucial: be businesslike but warm, succinct but not telegraphic, respectful, and never subtly reproachful. Avoid sarcasm, irony, and humour.
- It's best not to bother about phatic communication that 'oils the wheels' of sociability with sentiments such as 'Have a nice weekend', unless you are emailing a friend. Neither is it a good idea to start out with a compliment to someone whom you don't know, as that can be regarded as insincere.
- Avoid emoticons in professional exchanges. They are lame, potentially ambiguous, and unprofessional. Using them will mildly annoy some readers, and others may doubt your ability to convey the appropriate tone in a message if you need to rely on a 'smiley face'.
- Don't get drawn into back-and-forth emails. When you can see this happening, send an email that says: 'We appear to be talking at cross purposes; let's meet to work this out'.
- Reply with pertinent details to a request for a meeting: 'I'm available to meet with you next Tuesday 1 October. I'll see you in your office at 2 pm'.
- Avoid abbreviations in professional emails, except maybe very well-established ones such as *ASAP*, *COB*, and *FYI*. Not everyone will be familiar with *BTW* (by the way), *GR8* (great), *HTH* (hope that helps), *IMHO* (in my humble opinion), *pls* (please), *tnx* (thanks), and other much more obscure examples.

Structure and format
- Use a detailed subject line that unambiguously sets out your purpose and that is appropriate for your relationship with your reader (formal/informal). Readers scan for *who* and *what*. Aim for actionable motivation: for approval, for review, for action, for the record, as a reminder.
- Use an appropriate salutation, or weave your greeting into your opening. The days of 'Dear . . .' as a salutation have almost gone, but you may feel more comfortable using it to address your superiors. Because email messages are time-stamped, you can say 'Good morning, Jane'.

- Use a sign-off, such as 'Regards' or 'Cheers', that's appropriate in the circumstances.
- Create a standard signature block that gives all your contact details and use it at all times.
- Avoid the unprofessional motivational messages that some people include in their signature blocks, such as 'We come to serve' or 'Carpe diem'.
- Avoid flagging your emails with 'urgent' or 'high-priority' status. If it's that important, pick up the phone. If you can't do that, use a very strong subject line to get the recipient's attention.
- Avoid coloured type and huge or tiny point sizes. Generally avoid all caps. Always avoid 'frivolous' fonts, such as comic sans.
- If you want to communicate several messages on different topics to the same person, send several short emails with specific subject lines rather than a long one headed 'Various' or 'Three things'. This will make archiving and accessing easier.
- Avoid vague and/or gimmicky subject lines (e.g., 'We need to talk', 'Last chance!', 'Back in action', 'Monday', 'Ongoing', 'Don't miss out!').
- Use FAQs with dot-point answers when these would be helpful for your readers.
- Reply to emails at the top or inline (in the body of the email). The latter option is useful when you have been asked several individual questions, but make sure that you start your reply email with 'See inline', in case your readers think that you haven't responded to them.
- Deliberately keep the same subject line if it's a genuinely ongoing message string. Otherwise, change to an appropriately fresh subject line.
- If you can't answer a complex request quickly, send a short 'Very busy today. Will get back to you ASAP about this'.
- Turn on your out-of-office email message when you are going to be out of the office. In some organisations, staff turn on their out-of-office message when they go out to lunch. This seems a bit extreme. If possible, include alternative contact details when you will be out of the office for more than a day or so: it is worrying when you receive a message that the person you need a response from has gone on leave and they have failed to leave instructions about alternative arrangements in their absence.

- Don't rely on email for last-minute changes to meetings, unless your recipient is expecting to hear via email.
- Don't annoy recipients with attachments that they can't open automatically. However, for a significant amount of content, attachments work better than making your reader scroll.

Managing your inbox

One final piece of advice worth trying to follow, and which some people manage to do, is to clear your inbox every day.

Some people advocate archiving your emails once you have dealt with them, because it's often tricky to decide which folder to file a message in and even trickier to remember which folder you ended up filing it in. It's more efficient to archive, because you can then search easily.

Writing for social media in the workplace

Social media is just that—social. Social media has made companies, and the people within them, immediately accessible. It can function as a very powerful, direct, and effective portal to customers who, in turn, may expect to have an engaged relationship with you. As a workplace writer, you may be expected to contribute to the conversation by writing for your organisation's website, contributing to a blog that is hosted on the website, and/or communicating with customers via tweets and texts.

When writing for social media, you need to carefully manage your style and strategy, because you are presenting your brand to a potentially large audience, in a dynamic and potentially reactive way. Social media is a great way to amplify your brand, but it shouldn't replace quality writing on the core-brand platform of your website.

Organisational websites

These days, most organisations and businesses, no matter how small, have a website. It's rare for an organisation not to have a website, because the internet is the first place that people go to for information. Businesses use websites as the headquarters for their online presence; everything links back to their website, because running a business from a website is easy and flexible in terms of updating information. An organisation's website is a place for people to go if they have problems: they can get in touch with the organisation or other people using the organisation's services, for example, user forums. Some websites may host social media platforms such as Facebook and Twitter, but unless they do, they can't be categorised as social media.

Below are some of the purposes of an organisational website:
- To inform and communicate.
- To give an organisation the credibility of an online presence.
- To establish an organisation's 'brand'/image.
- To generate leads for the organisation to follow up by building an email database for marketing.
- To showcase and sell an organisation's products and services.
- To channel visitors to the information that the organisation wants them to see and the information that visitors are looking for.
- To serve as a repository of historical information about the company.
- To offer premium content and confidential information in a members'-only section.
- To recruit staff.

When designing a website, your company needs to consider the following questions:
- Who will be the target users? Current and future customers? Stakeholders/investors? Current and future staff? Anyone who is interested in researching the company, such as potential investors?
- Who else might read it? For example, potential employees and investors (so, write 'marketing' copy targeted at humans) and search engines (so, use content-rich keywords to improve your ratings).
- What will users want and what do they need to know? It's worth researching competitors' websites and even websites outside your market to see what others are doing well and not so well.
- How are readers most likely to arrive at the site? So, what are the major 'landing pages'/entry points?
- How will users act on the information provided on the website? If you are selling or promoting goods or services, you need to have a 'call to action'. An effective website contains many 'calls to action'—at the top, middle, and bottom of the page, on the homepage, and woven into blog posts.

Structure and content

There is no agreed-upon format/structure/architecture for websites, though websites using a particular platform, for example, WordPress, may well have a similar look. Many websites look alike because they are adhering to current trends. The one inarguable principle of website design is that 'Content is crucial'.

Users visit your website for its content, so your website has to make sense from their perspective, and it has to do this instantly. The design is there to allow users access to the content. Make sure that you communicate your credibility through your accurate, complete, current, and authoritative content. A website needs (inseparable) substance (content), structure, and style. It should not be merely a 'dump' for previously used paper documents.

Web usability guru Jakob Nielsen (1997) says that text on the Web is 'writing to be found' rather than prose to be read or experienced. In an article titled 'How users read on the Web', he says: 'They don't. People rarely read Web pages word by word; instead, they scan the page, picking out individual words and sentences in an F-pattern'.

Below is advice to follow in writing for an organisational website.

- Clearly indicate what business you are in, what services you offer, and who your clients are.
- Provide 'advance' organising devices that help your reader navigate through your website, such as a site map, short summaries, explanatory titles, meaningful headings and subheadings (these should be engaging, but not so abstract that your readers need to be clairvoyant), bolded keywords, and design navigation that creates consistency.
- Write for 'scannability' by highlighting headings, dot points, links, and 'chunks' of text, so that users don't have to read every word.
- Split up extended information into multiple pages with no more than 500 words on a page.
- Provide identifying information on every page of your site, as your reader may not have entered it through your homepage.
- Keep in mind that you are communicating, not just disseminating information. Establish credibility by crafting messages that resonate with readers and build your relationship with them.

- Use the inverted pyramid structure. Provide answers to the journalist's heuristic, 5 Ws and an H (what, when, where, who, why, and how), at the beginning.
- Aim to get your readers to take action, for example, to subscribe or to buy. Stir them to action and interaction, e.g., Register now!
- Use a 10-point (or larger, but not too large) sans serif typeface.
- Incorporate visuals such as photographs and infographics. Text without images may not be read.
- Archive documents in PDF files that retain their original formatting.
- Ensure that you have a search function.
- Provide internal links to avoid unnecessary duplication of information.
- Provide hyperlinks to external sites sparingly to support and deepen your content and as a reinforcement of, not a substitute for, your content. Links that open in a new tab or new page are best, so that readers still have your website open. This makes it more likely that they'll return to your website when they've finished with the link.
- Decide which content-rich keywords, relevant to your users, will most help your ranking by search engines such as Bing, Google, and Yahoo.
- Choose one keyword (called a 'title tag') for each page that a user could arrive at your site on and place it as close as possible to the top of the page. The title tag is the most important element on each page because it tells search engines what your page is about. Each page must have a different title tag.
- Create condensed, interrelated screen-sized chunks ('eye-bites') of text (no more than 75 words), with dot points (no more than seven), for reading of introductory pages.
- Include links that exemplify compelling, shareable, relevant content.
- Regularly update your site with fresh material for returning visitors. It is crucial to keep your website current so that your readers regularly return to it.

Frequently asked questions (FAQs)

- Place a list of FAQs at the top of the page with hyperlinks to the content below.

- Make them searchable (have a search icon at the top of the page).
- Use actual questions that people have asked, but edit them to ensure that they are clear and direct.
- Try to anticipate questions, or use a naïve focus group to generate drafts of questions.
- Include a back-to-the-top icon at the end of each question.
- Include a way for visitors to contact you. Many websites now have a contact form so they don't need to provide readers with the site owner's email address.
- Include an email question icon if you are willing to respond to email messages within a reasonably short time frame (two days).

Style

When it comes to writing style, draw on everything you know about writing.

- Use plain language (language that an intelligent layperson can understand) that supports the organisation's brand.
- Avoid hyperbole (a figure of speech that exemplifies exaggeration for effect) and marketese.
- Avoid jargon (management speak/bureaucratese/gobbledygook).
- Avoid (or use cautiously) abbreviations, acronyms and initialisms, contractions, colloquialisms, clichés, metaphors, humour, irony, puns, cuteness, and 'local' knowledge.
- Write in a style that's light(ish) and conversational (if that's appropriate), but professional and formal (if that's appropriate).
- Be precise and accurate.
- Be succinct. Use short, familiar words and not too many of them.
- Use 'strong' verbs in the active voice.
- Use short sentences (under 17 words).
- Use simple (not complex) sentences.
- Use present tense.
- Use second person—the stance of 'you'.
- Avoid using pronouns in case it's not clear what or whom they are referring to.
- Use short paragraphs that cover only one point and are around 50 words long.

- Avoid digressions and irrelevant information.
- Use 'normal' writing style for complex documents that your readers will print off.

A quality check
- Apply the 'So what?' test at all stages when revising your text. Ask yourself: Is this something my reader really needs to know? Am I making this point in the simplest possible way?
- Proofread systematically and meticulously on a printout (not onscreen).
- Carry out frequent and sustained authentic usability research on your website.

Blogs

A workplace blog (derived from the term 'weblog') is an online 'journal' that sits on a website. In Chapter 1, I discussed the benefits of keeping a journal of your private writing. In the late 1990s, when blogs first became common, diary-style blogs were popular, but since Facebook launched in 2004 much of this personal sharing has moved over to it. Many companies now feature one or more blogs on their website to support their social media activities internally and externally, by encouraging staff engagement, providing customer support, and building community.

A company blog, which can be written by one or more employees, exhibits a more personal, conversational style than the website, but follows many of the same principles of writing for organisational webpages that I have listed above. Blog posts need to be authentic, short, interesting, and valuable for readers. Blog posts need to have intriguing and/or challenging headlines—headlines that compel readers to click on them, such as 'How being too busy can make you less successful', or '7 career skills you can learn'. Images or graphics encourage engagement and sharing. Blogs can also feature links to relevant previous posts and other websites. Blogs need to be updated regularly.

Personal blogs
If you feel that you'd like to share your writing with the world, you could consider launching a personal blog. However, you must be able to commit to posting stories and updates regularly. Some people believe

that if you can't commit to regular (at least weekly) updates, you probably shouldn't launch yourself into the blogosphere. Most personal blogs are abandoned because bloggers run out of steam. Before launching a blog, examine your reasons for wanting to do so:

- Is it to practise your writing?
- Is it to reach out to and engage with readers who (you hope) will respond to your writing?
- Is it to inform, educate, entertain, reassure?
- Is it to record and share your learning experience (if you are a student) or your work experience (if you have a job)?
- Is it to sell/promote your own products, services, or self-published resources? This is booming as a reason for blogging.

Or perhaps you hope that a publisher will spot the blog's potential as a book? Several bloggers have followed this path to publishing success. Julie Powell, a writer living in Brooklyn, launched her blog, the *Julie/Julia Project*, to record how she set out to cook a different dish from Julia Child's classic cookbook, *Mastering the Art of French Cooking*, every day for a year. Her blog was transformed into a book and then into a film, *Julie & Julia* (2009). If you do decide to go ahead and launch a personal blog, you'll need to examine the potential of your 'digital self' and create a stockpile of posts. Follow the advice below to create and sustain a successful blog that readers regularly return to.

- Decide on the purpose and contents of your blog.
- Understand the blog genre—find blogs similar to what you'd like yours to be and analyse their style and format.
- Actively follow like-minded bloggers: this contributes to success in the blogging community as bloggers support and recommend one another.
- Consider which readers you want to attract (your demographic).
- Decide on a catchy blog name that will generate an appropriate URL and will pique readers' interest. Avoid commonly used words.
- Find a platform to host your blog, such as WordPress, Blogger, or Typepad.
- Decide on the style and tone of your writing: informal/formal? witty? whimsical? opinionated? authoritative? If you write humorous posts, be careful not to cross the line and offend readers.

- Decide how you are going to deal with comments. Respond to all of them? Respond to negative ones? Set up comment moderation, so you can select only the comments that you want to appear on your blog (this can also help to reduce trolling).
- Decide how you will evaluate the success of your blog. Google Analytics can count your followers and the comments on your site.
- The ProBlogger site provides great resources and much helpful advice on setting up and maintaining a blog.

Box 10.1 lists some of my favourite personal blogs.

BOX 10.1 **Favourite personal blogs**

What blogs do people follow? Ones that they enjoy reading. I like ones that cover my interests: books, writing and editing, publishing, education, politics, design, travel, food, jazz, film, and theatre. Here are my favourites:

1. *A Bloomsbury Life* at blogspot.com.au. This is a personal, lifestyle blog with one contributor, Lisa Borgnes Giramonti. Lisa doesn't blog regularly, but her site is lovely and she has some beautifully evocative photo essays on New Orleans and London.

2. *Lingua Franca* on *The Chronicle of Higher Education* site discusses writing, editing, grammar, and style. It features my favourite grammarian, Professor Geoffrey Pullum, and several other columnists who write provocatively and passionately about language, such as Lucy Ferriss and Ben Yagoda, whose work I have mentioned many times in this book. I check it a couple of times a week.

3. Another blog that I read regularly is Simon Thomas's *Stuck in a Book*. Simon blogs mainly about books, but regularly indulges in recaps of UK television shows such as *The Great British Bake Off*. He also blogs about books at *Shiny New Books*. His blog roll is tremendously tempting for anyone interested in books and reading.

4. Maria Popova maintains an amazing blog, *Brain Pickings*. She describes her blog as 'a cross-disciplinary LEGO treasure chest, full of pieces spanning art, science, psychology, design, philosophy, history, politics, anthropology, and more'.

I check these blogs regularly. Why? Because the writers' personalities come through so compellingly. Simon posts several times a week and I always read his posts, no matter how pushed I am for time.

If you're a gamer, a great site is David Kay's *Scent of a Gamer*. He has a note on his site to say that he updates it each weekend. How reliable is that?

Ideas for blog posts

Where will you get ideas for your blog posts? Follow Henry James's advice that I quoted in Chapter 1: 'Try to be one of those on whom nothing is lost'. Notice what's going on around you. Write it down in your journal so you'll remember it. Keep a running list of potential blog-post topics.

If it's going to be a struggle to come up with ideas, or you don't have lots of friends who are willing and able to guest-post for you, it might not be such a good idea to launch a blog.

Box 10.2 provides a list of common blog topics.

BOX 10.2 **Common blog topics**

books	lifestyle
business	music
family	parenting
fashion	photography
film	sport
food and wine	style and design
games	theatre
health	travel
hobbies	writing style and grammar

Characteristics of successful blogs

- They are friendly and engaging.
- They can be provocative and controversial and lead to intelligent debate (whether they are personal or professional blogs).
- They resonate with readers, particularly if the blogger regularly responds to comments.
- They have short, succinct posts that each cover one topic.
- Each post has an intriguing, descriptive title that draws readers in; before they click on it, they know whether or not they are interested.
- Posts are self-contained and coherent.
- Posts are somewhere between 250 and 800 words. (Some experts advocate an even lower word count.)
- Posts exude passion, energy, and personality, and have a distinctive voice and perspective (see Chapter 3).
- They are fresh and original, not clichéd and banal.
- They are clear and authentic and avoid broad, vague, and generic hype.
- They are aesthetically pleasing, with an attractive, well-designed layout.
- They are easy to navigate.
- They are scannable; that is, not every word has to be read, so they can be skim-read.
- They have headings and subheadings that are 'front-loaded' with strong keywords, as well as highlighted keywords, if necessary.
- They are authoritative and credible (with sources of information cited).
- Posts can be understood out of context if they turn up in news feeds and search results.
- They are of consistently high quality, with flawless grammar, syntax, punctuation, and spelling.
- If they use specialist jargon it is because all their readers are likely to be familiar with it.
- Their posts are rich with hyperlinks to earlier work or to other relevant material (though you don't want your readers to click too far away from your site and fail to return to you).
- Posts embed images, infographics, videos, and audio. You can embed media easily into your blog from most blogging platforms.
- They offer free 'content upgrades' in return for the email address of the follower. That way, the blogger can market to their audience

more intimately via email, while also being seen as an expert on their topic because they've provided great original content. An example of a content upgrade for a blog on blogging might be an article called '10 ways to increase blog traffic' that has a worksheet for a follower to fill in.
- They integrate easily with other social media such as Facebook and Twitter. Bloggers are highly active on these platforms for different purposes. For example, the social media site Periscope is very popular with bloggers who want a casual way to interact with their followers through video chats. Instagram is often used as a platform for 'behind the scenes' content, while Facebook is used for discussion and sharing content. These tools allow bloggers to grow their audience and engage current and new followers.

Format of blogs
Most blogs have similar design elements:
- a banner or masthead at the top of the page
- an attractive colour scheme and typeface
- a biography of the blogger in a sidebar
- a 'subscribe to this blog' button so that readers will receive notifications of new posts
- an invitation to comment and enter into a conversation with the blogger and other readers
- a list of the blogger's favourite links, including to other blogs (the blog roll)
- a search function
- an archive of all posts, some of which might include links to related posts to keep followers engaged with the blog
- social media icons on each post so that readers can follow the blogger on Twitter, etc.

Twitter

A more recent addition to social media platforms has been Twitter, a free microblogging platform that originated in the messaging protocols of mobile phones. Twitter allows its users to connect with others through brief text updates (tweets) that they post from various devices such as their computer, smartphone, or tablet through Short Message Service (SMS) text messaging, the Twitter website, email, Facebook, and other sites. Tweets essentially answer the question 'what's happening?' The 140 characters (even fewer than the number allowed in text messages) that tweets allow sounds easy, but the interface takes a bit of time to master. Twitter has taken over as the service for breaking news and has been a valuable source of information in its real-time updating of natural disasters such as hurricanes and floods.

Whereas Facebook users follow people whom they know, Twitter users follow those with similar political and professional interests whom they are not necessarily personally acquainted with. Twitter has more than half a billion users worldwide.

The Social Media Research Group at Queensland University of Technology has followed the tweeting phenomenon closely for several years. Researchers there estimate that Australia has close to three million 'tweeters'. If you are the designated expert in your organisation responsible for its social media presence, you'll need to be familiar with the Twitter platform.

The best tweets inform and entertain by exemplifying an engaging tone, flair, and wit. Twitter has its detractors. One high-profile critic is Frank Bruni, who, in a *New York Times* article called 'Tweet less, read more' (2013), laments the posting of 'unformed thoughts, half-baked wit or splenetic reactions' and instead touts the benefits of 'an activity that's in some ways the antithesis of texting and tweeting . . . the reading of fiction'. Many people would agree with Bruni.

To find engaging tweeters, go to the Twitter website and search for topics you are interested in. Find someone who tweets regularly on topics that interest you and check to see whose tweets they are following. You can then 'follow' people whose tweets interest you, and engage them by sending them a link to an article that you think will interest them.

You can also interact with people by responding to their tweets. Members of the public can use Twitter to interact immediately and directly with organisations.

Writing on Twitter

When writing a tweet, assume that all your tweets will one day be seen by someone who is considering employing you, and be conscious of the potential consequences of tweets in different contexts. Remember that not everyone has the same sense of humour as you. Avoid sarcasm, because it can backfire. One notorious case of unacceptable humour was that of public-relations professional Justine Sacco, who ruined her career with a racist tweet (Ronson, 2015). Hers was a personal tweet. Some organisations such as Australia's largest telecommunications company appoint staff to engage with customers by sending out tweets that are personal rather than scripted. These tweets generally alert readers to new posts on the organisation's blog, present tips on new products, update customers with ongoing news, etc. Staff also respond to incoming tweets. One tweetstorm that hit the headlines in 2016 occurred when a woman tweeted about an outage that she was experiencing. Her broadband was down and she had checked the telco's website, which revealed that the connection would be down for two days. She tweeted: 'I have a child who wants to watch TV, though'. She was shocked to get a tweet from the social media manager saying; 'Heya, I can appreciate that, I usually show my kid the outside world when there's no internet, it's tricky'. The mother was so outraged by what she regarded as a condescending response that she broadcast the reply, so, of course, the exchange went viral, with many people joining in her outrage.

Aim to create a quality message with a personable tone that achieves action and/or starts a conversation. Like other forms of social media, tweeting facilitates conversation and interaction.

Draft your tweet to be around 120 characters, so that if one of your followers wants to retweet it they can add a little text to it. Be as friendly and motivating as you can, particularly if you want readers to respond to or act on your tweet.

Researchers at Cornell University used an algorithm to parse the words and sentence constructions that result in some tweets getting more attention than others. They then created an online tool for predicting which tweets are likely to be the most popular. However, the researchers admitted that they were unable to factor humour into their calculations, and this is, of course, a crucial element in most popular tweets. Their advice is to use language that is familiar to the target audience, to mimic the abbreviated style of headline writers, and to ask followers to retweet (Kulp, 2015).

Other general advice is to write engaging content that speaks to your audience, shows off your personality, and includes a call to action. Including images is also recommended.

Many university and other sites offer guidance on tweeting: the London School of Economics and Political Science (LSE) has a helpful blog site. So does the digital media site Mashable, which also provides a downloadable PDF, *The Beginner's Guide to Twitter*. Both the LSE and Mashable sites provide their material under a Creative Commons licence.

The LSE suggests three styles of tweets:

1. *Substantive*. Large organisations tend to send out formal, corporate tweets in complete crisp sentences with few, if any, abbreviations. They usually have a headline that functions as a taster for a blog post or a relevant article of interest and a message that's understandable to all potential readers and written by an 'invisible' member of a team.
2. *Conversational*. These emanate from individuals. They can be personal and thus more relaxed, eclectic, and fragmented (not written in complete sentences), and use abbreviations. If a tweet emanates from a blog post, you need to carefully repurpose it before you post it.
3. *Middle ground*. These are a mixture of both styles, so, while they may reflect organisational culture, they can also convey personality without being as informal and conversational as the second type.

There are strong synergies between tweeting and blogging. Make sure that you put the Twitter share button on your blog and send out a tweet after each new blog post.

Why would people follow you on Twitter?
- Your relevant expertise?
- Your authoritative and valuable advice?
- Your interesting opinions?
- Your great stories and images?
- Your engaging and witty style?

Texting

Text messaging (texting) using Short Message Service (SMS) arrived on the social media scene in the 1990s after Nokia included it in its first mobile phones as a way for engineers to report problems (Self & Truss, 2008). It has always been popular among friends, but is now being used increasingly by companies for two-way communication with their customers. Millions of text messages are sent across the world every day. The author Will Self says that texting provides 'evidence, along with email, that we now live in the post-aural age, when an unsolicited phone call is, thankfully, becoming more and more understood to be an unspeakable social solecism, tantamount to an impertinent invasion of privacy' (Self & Truss, 2008). Email and texting have certainly been a boon for those afflicted with telephone apprehension.

In the early years of texting, many doomsayers predicted that it would cause the demise of Standard English. There were laments that 'young people would no longer be able to communicate normally but only in textspeak, and then only if they managed to avoid serious thumb injury' (Marsh, 2013a, p. 257). In 2007, John Humphrys warned that texters were 'vandals who are doing to our language what Genghis Khan did to his neighbours 800 years ago: they are destroying it. Pillaging our punctuation; savaging our sentences; raping our vocabulary. And they must be stopped'.

In opposition to Humphrys's view are the views of prominent linguists such as John McWhorter (2013) and David Crystal (2008). In a 2013 TED talk, McWhorter, of Columbia University, argues that 'texting is not a blight on the English language . . . rather, texting is a miraculous thing . . . a novel linguistic mode that's redefining the way we communicate with each other—for the better'. He says that texting 'shouldn't be characterised as written language, but as speech'. He calls texting 'fingered speech' and says: 'Now we can write the way we talk but still keep our ability to write like *The Economist*'.

Crystal says that people like to personally text 'because it's partly a game'.

Sociolinguist Lauren Collister (2015) argues that the way we communicate in texts, emails, and tweets is streamlining our language and updating it for the 21st century. Far from ruining the English language, she writes, 'textspeak' is modernising how we communicate with one another:

> And contrary to the idea that these innovations are corrupting language, they actually demonstrate a creative repurposing of symbols and marks to

a new age of technology. These evolutions of language are swift, clever, and context-specific, illustrating the flexibility of the language to communicate nonverbal meaning in a nuanced, efficient manner.

Conventions of workplace texting

If you use texting in the workplace to communicate with your customers, as opposed to texting with your friends, you need to adhere to certain conventions:

- It's best to keep texts to no more than 140 characters.
- Texts need to be appropriate for their context and their reader.
- Texts need to be action-oriented. Include a way for customers to respond, such as a phone number or website where they can get more information.
- Texts need to be professional, with clear, easy-to-read instructions about how your customer should respond. Tell them what to do next and how to do it. For example, if you text a customer about an appointment that needs to be confirmed, give them an easy and limited option such as 'respond *yes* if you still intend to keep the appointment or *no* if you need to change it'.
- Texts should be polite and friendly, with an upbeat tone. You need to achieve a balance between business-appropriate tone and the abbreviated style of texting.
- You can use abbreviations, but they need to be appropriate for your readers. Not everyone will be familiar with 'textese' such as *GR8*.
- Texts need to be timely, with a catchy lead.
- Use correct spelling and punctuation.
- Avoid the thesaurus syndrome in using nouns (see Chapter 3); for example, don't use *respond* but then vary that with *reply*.

The last word

The key to success with digital writing is understanding the platforms, how people use them, and what they want from them.

Understand social media etiquette (what is appropriate to share) and be accountable for your content. Anticipate how tone could be misconstrued, as happened in the example of the tweet that backfired in the telecommunications incident that I mentioned above, and that not everyone may read a joke as 'funny'. Remember that social media content is read by diverse people in diverse environments. Social media have revolutionised how we communicate with one another personally and professionally, but there can be mistakes, misunderstandings, dissatisfaction, and risks, so be aware of the potential consequences of any message that you send. A huge plus for graduates coming into the workplace is that a cursory scan of job sites reveals that opportunities abound for social media managers and content creators with skills in writing for social media platforms.

Activities

1. If you are a workplace writer, were you aware of the number of potential pitfalls in the use of email, as discussed earlier in this chapter? Have you experienced other challenges in using email for communication that you could add to the list?
2. Does your organisation use social media to communicate with its customers? If it does, what challenges has it faced?
3. Do you tweet? Who are your favourite tweeters? Analyse the content and style of some of their tweets to work out what makes them appealing to you.
4. Do you use new social media apps such as Snapchat? If you do, can you see why they may be more popular with teenagers than Facebook? Compare the features of Facebook and Snapchat.
5. Do you follow any blogs? If you do, which ones do you regularly read? What do you like about them? Analyse the content and style of some of your favourite blogs to work out what makes them appealing to you.
6. Do you blog? If you do, does your blog follow the principles suggested in this chapter? If you don't blog, what expertise do you have that you might be able to develop into a blog with some further research?
7. Many media stories have pointed to research on the negative effects of social media, particularly on teenagers. Explore this issue and write a short opinion piece appropriate for your journal, or perhaps for publication on a blog.
8. Read Joseph Bernstein's amusing article on Buzzfeed on the tilde ('The hidden language of the tilde', 2015, buzzfeed.com/josephbernstein/

the-hidden-language-of-the-tilde#.rizgJvkK8), a punctuation mark that I didn't cover in Chapter 6 but perhaps should have. Bernstein's article is a great example of the kind of lively and compelling writing that you may want to emulate when writing for social media. Analyse his style to see what makes it so engaging and write a paragraph in your journal.

9. Can you remember being impressed/excited by a website's design? Why? Find three or four websites for the same sort of organisation (e.g., airlines, banks, hotels, or universities). Compare the websites by constructing a matrix (see Figure 7.3 in Chapter 7) of their similarities and differences and see which one your matrix reveals as the best. You would need to consider features such as ease of navigation, usefulness and quality of content, and appropriateness of style.

11

How revising, editing, and proofreading work

> When you write, try to leave out the
> parts that readers tend to skip.
> ELMORE LEONARD

> Producing writing, then, is not so much filling
> a basin once, but rather getting water to keep
> flowing *through* it till it finally runs clear.
> PETER ELBOW

Writing with the intention of revising

Experienced writers follow the principle that we write with the intention of revising. To put it another way, we write our first draft so that we have something to revise.

Sir Arthur Quiller-Couch, the first professor of English at the University of Cambridge, gave the following sound advice in a lecture delivered at the university in 1914:

> If you require a practical rule of me, I will present you with this: Whenever you feel an impulse to perpetrate a piece of exceptionally fine writing, obey it—wholeheartedly—and delete it before sending your manuscript to press. Murder your darlings.

And here's the great and prolific comic novelist P.G. Wodehouse:

> I have never written a novel yet (except *Thank You, Jeeves*) without doing 40,000 words or more and finding they were all wrong and going back and starting again, and this after filling 400 pages with notes, mostly delirious, before getting anything in the nature of a coherent scenario. (2012, p. 149)

The cultural commentator Alain de Botton had this to say about revising when he came back to one of his own books several years after writing it:

> Rereading my book, I was struck by certain grammatical faults as well as inelegant turns of phrase. I could see sentences crying out to be amended and others to be added. I felt the wisdom of the remark that a work is never finished, it is only ever abandoned. (2006)

Quiller-Couch's advice to 'murder your darlings' has been echoed by many other writers, including Stephen King, who extended the principle in his wonderful book *On Writing* when he said: 'It's always easier to kill someone else's darlings than it is to kill your own' (2001, p. 213). Indeed it is; as H.G. Wells is alleged to have said: 'No passion in the world is equal to the passion to alter *someone else's* draft'.

Many people think that if you can talk, you can write, and if you can write, you can edit. They are mistaken. There's often a discrepancy between the kind of writing that people want to read and the way they themselves write. I have already mentioned a couple of times Henry James's dictum about being 'one of those on whom nothing is lost'. James Wood extends this to comment that neither should we be 'one of those people on whom everything is found' (2009, p. 80). In other words, sometimes nothing improves a text like a (metaphorical) sharpened pencil. In this chapter, I'll cover strategies that will help you to revise, edit, and proofread your own work and the work of others.

Revising

The term 'revising' (from the Latin 'to see back') literally means 're-seeing', so, when you revise a document, you 're-see' its overall shape and structure. Revising happens at the 'macro' (top) level, when you examine how your document is organised and what it 'says'. Revising is a multi-step, multi-strategy process that may prompt you to consider radical changes. So you revise to shape your meaning. Editing happens after you are satisfied with the overall structure of your document. Editing is the correcting and polishing of micro-level features. Proofreading is making the final checks before submitting your document.

Revising and editing are not necessarily linear processes; they can often be recursive—that is, you may loop back to an earlier stage of revising once you have started out on the editing process.

When, in talking or writing, people begin a sentence of more than about six words, they usually don't know what words will end it. The shape that they create as a first draft is not usually one that is perfectly acceptable to them. Peter Wason (1980) argues that writing is difficult for some people because 'they try to do two incompatible things at the same time: say something, and say it in the most acceptable way' (p. 130). To overcome the anxiety that this causes, he recommends 'satisficing'—making do with what comes out during the first draft. (See also the discussion of this portmanteau term in Chapter 3.)

Wason explains that to satisfice is to 'externalize your thoughts without regard to your expression in accordance with the belief that you don't know what you are trying to say until you've said it' (p. 130). He brushes aside the need for elaboration, connection, and perfection, and admonishes against rereading, tinkering, or prematurely altering. Many writers have reinforced Wason's comments. If we accept this advice, we accept the principle that 'writing is re-writing'.

Follow Peter Elbow's advice to:

> Write a lot and throw a lot away. Start writing early so you have time to discard a lot and have it metamorphose a lot and bubble and percolate. If you have three hours to write three pages, write it three times, instead of one page an hour. The essence of writing is easy come, easy go. (1973, p. 31)

Though articles and textbooks historically treated revision as a discrete activity at the end of a writing project, a more complex and accurate description has been developing for some time. Until the 1970s, writing researchers regarded writing as a linear process of prewriting, writing, and editing. In 1968, Donald Murray defined revision as 'what the writer does after a draft is completed to understand and communicate what has begun to appear on the page' (p. 87). In effect, the linear model of writing was displaced by a new 'recursive' model, whereby writers could move back and forth between processes and sub-processes. Composition was no longer regarded as a series of discrete, chronologically ordered tasks, but rather as a complex of recursive, embedded activities.

Jill Fitzgerald (1987) suggests that Murray's work on revision

> can be seen as a transition (a) from a time when revision received little or no theoretical attention to a time when the meaning of revision began to take shape, (b) from a longstanding view of alterations in text as relatively minor editorial changes to a new view of text changes as including major and/or meaty reconceptualizations of ideas and meanings, and (c) from a product-focused view of revision to an increasingly process-oriented one. (p. 482)

In an influential article about revision strategies of student writers and experienced adult writers, Nancy Sommers defined revision as 'a sequence of changes in a composition—changes which are initiated by cues and occur continually throughout the writing of a work' (1980, p. 380). This belief is echoed in Ann Berthoff's assertion that 'revision is *not a stage of composition but a dimension*' (1983, p. 95).

The research carried out by Sommers revealed that students were mainly concerned with vocabulary. According to Sommers, most of the students did not use the terms 'revision' or 'rewriting'. 'Students are under the misapprehension that the meaning to be communicated is already there [in the text], and all that is necessary is a better word' (p. 382). Experienced writers, in contrast, *did* revise, using the revising process to find the form or shape of their argument, as Sommers quotes one of her adult writers here:

> Revising: It means taking apart what I have written and putting it back together again. I ask major theoretical questions of my ideas, respond to those questions, and think of proportion and structure . . . I find out which ideas can be developed and which should be dropped. I am constantly chiseling and changing as I revise. (p. 384)

Another adherent to the belief that writing is rewriting is Toby Fulwiler, who observes that for novice writers such as students,

> learning to re-write is an alien activity that doesn't come easily. Many [university] students . . . assume that writing is essentially copying down what they've already been thinking . . . In contrast, I am convinced that revision is the primary way that both thinking and writing evolve, mature, and improve. So now, when I teach writing, I no longer leave revision to chance, happenstance, or writer whimsy. I not only encourage it, I provoke it, emphasizing where, when, and how to do it. (1992, p. 190)

As they explain their taxonomy for analysing revision, Lester Faigley and Stephen Witte underscore the conclusions of researchers such as Murray, Berthoff, and Sommers that revision cannot be separated from other aspects of composing, since expert writers 'move back and forth among the various activities of composing and . . . frequently review what they have written and make changes while in the midst of generating a text' (1981, p. 400).

A helpful heuristic for organising your revising and editing is the levels of edit, first developed as seven levels by Robert Van Buren and Mary Fran Buehler in 1980 at the Jet Propulsion Laboratory in Pasadena, California. I like to use five levels when revising and editing, as shown in Figure 11.1.

A valuable revising strategy to help you to consider the hierarchical structure of a document is to draw a retrospective outline of your draft as an issue tree (see Figure 7.4 in Chapter 7) or some other visual version

---

Revising at the **macro level**
Structure—how it is organised
Content—what it says

Editing and **proofreading** at the **micro level**
Style—how it says what it says
Format—how it is presented (layout/design)
Mechanics—grammar, spelling, punctuation

Figure 11.1 Levels of edit

of your document. This will show you the framework on which your document rests, and should indicate whether your framework is coherent and comprehensive. An outline can reveal structural problems, out-of-sequence sections, irrelevancies, redundancies, and non sequiturs (a non sequitur is a statement that does not logically follow a point that has just been made). An alternative strategy that will serve much the same purpose is to go through your document and drop out the headings to make a table of contents.

A third strategy, which you can do most easily on a computer, is to isolate the key/topic sentences in the order in which they occur in the document. Printing them out and reading through them will indicate the coherent progression (or otherwise) of the document.

It can take substantial rewriting and reorganisation to make your reasoning unassailable. Relying on the rhetorical appeals of ethos (your credibility), pathos (your readers' desires), and logos (rational argument) is a foolproof strategy for achieving persuasive content. You need to anticipate your readers' reservations and objections and counter them with impressive specific facts. Elbow reminds us that 'writing is not just getting things down on paper. It is getting things inside someone else's head' (1973, p. 76).

Editing

Once you are satisfied with the structure and content of your document, you can start editing it. The best thing an editor can do is help a writer to think. When you edit your work you are forced to think about what you have written.

Editing is polishing and sharpening successive drafts to achieve economical, dynamic prose. Editing eliminates mechanical and stylistic infelicities and gaucheries in grammar, syntax, punctuation, and choice of words to make prose cleaner, clearer, lighter, smarter, tighter, and brighter. Gail Hornstein (2009) advocates pruning your prose of weeds that choke sentences, using the analogy of thinning out carrots.

You need to be confident of your grammatical and syntactical knowledge, as well as your punctuation and spelling. Familiarise yourself with the errors that you commonly make, highlight these in your editing checklist or personal style sheet, and learn how to fix them.

The key strategy for editing is that of the editorial loop, also known by such terms as 'multistage revising', the 'systematic pass-through', and the 'calculated iteration'. You loop through your document several times, examining a different feature each time, remembering that good writing is as much a matter of subtraction as of creation.

David Shenk, in *The End of Patience*, suggests that 'responsibly editing enormous volumes of data down to digestible, contextual chunks is one of the most valuable services that human beings perform for other human beings' (1999, p. 39). John McPhee, the legendary writing teacher whom I have quoted several times in this book, has this to say about writing and editing: 'Writing is selection. You select what goes in and decide what stays out' (2014). He reminds us that sculptors 'address the deletion of material in their own analogous way'; Michelangelo is reputed to have said that every block of stone has a statue inside it, and it is the task of the sculptor to discover it.

Annotating your text can be very helpful at the editing stage. You could try the following strategies:

1. Mark headings and subheadings and try to write a short summary of each paragraph.
2. Ask yourself what you intend your reader to take away from each section.
3. Mark up your text, if it's on paper, with different highlighter pens: blue for 'reads well'; yellow, 'needs clarifying'; red, 'needs refining/revising'. If it's onscreen, use different colours to highlight.
4. Make notes: anticipate how a reader might respond to a text. Will they be bored, confused, annoyed, inspired, or distracted, or think that it's too technical?

As I recommended in Chapter 4, when you read writing that you like, try to work out how the writer has achieved those effects.

Specific strategies for editing

- Don't edit prematurely. Wait until you are satisfied that you have revised your global structure and that your content is comprehensive.
- Distance yourself from what you have written. Incubation is a big help. The longer the better, but at least a week.

- Assume the role of an objective reader with a 'cold' eye. Edit as if you had a contract with your reader to 'deliver the goods'.
- Use the editorial loop/the systematic pass-through, focusing on a different aspect each time.
- Examine every word. Keep in mind the concept of *le mot juste*.
- Delete anything that is not essential for your reader. Distil. Condense.
- Define any abstract or jargon terms.
- Eliminate ambiguity.
- Don't skip over sentences.
- Connect ideas to achieve smooth and strong transitions/cohesive ties within and between paragraphs.
- Construct helpful headings that are in parallel form.
- Insert previews of the material ahead, such as 'The following section presents strategies for proofreading'.
- Sum up regularly to confirm what you want your reader to understand.
- Break up long, rambling sentences into shorter sentences.
- Substitute dynamic verbs for heavy nouns, positive expressions for negative expressions (where appropriate), and active voice for passive voice (where appropriate).
- Be flexible. Be willing to consider changes suggested by readers of your document. Your metaknowledge is invaluable at this stage because you can decide whether or not to accept the suggested changes, and you will be doing this in an informed way.

Implementing the strategies above will ensure that your writing exemplifies 'plain language', as discussed below.

Plain language

For several decades, the movement to embrace plain language, or plain English as it is known in the UK, has been strong in government and legal circles in many countries (Petelin, 2010a). The International Working Group on Plain Language says: 'Communication is in plain language if its wording, structure, and design are so clear that the intended readers can easily find what they need, understand what they find, and use that information'.

In July 2015, Prime Minister David Cameron sent a letter to all civil servants in the UK urging them to 'be brief, simple, and jargon free' in the language used in their correspondence and not to 'hide bad news in complexities' (Taylor, 2015). This is not the first time that this has happened. Margaret Thatcher made the same request: 'I would like to see jargon and "officialese" banished forever', she told the civil service. 'Plain English must be the aim of all who work in government' (quoted in Taylor, 2015).

The benefits to an organisation in good will and cost savings of a commitment to clarity in the workplace are substantial:
- Call centres will receive fewer calls from customers.
- An organisation's documents and brand will be aligned.
- Users' problems can be solved more quickly.
- Customers will make fewer errors because information and instructions will be clearer.
- Compliance rates will be higher.
- Transparency of dealings will be clearer.
- Costs will be lowered because problems with customers will decrease.
- Equity and efficiency for staff will be more easily achieved.

The benefits to citizens can also be significant. A family court judge at a hearing on whether a child should be taken into care in Nottingham in the UK in 2015 said that the lack of plain English in a social worker's report resulted in its being so poorly written that it might as well have been 'in a foreign language'. The judge cited examples from the report, including the phrases 'imbued with ambivalence' and 'having many commonalities emanating from their histories', and wondered why the writer had asked her client 'to convey a narrative about her observations' rather than 'asked her to tell me' (Walden, 2015). The social worker's obfuscatory prose should have been weeded out in the editing process.

Consistency—levels of text

Consistency is crucial in all elements of your document. The following features are the key to a consistent document:
- semantic consistency—use consistent terminology
- syntactic consistency—use parallel structure for coordinate elements in sentences
- stylistic consistency—maintain your style throughout
- spatial consistency—standardise page layout

- mechanical consistency—standardise capitalisation, punctuation, spelling out of numbers, etc.
- structural consistency—ensure that the hierarchy of your heading levels is correct.

Proofreading

Mark Twain knew very well how hard it is to proofread effectively, particularly your own work. As he said in a letter to a friend in February 1898:

> You think you are reading proof, whereas you are merely reading your own mind; your statement of the thing is full of holes & vacancies but you don't know it, because you are filling them from your mind as you go along. Sometimes—but not often enough—the printer's proof-reader saves you—& offends you—with this cold sign in the margin: (?) & you search the passage & find that the insulter is right—it doesn't say what you thought it did: the gas-fixtures are there, but you didn't light the jets.

Proofreading is the final check in the writing process; neglecting this stage can damage your professional image and cancel out all your efforts to produce a perfect document. You may have created the most cogently argued essay, but if you have spelled your reader's name wrongly, you lose credibility immediately. Shakespeare may have spelled his name several different ways, but no one can get away with that these days.

Whenever you set out to proofread a document, **consider the consequences** of overlooking errors. Whether you have given your work professional attention will be immediately apparent to your reader.

In 2015, an English company, Taylor & Sons, claimed nearly £9 million in damages from a UK government agency, Companies House, which had incorrectly recorded it as being in liquidation. All of Taylor & Sons' credit agencies and 3000 suppliers revoked their services, resulting in the company collapsing and 250 people losing their jobs. A company called Taylor & *Son* had gone into liquidation six years earlier. Taylor & Sons won its High Court case, which had been caused by the failure of Companies House to carefully proofread. The UK government agency would have done well to remember the poet A.E. Housman's dictum: 'Accuracy is a duty, not a virtue'.

In November 2015, a copy of a 400-year-old Bible that omitted the word *not* from the seventh commandment, so that it read 'Thou shalt commit adultery', was sold in London for £31,250. The auctioneer, Bonhams, which did not disclose the owner of the Wicked Bible, had expected it, as one of the nine remaining copies, to sell for £15,000. So, a lack of proofreading paid off for someone in the end. This strategy is not to be relied upon, however!

Competence as a proofreader will enhance your credibility as a writer. Limit proofreading to the final stage of your writing process—after you have revised and edited. Premature proofreading, like premature editing, is a waste of time. Read through the whole document one final time before proofreading to make sure that the argument is coherent.

Reading is usually a process of anticipation and prediction, so at the proofreading stage it's important to avoid your normal reading process; otherwise, you will see only what you think you wrote—and fail to detect the minor errors that mar your work. You can proofread effectively only if you suspend anticipation while you read and don't merely read what you *think* you wrote, as Mark Twain warned in his letter to his friend that I quoted above. Modify your normal reading process of skimming, skipping, scanning, dipping, and browsing, and concentrate 100 per cent on your task. Detach yourself as best as you can. It is rare for anyone to be their own best editor.

Never set out to proofread if you are tired, bored, distracted by noise, anticipating a phone call, or likely to be interrupted. If you haven't the time to read the document critically and slowly, wait until you do. Give it your utmost concentration, accepting that it is a painstaking process. If you can feel yourself losing concentration, take a break. Be methodical, meticulous, even obsessive about detail. Use several strategic pass-throughs, systematically checking a different aspect each time, such as spacing, spelling, word use, sentence structure, consistency of headers and footers, as well as type size and punctuation. An earlier book of mine had a first print run with a chapter headed 'Deciding how to puctuate'.

Specific strategies for proofreading

Some people have a knack for proofreading—essentially they have an 'eye for detail'. Use the following strategies for finding typographical errors (typos), irregular spacing, omissions, and errors in punctuation and spelling that you have missed at an earlier stage in the revising–editing process. Most of these proofreading strategies can help you to reliably detect errors because they contravene your normal reading process by forcing you to slow down and be painstakingly methodical.

- Allow time to elapse between editing and proofreading the document. The passage of time (the longer the better) will allow you to forget to some extent what you wrote originally, so your ability to skim over and predict what you think you have said is impaired, and you are more likely to see what is actually on the page rather than what you think you wrote.
- Use proofreading aids such as a pointer (pen or pencil) to force yourself to look at each letter, each word, and each punctuation mark—noting what's there and what's not there. Or use a ruler or another sheet of paper and move it down your page line by line. Even printing or photocopying your document onto different-coloured paper can be useful in highlighting errors.
- Read your document aloud—to yourself or to someone else who has a duplicate copy. Oral reading requires attention to each word, punctuation mark, and space, so the listener is able to check for accuracy word by word. This strategy is particularly useful for eliminating incorrect doubling up of words, and for picking up whole sections that have been left out. Children learning to read often move their fingers along a line and move their lips to silently say the words. It's worth returning to these techniques when proofreading.
- Read in reverse order, sentence by sentence. Again, you can't predict too easily when you are reading backwards. The process slows you down, and you can't skip over bits, assuming that they are correct.
- Always double-check everything for accuracy: facts, names, spelling or choice of words, and any other detail, such as dates. Journalists who don't double-check their facts and thus cause their newspaper to print an apology soon learn the importance of this. The greatest spelling aid is doubt. It's not unusual to discover that you've been spelling a specific word wrongly for years. Spelling skills reside in the hand as well as in the brain, so writing out a troubling word can sometimes help you decide—though not if you've been spelling the

word incorrectly for years. This technique is nowhere near as reliable as using a dictionary and spell-checker.
- While spell-checkers are useful, they cannot be relied on to pick up much more than around 90 per cent of errors. For example, it's impossible for them to flag *casual* as an error for *causal*, *charges* as an error for *changes*, or *on* as an error for *of*.
- Read your draft more than once, concentrating on a different aspect each time, for example, consistency in your use of headings. You will find errors and omissions in second and subsequent strategic pass-throughs or loops that you did not see on your first reading. To do this you need to construct a proofreading checklist. It is also helpful to construct a style sheet to remind you of, for example, your policy on abbreviations, capitalisation, or how to write numbers. You may want to construct your own style sheet (see Chapter 8) or use the levels of edit detailed in Box 11.1 later in this chapter.
- Always double-check paired punctuation marks such as brackets to ensure that the closing bracket is included.
- Get other people to proofread your document, because you are often too close to your work to see errors. But don't rely solely on others. They usually lack the motivation that you have to ensure that your document is perfect, so you need to challenge them strongly by saying that you think your writing is superb. Also, as I discovered when this book was edited by those who had not been in my writing classroom, an experienced editor new to your work will question it much more thoroughly than someone who knows you and your work.
- If possible, always proofread word-processed material on a printout, because errors are much easier to spot on paper. If you have no choice but to proofread onscreen, scroll forwards or backwards only one line at a time, or scroll rapidly all the way through to check spacing. Other useful techniques are to triple your line spacing, create wide margins, or use an outlandish font, so that your document takes on a different appearance.
- Hypercorrection can also be a danger. This occurs when someone 'corrects'—with a pedantic but wrong suggestion—something that doesn't need correcting.

Using computers for writing and editing

Jane Tompkins, a university teacher and writer, presents the following testimony:

> The benefit [in using a computer to write] is not simply the ease with which you can revise, but rather in what it does to your process of composition. That is, the initial writing itself is freed up by the things the computer makes easy. (1995, p. 3)

Research since the early 1980s on using computers for writing has reported the following advantages:
- positive psychological effects (the cursor invites the writer to start typing)
- ease of free writing (i.e., writing without pausing to revise)
- writing as mosaic/patchwork (building up a document out of pieces such as the headings or writing the easiest bits first)
- elimination of drudgery (no need to retype)
- accumulation of accuracy (updating and correcting of details)
- ease of revising (shifting large chunks of text)
- ease of editing/polishing (spell-checkers, global 'search and replace')
- efficiency of cut-and-paste (boilerplating—reusing chunks of text, quotes, and references)
- usefulness of word counting, automatic documentation, generating outlines and indexes, formatting, and desktop publishing
- facilitation of collaborative writing. (Nobles & Paganucci, 2015)

Computer software with track changes and comments features is great for revising and editing onscreen. However, I never advocate using a grammar checker. They are notorious for introducing new errors and failing to identify errors that need correction.

Because, as discussed in Chapter 1, writing is at the heart of the economy, and compelling, coherent writing is central to the corporate world, reliable computerised editing would be highly valued in the workplace, particularly by staff who lack confidence in their writing competence. Style-analysis software has been developed as an alternative to long-discredited readability formulas that are still being applied to corporate writing (see Chapter 2). Because the software sells and had been so positively reviewed in the technical press, I was curious about just how well it measures up to the reviews, so I did some research. I ran an error-riddled workplace document through a computerised style-analysis program and compared the results to editing done on the same text by me, an experienced human editor. I concluded that this kind of software can, at best, flag only a small number of potential problems; at worst, it can fail to detect egregious errors and can introduce errors by making ungrammatical suggestions (Petelin, 2013). My belief that computers can count but they can't read is not shared by the American Educational Testing Service, which has a machine that can apparently grade 16,000 essays in 20 seconds (Winerip, 2012).

What happens in publishing?

How do the revising, editing, and proofreading practices that I have covered in this chapter so far mirror the practices in publishing companies? Reasonably closely, with small differences in terminology. The term 'revision' is replaced in publishing by 'structural' or 'substantive' editing, which concerns itself with restructuring, deleting, and expanding.

The other two dimensions, editing and proofreading, are much the same in the industry. The term 'editing' is replaced by the term 'copyediting' or 'stylistic' editing, which concerns itself with syntactical clarity; grammatical correctness; rhetorical appropriateness (writer–reader relationship, purpose of the text, context); headers and footers, captions on tables and figures, etc.; heading levels (coordinate and subordinate); and consistency of point of view. The term 'proofreading' carries over. As well as reading for typos, proofreaders are responsible for checking layout and design, pagination, cross-referencing, images and captions, front and end matter such as the table of contents, acknowledgements, index, the cover, the spine of a book, and its ISBN (International Standard Book Number).

Five levels of edit: checklist

The five levels of edit set out in Figure 11.1 above comprise the basis for a checklist that you can use during the revising, editing, and proofreading processes. Box 11.1 is a much more detailed version.

BOX 11.1 **Editing checklist**

Structure—how your document is organised
- What is the organising structure of your document?
- Does this structure help to make the purpose and message of the document clear?
- Is this structure clearly evident to the reader from the headings?
- Does your introduction clearly preview the structure?
- Does the document deal with all aspects outlined in the introduction?
- Is your document broken down into manageable sections that are 'signposted' for your reader?
- Do all parts of your document flow logically from one to the next with ideas in an appropriate sequence?
- Are all related ideas together and clearly identified?
- Have you regularly summed up the gist of your argument (if your document is long)?
- Does the conclusion comprehensively summarise the main points of the document?

Content—what your document says
- Is your title appropriate?
- Having read the document, what action will a reader take? (For example, file it for reference, base a decision on it, or act on it.) Do you think that your document will have the intended effect on your reader and generate the response you would like?
- Does the introduction clearly set out the context, or do you have preliminary phatic communication that is unnecessary in most cultural contexts (but not all)?
- Is your document convincing? Are your ideas fully explained and your arguments proved by supporting details and illustrations?
- If the intent of your document is persuasive, are your persuasive strategies effective? (For example, an effective sequence of ideas.)
- Have you identified the criteria that you used and qualified any tentative assertions you have made?
- Is there any evidence of unwarranted assumptions or bias that distorts your conclusions, or conclusions unjustified by the evidence?

- Have you included any irrelevant details or digressions?
- Is your material pitched at the appropriate level for its readers—that is, not too specialised, too superficial, or too pedestrian? (Do not underestimate or overestimate your readers.)
- If your document is one of a series (e.g., a progress report), have you made sure that you have incorporated all the developments that have occurred since the last report was written? (Clients are irritated by the inclusion of superseded material.)
- Have you checked to see that your document complies with your organisation's policy on the issues that you have discussed?
- Did you consider including appropriate graphic illustrations such as charts, graphs, tables, and infographics?

Style—how you say what you say

Paragraph construction
- Are your paragraphs adequately developed to support your major ideas?
- Are there too many ideas in any paragraph?
- Is there a new paragraph each time there is a shift in topic?
- Are there adequate linking words (e.g., *additionally, therefore*) between paragraphs?

Sentence construction
- Can each sentence be understood on the first reading?
- Are any sentences too short and choppy or overly simple?
- Are any sentences too long and complex, with bits awkwardly tacked on or intrusively embedded?
- Have you varied your sentence patterns to add interest to your writing?
- Have you used more active-voice verbs than passive-voice verbs?
- Have you avoided expletive constructions (*it is, there is/are*)?
- Have you minimised weak, linking verbs (*is, was*)?
- Is the order of words in any sentence inverted with the result that the sentence is illogical or difficult to understand (e.g., *Time was*

when we could rely on technology rather than *There was a time when . . .*)?
- Does every sentence coherently follow on from the one before?
- Have you avoided negative expressions, except where necessary?
- Have you generally avoided sentence fragments? Run-on sentences? Comma splices?
- Have you avoided inappropriate nominalisations and unwieldy noun strings (e.g., *industry benchmark correlation data*)?
- Is there parallel structure where you have parallel components?

Language use
- Have you used concrete and specific words rather than abstractions, whenever possible?
- Are all the words used correctly and unambiguously?
- Have you used words economically? Have you pruned verbose and redundant expressions?
- Are jargon or technical words used appropriately and defined where necessary?
- Have you avoided 'elegant variation' in using nouns (thesaurus syndrome) and used terminology consistently so that your reader is never puzzled by multiple terms for the same thing?
- Have you avoided abbreviations or acronyms that are not spelled out at the first use?
- Have you avoided clichés and archaisms?
- Is the writing non-discriminatory?

Tone
- Is your tone appropriate for your subject?
- Is your tone appropriate for the level of formality of your document?
- Is your tone appropriate for your reader?
- Is your tone courteous and considerate? Not too pompous? Not too colloquial?
- Does the document read as if it is written by a human? Does your personality as the writer come through? (If so, is this appropriate, or does it jar?)

Format
- Have you used the appropriate format (e.g., for a report)?
- Have you followed your organisation's style or, if you are a student, the style required by your lecturer? (If there isn't one set down, have you kept your own style sheet?)
- For hard-copy documents, have you followed guidelines for visual presentation with respect to paper quality, typeface and type size, margins, white space, headings, graphic material, highlighting, colour, and binding?
- If your work is online, have you followed the online format suggestions that I covered in Chapter 10?
- Is your document visually pleasing?
- Can your document be used for its intended purpose?
- Is your use of headings and numbering consistent?
- Are the pages numbered in the right order and bound in correctly?
- Is the document complete?
- Will your reader be able to find specific information easily?
- If your document is long (over five pages), have you included a table of contents?
- If a summary section is appropriate for this kind of document (e.g., a report), have you included one?

Mechanics
- Are there any grammatical errors or incoherent sentences?
- Are there any punctuation errors?
- Are there any spelling errors? Have you spell-checked and checked for confusable words (see Box 3.2 in Chapter 3)?
- Are there any typographical errors (typos)?

Box 11.2 lists specific features of your writing that you need to consider when you are editing. Many, but not all, of them are errors and/or infelicities (a feature of your writing that would make a reader in a formal, professional context unhappy) to look out for. Of course, good writing is more than an absence of errors, but it would be useful to check your writing against this list at the editing stage. I have grouped the items under headings: word use, grammar, sentence structure, paragraphs, punctuation, and mechanics.

BOX 11.2 **Error/infelicity/feature to consider**

Word use (diction/vocabulary)
acronyms and initialisms
ambiguity
archaisms
buzzwords and phrases
clichés
coined words (neologisms)
colloquial language
discriminatory language (ageist, racist, sexist)
equivocation
euphemism/dysphemism
foreign expressions
gaucherie (awkwardness)
glibness
gobbledygook (opaque, obfuscatory prose)
humour (inappropriate, lame)
hyperbole
inappropriate/mixed metaphors
intensifiers
jargon (unnecessary, inappropriate for readers)
loaded word(s)
malapropisms
missing words
negative expressions/connotations
nominalisations that can be 'unpacked' (converted back to a verb)
noun strings/adjective stacks
orality (speaking style)
purple prose (flowery, ornate)
redundant expressions
simplistic style (overly simple)
slang
spelling (confusable words)
thesaurus syndrome

tone problems (breezy, intimidating, overly casual, presumptuous)
vagueness
verbosity/verbiage/pomposity

Grammar
lack of agreement (subject–verb, pronoun–antecedent)
inconsistent use of person (moving from first person to second person or third person in a sentence)
incorrect pronoun case
incorrect use of tenses
one word or two ('breakup' or 'break up')?
wrong preposition

Sentence structure (syntax)
and-ness, is-ness, of-ness
awkward embedding of clauses
expletive constructions
faulty (or absent) parallelism
illogical statements
inelegance (awkwardness)
mixed/shifted constructions
modifiers (dangling, misplaced, squinting)
overreliance on passive voice
rambling, convoluted structure
repetitive sentence structure
run-on sentences
sentence fragments
syntactical complexity
weak transitions/lack of cohesive ties

Paragraphs
digressions
irrelevant sentences
lack of coherence
lack of cohesion
non sequiturs

statements unsupported by evidence
unclear central idea

Punctuation
apostrophe problems
comma splice
commas (serial and parenthetical)
contractions
emoticons and emoji (inappropriate)
hyphenation of compounds
other punctuation marks

Mechanics
capitalisation errors
dates/addresses (including websites)/telephone numbers in the wrong format
incorrect use of italics/roman/bolding
measurements/numbers (spell out up to and including ten)
spacing
symbol errors
time format errors

Typographical errors

Joseph Epstein published a witty essay in *The Weekly Standard* called 'Why cry over split milk?' (2010) in which he discusses typos. Here is the opening. You might like to find the essay and read it through to the end.

> I was reading along in an article in the *New York Times Magazine* about a woman who reacted to being fired from a rather cushy job by working out her depression through overeating, when I came upon the following sentence: 'I put the plate of peanut better, a half bottle of wine, a glass and a linen napkin on a tray and climbed back to my bedroom.' Ah, thought I, 'peanut better, what can be butter?'
>
> Why do people take such pleasure in discovering typographical errors—typos, in the trade term—especially in putatively august

publications? I confess I do. Is there a touch of Schadenfreude in it? Not so much 'see how the mighty have fallen' as 'see how sloppy, sadly incompetent, bereft of standards they have become.' Catching a typo heightens the reading experience, making a reader feel he is perhaps just a touch superior to the author, his or her editors, and, it does not go too far to say, the culture of our day.

My own pleasure in discovering typos is, alas, less than complete because of the typos readers have found—and too often reported to me—in my own published scribblings.

Epstein goes on to mention the number of people who send him messages about typos and suggest to him that they can be corrected in the second edition. Only when editing is absent is it noticeable. And when it's noticeable, readers can't resist telling you.

On the matter of typos, a reader of *The Chicago Manual of Style* sent the following note to its editors: 'Your copy editing leaves something to be desired. In section 8.64, the correct spelling is Baudelaire, not Beaudelaire. Also, you might want to add a place on the website to suggest corrigenda'.

The reader received the nicely sarcastic reply below:

Thank you for taking the time to write. We depend on the kindness of our readers—and reader kindness overflowed when this typo made it into print. The error will be corrected in the next printing of the manual. You will find a place to send comments just above the place where you submit questions. Perhaps in future revisions of the Web page we can add a place for corrigenda—and what the heck—while we're at it, one for chastisement.

The last word

Box 11.3 provides a list of useful websites with further information about editing and grammar. You may want to use them to flesh out some of the concepts in this book, particularly those around grammar, syntax, word use, and punctuation. I regularly read *The Chronicle of Higher Education* blog *Lingua Franca*, the *New Yorker* blogs, and Opinionator on the *New York Times* site. The most comprehensive site is Richard Nordquist's grammar.about.com.

> BOX 11.3 **Useful usage sites**
>
> bartleby.com/141/
> chicagomanualofstyle.org
> chompchomp.com
> chronicle.com/blogs/linguafranca/
> dailywritingtips.com
> english.stackexchange.com
> etymonline.com (Online Etymology Dictionary)
> grammar.about.com
> grammar.quickanddirtytips.com
> languagelog.ldc.upenn.edu/nll/
> theoatmeal.com
> owl.english.purdue.edu/
> oxforddictionaries.com/words/grammar
> subversivecopyeditor.com
> throwgrammarfromthetrain.blogspot.com.au/
> worldwidewords.org

Activities

Answers are at the back of the book.

1. In her book *Problem-Solving Strategies for Writing* (1981), Linda Flower presents a strategy for making sentences more dynamic. She calls it 'lowering the noun:verb ratio'.

    Here is her example sentence marked with the *nouns* and **verbs**:

    > The *effect* of the *overuse* of *nouns* in *writing* **is** the *placing* of excessive *strain* upon the inadequate *number* of *verbs* and the resultant *prevention* of the *flow* of *thought*.

    The ratio of nouns to verbs is 11:1. In her rewrite, in which she replaces the weak verb **is** with two strong verbs, the ratio drops to 7:2:

    > *Using* too many *nouns* in *writing* **places** *strain* on *verbs* and **prevents** the *flow* of *thought*.

Note that *using* and *writing* are verbal nouns, so have been counted as nouns.

Find some sentences that you have written that you suspect may benefit from this exercise and see if you can reduce the noun:verb ratio as Flower has done.

2. In Chapter 8, I mentioned getting a surprisingly error-riddled letter from a bank. Read the letter and its background and then write a polite and apologetic letter to me.

The bank's letter:

Dear Mrs Petelin,

MASTERCARD ACCOUNT NO. 1234567

We refer to your enquiry regarding a disputed amount of $494.31 debited to your account from

BUSYTOWN HOTEL, BUSYTOWN, CALIFORNIA

As previously advised, action was taken to credit your account pending receipt of the vouchers from the merchant's bank.

The merchant's bank have now supplied us with two vouchers which are enclosed for your perusal.

Unfortunately we are unable to assist you any further as rental/lodging agreements are subject to final audit.

As details appear valid, we wish to advise you that action will be taken to reprocess $494.31 to your Account. If you still dispute this matter, the only avenue for you to try and retreive $494.31 is directly from the merchant.

If this proves unsuccessful you may seek the assistance from the EMBASSY.

We apologise for the inconvience.

Yours sincerely,

Customer Services

The background to the bank's letter:
Prior to participating in a conference, I sent my HillEnd Bank MasterCard number to the Busytown Hotel to guarantee a room reservation. I stayed

at the hotel for three nights. On checking out, I paid my account with the same credit card I had used to guarantee my reservation.

Several months later, I noticed that I had been charged an identical amount twice for my stay at the hotel. I rang the bank, explained to them how I believed the error had occurred, and asked them to deposit the second amount back into my account. They did.

Nearly a year later, I received the letter above out of the blue. It was accompanied by a photocopy of the slip I had signed on checking out and a hand-filled-in slip with no signature on it that said 'signature on file'.

3. The following sentences will test your ability to edit at the sentence level. Identify and correct the problem in each sentence.
    a) People are always impressed by her smooth manner, elegant clothes, and being witty.
    b) The rural towns are dying. One of the problems being that young people are leaving.
    c) Having argued all morning, a decision was finally reached.
    d) The situation is quite different than that of previous years.
    e) The army moved my partner and I to Melbourne last year.
    f) It is late in his term and inflation is worse and no one has a solution.
    g) When a person moves every year, one cannot expect them to develop civic pride.

Acknowledgements

I owe thanks to the University of Queensland, which granted me a semester's leave to write this book. The book is based on my long experience of teaching and researching writing and editing in Brisbane, Hong Kong, London, and New York. Over the years, my life has been enriched by encounters with so many wonderful graduates of my classes, particularly Krista Berga, Harry Brumpton, Simon Chester, Kerryn Colen, Kate Cowen, Carody Culver, Kate Cuthbert, Marianne de Pierres, Shastra Deo, Sally Dillon, Paul Dunne, Kim Ellis, Jason Emmett, Sonya Faint, Fiona Louise Fleming, Candice Fox, Justine Gannon, Caroline Gardam, Amber Gwynne, Rebeccca Harris, Margaret Heaslop, Damian Kington, Adam LeBrocq, Melanie Lord, Craig McAnulty, Corrie Macdonald, Caroline McKinnon, Hawys McManus, Rosie Morley, Richard Newman, Candice Poole, Megan Porter, Justine Ryan, Dean Saunders, Jodi Simpson, Kate Stevens, Kate Watson, Louise White, Ben Wilson, Tony Wilson, Lee Winston, and countless others.

I want to thank the students who have given me permission to share their work in the book: Kirstie Asmussen, Melanie Bayes, Jessica Miller, Richard Newman, Megan Porter, and Deānne Sheldon-Collins.

I also want to thank the thousands of students from more than 200 countries and territories who participated in WRITE101X English Grammar and Style, a massive open online course (MOOC) offered by edX, which I developed and presented in 2014, 2015, and 2016.

I am grateful to Professors David Crystal, Mignon Fogarty, and Geoffrey Pullum, who so kindly talked to me about grammar in Oxford, Cambridge, and Edinburgh, and Dr Harry Ritchie, whom I interviewed in London.

I also owe thanks to my current writing colleagues at the University of Queensland and earlier at the Queensland University of Technology: Carrie Finn, Mike Lefcourt, Mary-Rose MacColl, Rod Miller, Peta Mitchell, Gabrielle O'Ryan, Josephine Robertson, Gerard Ross, and Kim Wilkins. Vanessa Dunn and Joanne Nelson provided great collegiality for many years in the corporate sphere, as did Lelia Green, Shirley Leitch, David McKie, and Judy Motion in the academic arena.

I am grateful for the support of my academic colleagues in Hong Kong—Valentina Chan, Patrick Ng, Cindy Ngai, Daniel So, Doreen Wu—and in New York: Michael Goodman and Tina Genest.

It is impossible to exaggerate Clara Finlay's exemplary editorial work on this book. Her contribution was painstakingly monumental, as was that of the proofreader, Elizabeth Keenan. Elizabeth Weiss and Angela Handley have provided splendid support throughout the process of publishing this book.

Answers to the activities

Chapter 3: How words work
2. archaic
3. thesaurus syndrome
4. inappropriate tone

Chapter 4: How sentences and form-class words work
1. There are thousands of potential sentences.
2. verbal phrase
3. The room *alarmed* him.
   They finally *reached* the end of the road.
4. I *have* attached a short note to this document. While a clean uncluttered copy for submission *was* desired, upon final draft yesterday, errors *were* still found.
5. Time *has* not *permitted* the production of a final, polished draft. I *have edited* all of the errors that were able to be located. I *appreciate* that this *mars* the presentation.
6. Time has not permitted the production of a final, polished draft. I have edited all of the errors that *were able to be located*. I appreciate that this mars the presentation.
7. None of them. *Ran* is a verb that's followed by the prepositional phrase *up the hill*.
8. This is a ridiculously *easy* test.

The robots stared at the *strange* phenomenon.
Avoid *unnecessary* and *clichéd* adjectives.
A *creative* use of adjectives can enhance your writing.
9. a *black* cat, the city *proper*, the heir *apparent*, a *gloomy* outlook, the *sheer* richness of the material
10. *Happy* and *interesting* can each be compared, so they are not absolute.
11. This is a *ridiculously* easy test.
    I would *certainly* have loved to be there.
    Something had to *drastically* change.
    We ask you to stay *safely* in your seats.
    Drive *safe*.
12. Writers write books, while readers read books.
13. The director addressed the meeting.
14. comma splice
15. periodic
16. complex
17. verb
18. dangling (or unattached)
19. squinting (or ambiguous)
20. lack of parallel structure
21. Here is a course of action that I believe should be taken.
    There was only one thing that needed to be taken seriously.

Chapter 5: How structure-class words and paragraphs work

2. a) iii) A paragraph is a group of sentences relating to a central idea and appearing in a logical sequence.
   b) i) states the central idea or focus of the paragraph
      ii) tells the reader what to expect
   c) ii) reinforce the main idea
      iii) lead the reader logically through a series of points
   d) i) remind the reader what the paragraph was about
      ii) summarise the paragraph's main points
      iv) provide a logical link to the next paragraph
   e) true
   f) ii) cohesive ties
   g) i) plan what they are going to write
      ii) decide on the most coherent sequence of ideas

       iii) be mindful that too many long paragraphs may overwhelm a reader visually
       v) develop the main idea by amplifying, elaborating, and reinforcing
- h) i) summarising
- i) iii) however
- j) i) an introductory clause
  - ii) a pronoun linking to an antecedent
  - iii) a parallel list
  - iv) phrasal verbs
  - vi) an adjective

3. COHESIVE TIES = TRANSITIONAL DEVICES = GLUE
   - Central concept, key words and repeated words—shown in *italic*. Note that the key concept occurs 13 times.
   - Connecting words—shown in **bold**.
   - Pronouns—shown in ***bold italic***.
   - Summary words.
   - Repeated sentence patterns and parallelism—shown in square brackets.
   - Examples—shown in CAPITALS.
   - Explanations—marked by underlining.
   - Sentence structure—all the sentences in this paragraph.
   - Logical sequence—the sequence in this paragraph is logical.
   - Punctuation—indicating the structure of each sentence.

   Plain language, **still** called '*plain* English' in the United Kingdom, has been the focus of extensive discussion, research, **and** legislation **since** the 1960s IN THE USA, THE UK, CANADA, AND AUSTRALIA. **More recently**, the *plain language* movement has been taken up in Europe, **where** FRANCE, ITALY, GERMANY, DENMARK, THE NETHERLANDS, PORTUGAL, AND SWEDEN have adopted *plain language*. Other countries **such as** MEXICO have adopted ***it***, **as well as** NEW ZEALAND, SINGAPORE, HONG KONG, AND SOUTH AFRICA.

      [The key principle of *plain language* is that the intended reader can use the document for ***its*** intended purpose. The key aims of *plain language* are that the reader can understand **and** use the document.]

      The researcher Garner regrets that the set phrases '*plain language*' **and** '*plain English*' contain the word '*plain*', **because** *he* thinks that *it* suggests the idea of 'drab and ugly'. **However**, the term has no serious competitor, **so** advocates of *plain language* need to be prepared to explain what they mean by *it*. Another researcher, Balmford, argues that the term '*plain language*' is inaccurate **because** it places too much emphasis on words and sentences. **He** says that *plain language* involves elements of the whole document: content, language, structure, **and** design. No *plain-language* proponent would argue with *his* statement.

4. a) to h), inclusive, are all correct.
    i) Bob and *I* travel a good deal.
    j) He gave the flowers to Jane and *me*.
    k) Let's you and *me* go to the library.
    l) *We* travellers like comfort.
    m) They provided vouchers for *us* passengers.
    n) They like movies more than *I* do.
    o) Eating vegetables keeps them—John and *him*—healthy.
    p) *She* and *I* went to dinner.
    q) Susan and *I* are twins.
    r) when it comes to *us* girls
    s) between you and *me*
    t) Why is the government not listening to *us*, the people?

5. a) I have no qualms *about* the project's aims.
    b) a hotbed *of* gossip
    c) fluent *in*
    d) suitability *of* or *for* an event
    e) take umbrage *at*
    f) dance *to* or dance *with*
    g) devastated *by*
    h) drizzle *over* or drizzle *down*
    i) parallel *with* or parallel *to*
    j) conform *with* or conform *to*
    k) an aversion *to*
    l) cater *to* or cater *for*
    m) smitten *with* or smitten *by*
    n) adapt *from* or adapt *to*

Chapter 6: How punctuation works

7. a) That which is is. That which is not is not. Is that not it? It is. (If you say the words out loud, you can sense how to punctuate this example. I wouldn't put a comma between *is* and *is* or between *is not* and *is not*, because, if you do, you are separating a subject from its verb with a comma. See sentence b for the same problem.)
    b) His grasp of the world of economics found him writing for the financial pages. (Don't separate a subject from its verb with a comma unless you have a comma pair. For example, *We, that is to say our team, won the trophy.*)
    c) The lecturer asked if we had done our reading. (Don't use a question mark unless you ask a direct question. The sentence is a statement.)
    d) Improvement works may affect your journey, particularly at weekends. (You need a comma to separate the closing phrase from the main part of the sentence.)
    e) Check before you travel; look for publicity at stations. (You have two sentences closely connected. The original sentence was a fused or run-on sentence. Use a semicolon, as shown, or, perhaps, a full stop to separate the two sentences.)
    f) The Pet Shop Boys have loads of fans, including me. (You need a comma to separate the closing phrase from the main part of the sentence.)
    g) We suspect, however, that those names are pseudonyms. (You need a comma pair around *however* because it is an 'aside'.)
    h) The food arrived; however, it looked inedible. (This is much the same structure as sentence e).)
    i) Though usually happy, people get sad sometimes. (You need a comma after *happy* to prevent overreading.)
    j) Coincidentally, several visitors arrived at the door. (You need a comma after the introductory sentence element.)
    k) Mary, whereas her teacher had had 'had', had had 'had had'. 'Had had' was approved by her teacher. Or, Mary, whereas her teacher had had 'had had', had had 'had'. 'Had' was approved by her teacher.
    l) As the work pressure becomes more intense, your partner may become preoccupied, apprehensive, and worried about their prospects. (You may decide not to put a comma after 'apprehensive', so you have a phrase 'apprehensive and worried'.)

m) Note: this sentence does not require any internal punctuation, because there is no break in its structure. However, you could punctuate it as follows: This university prides itself on its unique ability to offer students, of just about every profession, a balance of theory and practical experience to prepare them for careers in the real world.

n) Study may be undertaken in the fields of marketing; strategic management; or writing, editing, and publishing. (As in some of the earlier sentences, the serial comma after *editing* is optional.)

8. a) Only in recent years have I improved my writing skill.
   b) The curtain, which had been exposed to the sun, was badly faded.
   c) Johnny Depp is a wonderful guy; he has so many talents.
   d) Our favourite films are the films made by Video Arts.
   e) Please make a list of staff eligible for leave.
   f) The software they chose had one advantage: it was easy to use.
   g) She produced a large, expensive, glossy brochure.
   h) The comma splice is a common error; it is a fault of many writers.
   i) She said: 'Thank you for your help'.
   j) I wish to heartily thank the members of the Working Party, who, within tight time constraints imposed by vacation schedules, have worked constructively, diligently, and harmoniously on this extensive task. (The serial comma after 'diligently' is optional.)

9. a) the boy's nose
   b) the mice's tails
   c) Jenny's books
   d) James's father
   e) the men's wives
   f) the ladies' husbands
   g) It's yours, isn't it?
   h) seven weeks' holiday (the apostrophe is optional)
   i) a minute's silence
   j) John's and Mary's books
   k) John and Mary's house
   l) Sydney's beaches
   m) the Joneses' house
   n) Brisbane Writers Festival/Queensland Writers Centre
   o) the companies' line of work

p) Decisions generally follow.
q) Jones's approach
r) Astrophysics's gain is linguistics's loss. (If you find this too awkward, you could write: The gain of astrophysics is the loss of linguistics.)
s) Whose is this book?
t) QANTAS's flight schedules
u) SBS's programming
v) One must choose one's words carefully.
w) There are three l's in lollipop.
x) The 1980s were good years.
y) In the 21st century, fewer writers are using and's and but's.
z) Las Vegas's obvious disdain for the written word

Chapter 11: How revising, editing, and proofreading work

2. The HillEnd Bank letter reworked (overleaf). Note the spelling errors in the original: retrieve, unsuccessful, and inconvenience.
3. a) People are always impressed by her smooth manner, elegant clothes, and wit.
   b) The rural towns are dying, one of the problems being that young people are leaving.
   c) Having argued all morning, the committee finally reached a decision.
   d) The situation is quite different from that of previous years.
   e) The army moved my partner and me to Melbourne last year.
   f) It is late in his term, inflation is worse, and no one has a solution.
   g) When a person moves every year, you cannot expect them to develop civic pride.

Dear Mrs Petelin

MASTERCARD ACCOUNT NO. 1234567

I refer to your enquiry regarding a disputed amount of $494.31 debited from your account for a stay at the Busytown Hotel, Busytown, California.

As we informed you previously, we credited your account while waiting for the vouchers from the hotel's bank.

The bank has now supplied us with two vouchers, which we have enclosed. As details appear valid, we wish to advise you that we will deduct $494.31 from your account. If you do not agree with this decision, you can try to retrieve $494.31 directly from the hotel. If this is unsuccessful, you could contact the Californian High Commissioner for assistance.

Unfortunately, we are unable to help you any further because accommodation-cost agreements are the business of the hotel.

We apologise for the inconvenience.

Yours sincerely

Customer Services

Further reading

Chapter 1: How writing works

Brandt, D. (2012, October 18). 'Deborah Brandt on how "writing has become the work of our time"'. Retreived from youtube.com/watch?v=V79Shf6FKSY

Popova, M. (n.d.). 'Famous writers on the creative benefits of keeping a diary'. Retreived from brainpickings.org/2014/09/04/famous-writers-on-keeping-a-diary/. If you read and/or write for pleasure, you might like to check up on the advice offered by your favourite authors in the list below, which you can find on Maria Popova's site. Authors include Margaret Atwood, Ray Bradbury, Raymond Chandler, Leonard Cohen, Joan Didion, Annie Dillard, William Faulkner, F. Scott Fitzgerald, Neil Gaiman, Ernest Hemingway, Jack Kerouac, Stephen King, Ursula Le Guin, Elmore Leonard, C.S. Lewis, Alice Munro, Vladimir Nabokov, Joyce Carol Oates, David Ogilvy, Susan Orlean, George Orwell, Ann Patchett, John Updike, Kurt Vonnegut, and David Foster Wallace.

Pullum, G. (2014, November 10). 'UQx WRITE101x Interview with Geoffrey Pullum'. Retrieved from youtube.com/watch?v=AruB5h3MWJE (Pullum talks about the upsurge in writing with the rise of the internet)

Chapter 2: How reading works

See Electric Lit's very detailed infographic 'The science of speed reading' (2015, April 18) at electricliterature.com/infographic-the-science-of-speed-reading/

Chapter 3: How words work

Ferriss, L. (2011, August 21). 'I'm relatable, you're relatable'. *Chronicle of Higher Education*. Retrieved from chronicle.com

McWhorter, J. (2013, March 29). 'Washington's favorite, weaselly new verb'. Retrieved from tnr.com

Mogollón, O. (2013, July 1). 'The history of English in ten minutes'. Retrieved from youtube.com/watch?v=njJBw2KlIEo

Pullum, G. (2015, February 11). 'Comprise yourself'. *The Chronicle of Higher Education*. Retrieved from chronicle.com

Wilson, P. (n.d.). Academic writing in British English. Retrieved from hull-awe.org.uk/index.php/Category:AmE

Yagoda, B. (n.d.). 'Not one-off Britishisms'. Retrieved from britishisms.wordpress.com/list-of-entries/

Yankovic, 'Weird Al' (2014, July 15). 'Word Crimes'. Retrieved from youtube.com/watch?v=8Gv0H-vPoDc

Chapter 4: How sentences and form-class words work

See my interview with 'Grammar girl' Professor Mignon Fogarty at youtube.com/watch?v=JJa7IIrvvAU

Chapter 5: How structure-class words and paragraphs work

There's a witty video on grammar featuring Rowan Atkinson and the headmaster at youtube.com/watch?v=tTv5ckMe_2M

Garber, M. (2013, November 19) 'English has a new preposition'. *The Atlantic*. Retrieved from theatlantic.com. In this article, Megan Garber talks about the new use of *because* as a preposition.

Nordquist, R. (2016, February 24). '"Oh, wow!": Notes on interjections'. Retrieved from grammar.about.com

Pullum, G. (2013b, February 5). 'Being a preposition'. *The Chronicle of Higher Education*. Retrieved from chronicle.com

Chapter 6: How punctuation works

Crezo, A. (2012, October 5). '13 little-known punctuation marks we should be using'. Retrieved from mentalfloss.com

Curzan, A. (2013, March 14). 'Commas and feelings'. *The Chronicle of Higher Education*. Retrieved from chronicle.com

Dolnick, B. (2012, July 2). 'Semicolons: A love story'. *The New York Times*. Retrieved from nytimes.com

Economist, the (S.H.) (2014, October 1). 'The rise and fall of the interrobang'. *The Economist*. Retrieved from economist.com

Ferriss, L. (2013, March 29). 'Auto-da-fé for the façade of diacritics'. *The Chronicle of Higher Education*. Retrieved from chronicle.com

Ferriss, L. (2013, May 29). 'The battle[']s joined'. *The Chronicle of Higher Education*. Retrieved from chronicle.com

Ferriss, L. (2014, January 29). 'Cannibal commas'. *The Chronicle of Higher Education*. Retrieved from chronicle.com

Ferriss, L. (2015, April 27). 'Apostrophe, where is thy comma?' *The Chronicle of Higher Education*. Retrieved from chronicle.com

Houston, K. (2013, September 24). '8 punctuation marks that are no longer used'. Retrieved from huffingtonpost.com

Norris, M. (2014, April 12). 'In defense of "nutty" commas'. *The New Yorker*. Retrieved from newyorker.com

Norris, M. (2014, February 23). 'Holy writ'. *The New Yorker*. Retrieved from newyorker.com

Press Association (2014, February 6). 'Council reverses the ban on apostrophes'. *The Guardian*. Retrieved from theguardian.com

Shepherd, J. (2011, October 27). '14 punctuation marks you never knew existed'. Retrieved from buzzfeed.com

Soffe, E. (2015, September 23). 'Perfect your punctuation'. Retrieved from ted.com

Walsh, J. (2013, June 14). 'The plucky punctuators fighting against apostrophe catastrophes'. *The Independent*. Retrieved from independent.co.uk

Yagoda, B. (2011, May 12). 'The rise of "logical punctuation"'. *Slate*. Retrieved from slate.com

Chapter 7: How structure and design work

Barrett-Forrest, B. (2013, April 28). 'The history of typography: Animated short'. Retrieved from youtube.com/watch?v=wOgIkxAfJsk

Norvig, P. (n.d.). 'The making of the Gettysburg PowerPoint presentation'. Retrieved from norvig.com/Gettysburg/making.html

References

Adler, N. (2016, January 13). 'Want to be an outstanding leader? Keep a journal'. *Harvard Business Review*. Retrieved from hbr.org

Adorno, T. (1990, Summer). 'Punctuation marks'. *The Antioch Review*. Retrieved from review.antiochcollege.org

American Psychological Association (2010). *Publication Manual of the American Psychological Association* (6th edn). Washington, DC: Author

Anderson, H. (2012, November 14). 'In praise of the cliché: At the end of the day, sometimes you've just got to think inside the box'. *Prospect*. Retrieved from prospectmagazine.co.uk

Asimov, I. (1974). *Before the Golden Age: A science fiction anthology of the 1930s*. New York: Doubleday

Baron, D. (2015, September 4). 'What's your pronoun?' *The Web of Language*. Retrieved from illinois.edu/blog/view/25

Baron, N. (2015, February 4). 'Reading On-screen Versus Paper'. Retrieved from blog.oup.com

Barthes, R. (1984) [1977]. *Image, Music, Text* (S. Heath, selected & trans.). London: Fontana

Bartholomae, D. (1985). 'Inventing the university'. In M. Rose (ed.), *When a Writer Can't Write: Studies in writer's block and other composing-process problems* (pp. 134–65). New York: Guilford

Bauch, C. (2010, October 21). '10 authors against adjectives'. Retrieved from flavorwire.com

Bazerman, C. (1989). *The Informed Reader: Contemporary issues in the disciplines*. Boston, MA: Houghton Mifflin

Bennett, A. (2007). *The Uncommon Reader: A novella*. London: Faber & Faber

Bennett, A. (2010). *A Life Like Other People's*. London: Faber & Faber

Bercovici, J. (2010, December 9). 'Who coined the term "social media"? Web pioneers compete for credit'. *Forbes Magazine*. Retrieved from forbes.com

Berthoff, A. (1983). 'Response to Richard Gebhardt'. *College Composition and Communication*, 34: 95

Bitzer, L. (1968). 'The rhetorical situation'. *Philosophy and Rhetoric*, 1: 1–14

Bizzell, P. & Herzberg, B. (eds) (1990). *The Rhetorical Tradition: Readings from classical times to the present*. Boston, MA: Bedford Books

Booth, T.Y. (1986). 'I.A. Richards and the composing process'. *College Composition and Communication*, 37(4): 453–65

Botton, A. de (2006, March, 25). 'Once good; twice better'. *The Australian*. Retrieved from theaustralian.com.au

Brandt, D. (2012, October 18). 'Deborah Brandt on how "writing has become the work of our time"'. Retrieved from youtube.com/watch?v=V79Shf6FKSY

Brandt, D. (2015). *The Rise of Writing: Redefining mass literacy*. Cambridge, UK: Cambridge University Press

Brodkey, L. (1990). *Academic Writing as Social Practice*. Philadelphia, PA: Temple University Press

Brown, C. (2003, December 13). 'The temple of whom (singularly possessive)?'. *The Spectator*. Retrieved from spectator.co.uk

Bruni, F. (2013, December 31). 'Tweet less, read more'. *The New York Times*. Retrieved from nytimes.com

Burke, K. (1941). *The Philosophy of Literary Form: Studies in symbolic action* (3rd edn). Berkeley, CA: University of California Press

Burke, K. (1950). *A Rhetoric of Motives*. Berkeley, CA: University of California Press

Burnham, S. (1994). *For Writers Only*. New York: Ballantyne Books

Carr, N. (2011). *The Shallows: What the internet is doing to our brains*. New York: Norton

Chivers, T. (2014, March 19). 'Are "Grammar Nazis" ruining the English language?' Retrieved from telegraph.co.uk.

Churchill, W. (1996) [1930]. *My Early Life: 1874–1904*. New York: Simon & Schuster

Colangelo, A. (2015, September 1). '10 tips for Dyson Heydon on how to use email'. *The New Daily*. Retrieved from thenewdaily.com.au

Collister, L. (2015, April 6). 'Textspeak is modernizing the Egnlish language (*English)'. *The New Republic*. Retrieved from newrepublic.com

Connors, K. & Bayley, S. (eds) (2007). *Eye Rhymes: Sylvia Plath's art of the visual*. Oxford: Oxford University Press

Cross, G. (2011). *Envisioning Collaboration*. Amityville, NY: Baywood Publishing

Crystal, D. (2008, July 8). '2b or not 2b?' *The Guardian*. Retrieved from theguardian.com

Crystal, D. (2014, November 5). 'UQx WRITE101x Interview David Crystal'. Retrieved from youtube.com/watch?v=8wrzJ0qqZHg

Curzan, A. (2014, March 6). 'Perfect!' *The Chronicle of Higher Education*. Retrieved from chronicle.com

D'Agostino, F. (2014. September 23). 'UQx WRITEx101x 1.5.1.1 Interview with Fred D'Agostino'. Retrieved from youtube.com/watch?v=B7fPCv4hgHo

Deacon, M. (2013, April 9). 'How P.G. Wodehouse influenced Game of Thrones'. *The Telegraph*. Retrieved from telegraph.co.uk

Denham, R.D. (ed.) (2001). *The Diaries of Northrop Frye, 1942–1955*. Toronto: University of Toronto Press

Didion, J. (1976, December). 'Why I Write'. *The New York Times*. Retrieved from nytimes.com

Dugdale, J. (2015, July 18). 'Comma chameleon: Harper Lee novel title change'. *The Guardian*. Retrieved from theguardian.com

Elbow, P. (1991). 'Reflections on academic discourse: How it relates to freshman and colleagues'. *College English*, 53(2): 135–55

Elbow, P. (1973). *Writing Without Teachers*. New York: Oxford University Press

Elbow, P. (1998). *Writing With Power*. New York: Oxford University Press

Elgot, J. (2015, August 29). 'From relationships to evolutions: Seven ways Facebook has changed the world'. *The Guardian*. Retrieved from guardian.com

Epstein, J. (2010, May 10). 'Why cry over split milk?' *The Weekly Standard*. Retrieved from weeklystandard.com

Faigley, L. & Witte, S. (1981). 'Analyzing revision'. *College Composition and Communication*, 32: 400–14

Faigley, L. & Hansen, K. (1985). 'Learning to write in the social sciences'. *College Composition and Communication*, 36(2): 150–9

Farrelly, E. (2015, December 9). 'Don't fall for Wiki-denial: There's nothing wrong with Wikipedia'. *The Age*. Retrieved from theage.com.au

Fish, S. (1980). *Is There a Text in This Class? The authority of interpretive communities*. Cambridge, MA: Harvard University Press

Fisher, J. (2006). *The Writer's Quote Book*. New Brunswick, NJ: Rutgers University Press

Fitzgerald, J. (1987). 'Research on revision in writing'. *Review of Educational Research*, 57(4): 481–506

Flower, L. (1981). *Problem-solving Strategies for Writing*. Orlando, FL: Harcourt Brace Jovanovich

Franklin, R. (2005, July 10). 'How to read a book'. *The New York Times*. Retrieved from nytimes.com

Frost, R. (1939). 'The figure a poem makes'. In M. Richardson (ed.), *The Collected Prose of Robert Frost*. Cambridge, MA: Harvard University Press

Frow, J. (2007). 'Reproducibles, rubrics, and everything you need: Genre theory today. *Proceedings of the Modern Language Association*, 22(5): 1626–34

Fulwiler, T. (1987). *The Journal Book.* Portsmouth, NH: Heinemann
Fulwiler, T. (1992). 'Provocative revision'. *The Writing Center Journal,* 12(2): 190–204
Gaiman, N. (2006). *Fragile Things.* New York: Harper Collins
Gardner, H. (2011). *Leading Minds: An anatomy of leadership.* New York: Basic Books
Gardner, J., Kittredge, G., & Arnold, S. (1902). *The Mother Tongue: Book III, Elements of English composition.* Boston: Ginn & Company
Geertz, C. (1988). *Works and Lives.* Stanford, CA: Stanford University Press
Gibaldi, J. & Achtert, W.S. (2009). *The MLA Handbook for Writers of Research Papers* (7th edn). New York: Modern Language Association of America
Giraldi, W. (2015, April 19). 'Why we need physical books'. *The New Republic.* Retrieved from newrepublic.com
Gordon, K.E. (1984). *The Deluxe Transitive Vampire: The ultimate handbook for the innocent, the eager, and the doomed.* New York: Pantheon Books
Gowers, E. (1954). *The Complete Plain Words.* London: Penguin Books
Gowers, R. (2014). *Plain Words.* London: Penguin Books
Graff, G. & Birkenstein, C. (2010). *They say/I say: The moves that matter in academic writing* (2nd edn). New York: W.W. Norton & Company
Graves, R. & Hodge, A. (1944). *The Reader Over Your Shoulder.* New York: Macmillan
Green, E. (2014, April 24). 'The origins of office speak'. *The Atlantic.* Retrieved from theatlantic.com
Hoberman, J. (2005, October 18). 'Get reel'. *The Village Voice.* Retrieved from villagevoice.com
Hornstein, G. (2009, September 7). 'Prune that prose'. *The Chronicle of Higher Education.* Retrieved from chronicle.com
Huddleston, R. & Pullum, G. (2002). *The Cambridge Grammar of the English Language.* Cambridge, UK: Cambridge University Press
Humphrys, J. (2007, September 24). 'I h8 txt msgs: How texting is wrecking our language'. *The Daily Mail.* Retrieved from dailymail.co.uk
Isard, H. (2015). 'Where writers write'. Retrieved from anothermag.com
Jabr, F. (2014, September 3). 'Why walking helps us think'. *The New Yorker.* Retrieved from newyorker.com
James, H. (1944) [1884]. 'The Art of Fiction'. In L. Edel (ed.), *Literary Criticism (Volume One): Essays on literature, American and English writers.* New York: Library of America
Jenkins, H., Ito, M., & boyd, d. (2016). *Participatory Culture in a Networked Era: A conversation on youth, learning, commerce, and politics.* Cambridge, MA: Polity Press
Kellaway, L. (2015, January 6). 'Most irritating business phrases of 2014'. Retrieved from bbc.com

King, S. (2001). *On Writing: A memoir of the craft*. New York: Pocket Books

Klinkenborg, V. (2009, May 16). 'Some thoughts on the lost art of reading aloud'. *The New York Times*. Retrieved from nytimes.com

Kulp, P. (2015, February 18). 'This tool could make your tweets more popular'. Retrieved from mashable.com

Lahey, J. (2014, September 9). 'How Stephen King teaches writing'. *The Atlantic*. Retrieved from theatlantic.com

Larson-Walker, Lisa. (2014, December 2). 'Will we use commas in the future?' Retrieved from slate.com

Lee, H. (1996). *The Novels of Virginia Woolf*. New York: Knopf

Leonardi, S. (1989). 'Recipes for reading: Summer pasta, lobster à la Riseholme, and Key Lime pie'. *Publications of the Modern Language Association*, 104: 340–7

Lewis, G. & Slade. C. (1994). *Critical Communication*. Sydney: Prentice Hall

Lutz, W. (n.d.). 'Life under the Chief Doublespeak Officer'. Retrieved from dt.org/html/Doublespeak.html

McCarthy, L. (1987). 'A stranger in strange lands: A college student writing across the curriculum'. *Research in the Teaching of English*, 21: 233–65

McCrum, R. (2012, November 27). 'Against type: Writers with other careers'. *The Guardian*. Retrieved from theguardian.com

McPhee, J. (2013a, January 14). 'Structure: Beyond the picnic-table crisis'. *The New Yorker*. Retrieved from newyorker.com

McPhee, J. (2013b, April 29). 'Draft no. 4'. *The New Yorker*. Retrieved from newyorker.com

McPhee, J. (2014, September 14). 'Omission'. *The New Yorker*. Retrieved from newyorker.com

McPhee, J. (2015, March 9). 'Frame of reference'. *The New Yorker*. Retrieved from newyorker.com

McWhorter, J. (2013b, February). 'Txting is killing language. JK!!!'. Retrieved from ted.com

Manguel, A. (2010). *A Reader on Reading*. New Haven, CT: Yale University Press

Marsh, D. (2013a). *For Who the Bell Tolls: One man's quest for grammatical perfection*. London: Guardian Books/Faber & Faber

Marsh, D. (2013b, October 1). '10 grammar rules you can forget'. *The Guardian*. Retrieved from theguardian.com

Menand, L. (2008, October 20). 'Thumbspeak. Is texting here to stay?' *The New Yorker*. Retrieved from www.newyorker.com

Mount, H. (2013, April 15). 'If you don't know grammar, you can't write English'. *The Telegraph*. Retrieved from telegraph.co.uk

Mount, H. (2014, May 31). 'Commas and colons: Without them, we're sunk'. *The Telegraph*. Retrieved from telegraph.co.uk

Mullin, B. (2015, December 1). 'The Washington Post will allow singular "they"'. Retrieved from poynter.org

Murakami, H. (2008, June 9). 'The running novelist'. *The New Yorker*. Retrieved from newyorker.com

Murray, D. (1968). *A Writing Teacher Teaches Writing*. New York: Houghton Mifflin

Nelson, J. (1990). 'This was an easy assignment: Examining how students interpret academic writing tasks'. *Research in the Teaching of English*, 24(4): 362–96

Nguyen, A. (2015, September 16). 'The biggest writing mistakes new graduates make'. *BBC Capital*. Retrieved from bbc.com

Nichol, M. (n.d.). 'Interjections'. Retrieved from dailywritingtips.com

Nielsen, J. (1997). 'How users read on the web'. Retrieved from nngroup.com

Nobles, S. & Paganucci, L. (2015). 'Do digital writing tools deliver? Student perceptions of writing quality using digital tools and online writing environments'. *Computers and Composition*, 38: 16–31

Nordquist, R. (2015, February 8). 'Pros on prose: The best advice on writing'. Retrieved from grammar.about.com

Nunberg, G. (2016, January 13). 'Everyone uses singular "they", whether they realize it or not'. Retrieved from npr.org.

Olivier, A. (ed.) (1977). *The Diary of Virginia Woolf*. London: Harcourt Brace Jovanovich

Pareles, J. (1997, June 26). 'Songs to unite heaven and earth'. *The New York Times*. Retrieved from nytimes.com

Parks, T. (2014, December 3). 'A weapon for readers'. *The New York Review of Books*. Retrieved from nybooks.com

Petelin, R. & Durham, M. (1992). *The Professional Writing Guide: Writing well and knowing why*. Sydney: Allen & Unwin

Petelin, R. (2002). 'Managing organisational writing to enhance corporate credibility'. *Journal of Communication Management*, 7(2): 172–80

Petelin, R. (2010a). 'Plain language: Issues and initiatives'. *Corporate Communications*, 15(2): 205–16

Petelin, R. (2010b, February). 'Clichés: Are they all bad?' *Queensland Writers Centre Newsletter*, p. 14

Petelin, R. (2013). 'Enhancing the quality of corporate writing: The efficacy of editing software'. *Proceedings of the Annual Conference of Corporate Communication International*, 4–7 June, New York: City University

Peters, P. (2007). *The Cambridge Guide to Australian English Usage*. Cambridge, UK: Cambridge University Press

Pinker, S. (2014, August 15). '10 "grammar rules" it's OK to break'. *The Guardian*. Retrieved from theguardian.com

Press Association (2014, February 7). 'Council reverses its ban on apostrophes'. *The Guardian*. Retrieved from theguardian.com

Prose, F. (2006). *Reading Like a Writer: A guide for people who love books and for those who want to write them*. New York: Harper Perennial

Pullman, P. (2002, December 28). 'Voluntary Service'. *The Guardian.* Retrieved from theguardian.com

Pullum, G. (2013a, November 27). 'Not whether, but when'. *The Chronicle of Higher Education.* Retrieved from chronicle.com

Pullum, G. (2013b, February 5). 'Being a preposition'. *The Chronicle of Higher Education.* Retrieved from chronicle.com

Pullum, G. (2014, November 10). 'UQx WRITE101x Interview with Geoffrey Pullum'. Retrieved from youtube.com/watch?v=AruB5h3MWJE

Pullum, G. (2015, February 11). 'Comprise yourself'. *The Chronicle of Higher Education.* Retrieved from chronicle.com

Putnis, P. & Petelin, R. (1999). *Professional Communication: Principles and applications.* (2nd edn). Sydney: Pearson

Quiller-Couch, A. (1916). 'On the art of writing'. Retrieved from bartleby.com

Rabinovitch, S. (2007, September 21). 'Thousands of hyphens perish as English marches on'. Retrieved from reuters.com

Randle, C. (2015, May 15). 'Lynda Barry: What is an image?' *The Guardian.* Retrieved from theguardian.com

Reisz, M. (2014, March 13). 'John Carey: The constant reader'. *Times Higher Education.* Retrieved from timeshighereducation.com

Rich, M. (2007, November 25). 'A good mystery: Why we read'. *The New York Times.* Retrieved from nytimes.com

Ritter, R. (2002). *The Oxford Guide to Style.* Oxford: Oxford University Press

Roberts, S. (2008, February 18). 'Celebrating the semicolon in a most unlikely location'. *The New York Times.* Retrieved from nytimes.com

Roosevelt, T. (1916). 'Origin of weasel words'. *The New York Times.* Retrieved from nytimes.com

Rosman, K. (2015, June 7). 'Me, myself and Mx'. *The New York Times.* Retrieved from nytimes.com

Rubin, R.B., Rubin, A.M., & Piele, L.J. (1993). *Communication Research: Strategies and sources* (3rd edn). Belmont, CA: Wadsworth

Safire, W. & Safir, L. (1992). *Good Advice on Writing.* New York: Simon & Schuster

Sayers, D.L. (1972) [1928]. *Lord Peter: A collection of all the Lord Peter Wimsey stories.* New York: Harper & Row

Scott, K. (2015, April 22). 'Jon Favreau shares five lessons from President Obama'. Retrieved from today.duke.edu

Scruby, H. (1987). *Waynespeak.* Sydney: Watermark Press

Self, W. & Truss, L. (2008, July 5). 'The joy of text: Will Self and Lynne Truss on the horrors of text speak'. *The Guardian.* Retrieved from theguardian.com

Selzer, J. (1989). Arranging business prose. In M. Kogen (ed.), *Writing in the Business Professions* (pp. 37–64). Urbana, IL: National Council of Teachers of English

Shenk, D. (1999). *The End of Patience: Cautionary notes on the information revolution*. Bloomington, IN: Indiana University Press

Simons, M. (2003, March 15). 'Unaccustomed as I am'. *The Sydney Morning Herald*. Retrieved from smh.com.au

Snooks & Co. (2002). *Style Manual: For authors, editors and printers* (6th edn). Brisbane: John Wiley & Sons

Sommers, N. (1980). 'Revision strategies of student writers and experienced writers'. *College Composition and Communication*, 31: 378–88

Stein, G. (1971) [1935]. *Lectures in America*. Boston, MA: Beacon Press

Taylor, D.J. (2015, July 18). 'Er, inexecutable jargon'. *The Independent*. Retrieved from independent.co.uk

Thomas, L. (1979). *The Medusa and the Snail*. New York: Viking

Tompkins, J. (1995). 'The politics of writing'. *Journal of Advanced Composition*, 15(1): 1–17

Toulmin, S. (1958). *The Uses of Argument*. Cambridge, MA: Cambridge University Press

Toulmin, S., Reike, R. & Janik, A. (1984). *An Introduction to Reasoning*. New York: Macmillan

Truss, L. (2003). *Eats, Shoots and Leaves*. London: Profile Books

Tufte, E. (1983). *The Visual Display of Quantitative Information*. Cheshire, CT: Graphics Press

Usher, S. (ed.) (2013). *Letters of Note*. London: Canongate

Van Buren, R. & Buehler, M.F. (1980). *The Levels of Edit*. Jet Propulsion Laboratory, Pasadena, CA: California Institute of Technology

Van Maanen, J. (1988). *Tales of the Field: On writing ethnography*. Chicago, IL: University of Chicago Press

Walden, C. (2015, August 4). 'The perils of jargon: A plea to speak in plain English'. *The Telegraph*. Retrieved from telegraph.co.uk

Wallace, D.F. & Garner, B.A. (2013). *Quack This Way: David Foster Wallace and Bryan A. Garner talk language and writing*. Dallas, TX: RosePen Books

Wallace, D.F. (2012, November 6). 'The nature of the fun: David Foster Wallace on why writers write'. Retrieved from brainpickings.org

Wason, P. (1980). 'Specific thoughts on the writing process'. In L. Gregg & E. Steinberg (eds), *Cognitive Processes in Writing* (pp. 129–137). Hillsdale, NJ: Lawrence Erlbaum

Waxman, N. (1996). 'Cooking dumb, eating dumb'. In K. Washburn and J. Thornton (eds), *Dumbing Down: Essays on the strip mining of American culture* (pp. 297–307). New York/London: W.W. Norton

Williams, J. (1995). *Style: Toward clarity and grace*. Chicago, IL: University of Chicago Press

Winerip, M. (2012, April 22). 'Facing a robo-grader? Just keep obfuscating mellifluously'. Retrieved from nytimes.com

Wodehouse, P.G. (2012). *In His Own Words*. London: The Overlook Press
Wood, J. (2009). *How Fiction Works*. New York: Picador
Wordsworth, D. (2012, July 7). 'It's cruel not to teach children grammar'. *The Telegraph*. Retrieved from telegraph.co.uk
Wright Mills, C. (1977) [1959]. *The Sociological Imagination*. Harmondsworth, UK: Penguin
Wurman, R.S. (1989). *Design Quarterly*, 145: 1–32
Wurman, R.S. (2001). *Information Anxiety 2*. Indianapolis, IN: Que Books
Yagoda, B. (2004, February 20). 'The adjective: So ludic, so minatory, so twee'. *The Chronicle of Higher Education*. Retrieved from chronicle.com
Yagoda, B. (2012a, April 9). 'Fanfare for the Comma Man'. *The New York Times*. Retrieved from nytimes.com
Yagoda, B. (2012b, May 25). 'Some comma questions'. *The New York Times*. Retrieved from nytimes.com
Yagoda, B. (2013, October 3). 'Is the internet good for writing? Part 1: Affirmative'. *The Chronicle of Higher Education*. Retrieved from chronicle.com
Yagoda, B. (2014, April 29). 'The commas suit ya'. *The Chronicle of Higher Education*. Retrieved from chronicle.com

Index

abbreviations, 46, 133, 171, 235, 244, 250, 259, 261, 276, 281
abstract, 29, 154, 222
abstract words, 45, 92, 248, 271
abstract nouns, 102
academic research writing, 206-36
   academic research, 208-9
   academic style, 187, 212, 231, 233
   academic writing, 210-12
   annotated bibliography, 206-7, 224-5
   assessment criteria, 235-6
   choosing a research question, 215-16
   choosing a topic, 215
   critical reasoning, 212-13
   documentation styles, 223-4
   end-of-text citations, 224
   evaluating sources, 218
   heuristic for research, 214
   incorporating source materials, 220
   in-text citations, 224
   linking sources, 217
   literature review, 206-7, 226-34
   paraphrasing, 222
   plagiarism, avoiding, 222-3
   'practical argument', 213-14
   presentation of academic documents, 233-4
   quoting verbatim, 221
   recording information from sources, 219
   research paper, 206-7, 226-34
   research thesis, 229
   summarising, 222, 231
   syllogism, 213
   understanding the field, 216
   university documents, 208
acronyms, 46, 250, 281, 283
active voice, 88, 89, 90, 121, 232, 235, 237, 250, 271
adjectives, 95-8
   absolute/uncomparable/ungradable, 97
   attributive/associative/affiliative, 143
   comparison of, 97
   coordinate, 98
   irregular, 97
   predicative, 95
   sequence of, 98
   stack, adjective, 94

adverbs, 98–100
　absolute, 99
　comparison of, 99
　conjunctive, 119–20
　placement of, 100
allusion, 28, 46–7
American Psychological Association (APA), 223–4
Americanisms, 47
analogy, 3, 47, 48, 269
analysing sentences, 120–1
'and-ness', 82, 284
annotated bibliography, 206–7, 224–5
annotating text for editing, 270
antecedent, 109, 111, 112, 113, 127, 284, 294
antonym, 38
arcane words, 48
archaic words (archaisms), 49, 69, 85, 281, 283, 292
article in grammar (definite and indefinite), 76, 115
Australian Government Publishing Service *Style Manual*, 142, 143, 195, 223
author–date system, 223
author–short title system, 223
avocation, 3, 4

biased/loaded words, 49
bibliography, 224
blogs, 251–6
　format of, 256
　origin of, 251
　personal, 251–4
brainstorming, 157
Britishisms, 47–8
buzzwords, 49–51, 283

calculated iteration, 270
capitalisation, 169, 194, 273, 276, 285
cardinal numbers, 115

case, 93–4
　appositive, 93
　complement, 93
　object, 93
　subject, 93
charts, 166, 169, 170, 195, 280
Chicago Manual of Style, 171, 195, 286, 287
circumlocution, 60
citation, 164, 224
clarity, 3, 14, 41, 67, 170, 272, 278, 310
clauses
　awkward embedding of, 284
　in complex sentences, 81
　in compound sentences, 80
　connected by conjunctions, 118
　connected by conjunctive adverbs, 119
　dependent (subordinate) clause, 79
　FANBOYS separating independent clauses, 134
　independent (main, principal) clause, 79
　modified by adverb, 98
clichés, 50, 51, 96, 201, 235, 250, 281, 283, 308
coherence, 32, 124, 284
cohesive ties (transitional expressions), 30, 78, 117, 124, 126, 127, 271, 284, 293, 294
coined word (neologism), 38, 39, 52, 63, 82, 91, 150, 170, 239, 283, 303
colloquial and slang words, 10, 52, 69, 180, 233, 235, 250, 281, 283
comma splice, 80, 105, 137, 148, 281, 285, 293, 296, 297
complement, 20, 53, 84, 86, 93, 95, 108, 109, 169
concrete words, 6, 45, 92, 281
confusable words, 52–4, 243, 252, 282, 283
conjunctions, 117–19
　coordinating, 118

correlative, 119
subordinating, 118
conjunctive adverbs, 119–20
connotation, 49, 54, 283
consistency (levels of text), 65, 272–3, 135, 168, 193, 194, 225, 248, 274, 276, 278
contractions, 141, 235, 250, 285
copular/linking verb, 84
creative writing, 20, 24, 37, 42, 45, 47, 52, 58, 63, 74, 97, 123, 131, 137, 159, 164, 177, 231; *see also* writing
credibility, 44, 52, 73, 166, 178, 186, 195, 200, 209, 217, 247, 248, 269, 273, 274, 308

dash hybrid, 132
dates, for format, 115, 193, 194, 275, 285
debasement /transformation of words, 54–5
defensive/apologetic words, 55
definite article *see* article
denotation, 47, 54
descriptivism, 74
design, 166–74
  briefing a designer, 171–2
  clip art, 170
  data visualisation, 170
  design sites, 173–4
  floating baseline, 168
  font, 167
  illustrative material, 169–71
  indentation, 167
  InDesign, 171, 173, 189
  infographic, 170
  interparagraph spacing, 168
  leading, 167
  PowerPoint, 170
  typeface, 167
  typography and layout, 167–9
desktop publishing, 171, 189, 277
determiners, 78, 107, 114–15, 124

diacritics, 192, 301
diagrams, in documents, 157, 166, 195, 197
dictionaries, 38, 39, 55–6, 66, 68, 77, 153
digital object identifier (DOI), 219
digital writing, 238–63
  early years, 240–1
  email, 241–6
  email inbox, 246
  organisational websites, 246–51
  personal blogs, 251–4
  rise of social media, 238–40
  social media in workplace, 246
  texting, 259–61
  Twitter, 256–9
direct objects, 85, 90, 121
discriminatory (non-inclusive) language, 56–7, 114
documentation, 159, 168, 177, 193, 196, 219, 220, 223, 236, 237
documentation style, 223–4
  author–date system, 223
  author–short title system, 223
  numbered notes system, 223–4
document testing *see* usability testing
double-entry journal, 8–10, 20
doublespeak, 57, 58, 62, 307

editing, 266, 268, 269–71, 278–85
  editing checklist, 279–82
  typographical errors (typos), 285–6, 243, 275, 278, 282
elegant variation *see* thesaurus syndrome
email, 241–6
  content, 242–3
  purpose, 242
  structure and format, 244–6
  style, 243–4
emoticon/emoji, 39, 244, 285
equivocation, 58, 62, 63, 232, 283
ethos, 41, 44, 136, 166, 269
etymology, 39, 287

euphemism and dysphemism, 58, 62, 283
exclamation *see* interjection (exclamation)
expletive (four-letter word), 58
expletive (grammatical), 108, 111, 112, 280, 284

F-pattern, 248
Facebook, 28, 39, 57, 125, 165, 238, 239, 240, 247, 251, 256, 257, 262, 305
FANBOYS, 80, 118, 134
FAQs, 46, 245, 249
figures of speech, 47, 61, 63, 68; *see also* allusion; analogy; hyperbole; metaphor; oxymoron; simile
final position in a document, 155
first draft, 13, 15, 63, 230, 264, 266
first person, 10, 231, 235, 284
first position in a document, 155
floating baseline, 169
flow chart, 156, 157, 165, 185
fonts, 167, 245, 276
foreign expressions, 59, 283
form-class words (open, lexical), 77–8, 84–100
   adjectives, 95–8
   adverbs, 98–100
   nominalisations, 94–5, 232–3
   nouns, 91–3
   noun strings *see* adjective, stack
   verbs, 84–91

gaucheries, 269
genre blurring, 233
genre (generic) conventions and expectations, 3, 30, 176–7
gerund, 70, 85, 86, 87, 113, 114
given-new contract, 155
gobbledygook, 59–60, 250, 283
gold-collar workers/knowledge workers/ information architects, 2
grammar, 70–129
   glamour of, 72
   non-standard, 3, 71, 73, 75, 76
   parts of speech, 74–7; *see also* word classes
   'real' rules of grammar, 75–6
   syntax, 71, 78
   traditional grammar, 74–7
   why study grammar? 71–4

hard copy, 33, 206, 216, 236
Harvard comma, 135
headings
   in academic papers, 227
   as advance organisers, 166
   to clarify structure, 279
   in columns, 171
   consistency of, 236, 276, 282
   in documents, 153, 277
   for front loading, 255
   hierarchy of, 273, 278
   to highlight, 248
   levels of, 29
   as an outline, 161
   parallel forms of, 29, 281
   point size, 167
   in a report, 182
   for revising and editing, 269
   as signposts, 233
   spacing in, 168
   underlining in, 167
heuristic, 12, 63, 94, 154, 214, 234, 249, 268
heuristic (journalist's), 12, 249
humour, 11, 36, 44, 61, 159, 201, 202, 237, 244, 250, 258, 283
hyperbole (hyperbolically), 69, 137, 167, 250, 283
hyperlinks (hyperlinked), 182, 249, 255

idioms, 59
inclusive (non-discriminatory) language, 56–7, 114

INDEX

incubation, 230, 265, 270
indefinite article *see* article
indirect object, 85, 86, 90, 121
infelicities, 36, 269, 282
information architecture, 150
information design, 171, 173, 174
information society/knowledge economy, 1, 239
initialism, 39, 46, 250, 283
Instagram, 238, 256
instructions for documentation, 196
instructions plan sheet, 197
intensifier, 59, 66, 283
interjection (exclamation), 76, 77, 78, 107, 120, 124, 140
interpolation, 221
interpretive community, 22–3
interrobang, 132
intuitive sense of grammar, 72
inverted pyramid, 154, 249
irony, 44
'is-ness', 82, 106, 284
italics, 143, 144, 167, 194, 220, 285
iteration, 13, 270; *see also* recursivity

jargon, 59, 60, 91, 180, 186, 202, 210, 211, 235, 237, 250, 255, 271, 272, 281, 283, 309, 310
journal, keeping a, 2, 6–11
journalist's heuristic, 12, 249

knowledge/information economy, 1, 239

landing page, 247
Latin, 1, 3, 32, 39, 44, 52, 59, 60, 75, 86, 91, 92, 111, 115, 116, 126, 140, 208, 265
leading, 167, 168, 169
levels of edit, 268
like, as a preposition, 117
linearity, 13
linking verb *see* copular/linking verb

literary competitions, 24
literature review, 206–7, 226–34
loaded words *see* biased/loaded words
logomisia, 39
logos, 166, 269
London School of Economics and Politics (LSE), 259
loose sentence structure, 81

macro level, 268
malapropism, 60, 61, 283
Mashable, 259
metaknowledge, 12, 17, 165, 271
metaphor, 47, 61, 68
micro level, 268
millennials, 240
mind mapping, 163
mispronunciation, 67
mnemonic, 80, 153
Modern Language Association (MLA), 173, 195, 223, 224, 306
modifiers, 82–4, 284
  ambiguous/squinting, 83
  dangling/hanging/unattached, 83
  misplaced, 83
mood
  imperative, 97
  indicative/declarative, 97
  interrogative, 97
  subjunctive, 97
mot juste, le, 38, 45, 56, 271
multistage revising, 270

negative expressions, 62, 271, 281, 283
netiquette, 242
New Critics, 22, 23
nominalisation, 94–5, 232–3
non-discriminatory language, 56–7, 114
non-standard English, 3, 71, 73, 75, 76
noun strings, 94–5, 233
noun:verb ratio, 287
nouning, 62

nouns, 91–5
  abstract, 92
  collective, 92–3
  common, 92
  concrete, 92
  plural, 91
  proper, 92
  singular, 91
nuance, 62, 68

obsolete words, 49
'of-ness', 82, 94, 284
'old-before-new' principle *see* given-new contract
online reading, 33
oral style, 201
orality, 1, 283
ordinal numbers, 115
organisational storytelling, 37
organisational websites, 246–51
orphan, 179
outlining on a computer, 163–5
Oxford comma, 135
oxymoron, 47, 63, 100

paragraphs, 112–24
  body of paragraph, 122
  cohesion in paragraphs, 124
  conclusion of paragraph, 122
  length of paragraph, 123
  topic sentence of paragraph, 122
parallel structure (parallelism), 29, 82, 83, 106, 119, 127, 144, 233, 271, 272, 281, 293
paraphrasing, 222
parse (parsing), 54, 55, 120, 121, 258, 284
parts of speech, 77; *see also* word classes
passive voice, 88, 89, 90, 103, 106, 232, 237, 271, 280, 284
pathos, 166, 269
periodic sentence structure, 81

Periscope, 256
person (1st, 2nd, 3rd), 10, 89, 108, 11, 120, 121, 122, 231, 235, 237, 250, 284
persona, 31, 41, 44, 45
phrases, 78–9
  absolute, 79
  adjectival, 79
  adverbial, 79
  appositive, 79
  loaded, 49
  noun, 79
  pompous, 49
  prepositional, 79, 115
  redundant phrases, 64
  verb phrase, 77, 86, 103
  verbal phrase, 87
placement of adverbs, 100
plagiarism, 222, 223, 234
plain language (plain English), 127, 128, 226, 250, 271, 294, 295, 308
point size, 167, 169, 245
polemical language, 63
portmanteau words, 39, 63, 170, 242, 266
possessive case with gerund, 114
possessive case of nouns, 141–2
possessive case of pronouns, 151
power, in writing, 2, 12, 15, 38, 58, 72, 146
PowerPoint, 170
précis, 45
prepositional verbs, 117
prepositions, 115–17
  ending a sentence with, 116
  superfluous, 117
prescriptivism, 74
primary sources, 219
pronouns, 108–14
  agreement and reference, 111, 113
  antecedent, 111–12
  case, 108

demonstrative, 108, 112
distributive, 110, 12
expletive, 111, 112
indefinite, 110, 112
intensive (emphatic), 110, 112
interrogative, 109, 112
non-discriminatory (gender-neutral), 114
person, 108, 111
possessive case, 151
possessive case with gerund, 114
reciprocal, 111, 112
reflexive, 110, 112
relative, 109, 112
singular 'they', 56–7, 114
'that creep', 110
'that' versus 'which', 109–10
'who' versus 'whom', 113
proofreading, 266, 268 273–6, 285–6
publishing, 278
punctuation, 130–46
apostrophe, 141–3
bulleted/dot-point lists, 144–5
colon, 137
comma, 133–7
comma handles, 136
comma misuse, 136–7
dash, 138–9
'Dear John' letter, 131–2
dot-point lists, 144–5
ellipsis, 44
em dash, 138
en dash, 138–9
exclamation mark, 140
floating bullet symbols, 145
full stop, 122
hyphen, 139
punctus percontativus, 132
question mark, 140
quotation marks/inverted commas, 143–4
round brackets/parentheses, 139–40
semicolon, 137–8
serial comma (Oxford, Harvard), 135, 144, 145, 147, 285, 297
slash, 144
square brackets, 140
vocative comma, 135
puns, 63, 250
purple prose, 283

reading, 18–36
aloud, 19
close reading, 31
critical reading, 30
deep reading, 33
online reading, 33
readability formulas, 31–2
'reading' path, 14, 29, 165
skim reading, 31–2
speed reading, 32, 300
'to do', 22, 150–1
'to learn', 22, 151
value of reading, 18, 19, 73
'real' rules, 75–6
recursive (recursivity), 2, 13, 165, 166, 227, 266, 267
redundancy, 40, 64
references list, 224; *see also* documentation style
research paper, 206–7, 226–34
research thesis, 228–9
revising, 264–9, 279–80
Rhetoric (rhetorical), 3, 13, 14, 44
rhetorical appeals (ethos, pathos, logos), 269
rhetorical question, 132
rhetorical situation, 151
'Royal we', 233

sans serif typeface, 167, 249
sarcasm, 44
satisfice, 13, 63, 266
scannability, 248

scanning, 274
schemata, 21
Scrabble, 40
search engine, 247, 249
second person, 235, 250, 284
secondary sources, 219
self-efficacy, 14
sentence, 79–84
   analysing, 120–1
   fragment, 80, 144
   complex, 81
   compound, 80
   compound-complex, 81–2
   shifted construction, 83–4
   simple, 80
   topic sentence, 122
sequence of adjectives, 98
serial comma, 135
serif typeface, 167, 249
shibboleths, 75
short message service (SMS), 257, 259
simile, 47, 61, 68
singular 'they', 56–7, 114
Slack, 241
Snapchat, 250, 262
snowball effect, 217
'so what?' test, 251
social media, 2, 239–40, 246, 251, 261–2
Social Media Research Group, 257
spelling
   checks of spelling, 138
   correct spelling, 220, 255, 261, 269, 275
   errors in spelling, 230, 231, 282, 286, 298
   North American versus Australian/British spelling, 48
   spelling out of numbers, 273
   unreliable spelling rules, 64
spoken communication, 67, 131
standard English (Grammar), 2, 67, 71, 73, 74, 78, 243, 260

structure, 151
   of an academic paper, 229, 223
   checklist for academic paper, 235
   checklist for editing, 279
   containment, 151–2
   in documents, 150–66
   in email messages, 244
   essay, generic, 177
   flow chart, 157
   formulaic structure, 126
   headings to clarify structure, 29
   hierarchical, 14, 74, 161, 268
   inverted pyramid structure, 164, 249, 267
   issue tree, 157, 160–1
   LATCH, 153–4, 165
   logical, coherent, cohesive, focused, 11, 24, 29, 157
   matrix, 157, 159
   mind map, 157, 158, 164
   numbered outline, 157, 162
   for an outline, 156
   outlining on a computer, 160–4
   paragraph structure, 122
   parallel structure, 29, 83, 146, 233, 281
   poor structure, 150
   proposal flow chart, 185
   punctuate to reveal structure, 130, 133
   for a reader, 151
   readers structuring data, 21
   reading path, 29
   for revising global structure, 264, 271
   for science papers, 164
   sentence structure, 2, 32, 71, 78, 80, 81
   sequence, 151–2
   for social science papers, 164
   for a speech, 201
   structuring information, 3
   taxonomy, 52
   tree structure, 163

typology, 52
of websites, 248
structure-class words (closed, grammatical, or function words), 77–8, 107–21
   conjunctions, 117–19
   conjunctive adverbs, 119–20
   determiners, 78, 107, 114–15, 124
   prepositions, 115–17
   pronouns, 108–14
   pronouns, agreement, 111, 113
style, 11, 41–2, 280
   academic, 187, 212, 231, 233
   BuzzFeed style manual, 195
   Chicago Manual of Style
   CIA style manual, 195
   Coleridge's test for, 41
   creative writing style, 42
   Economist style manual, 195
   email style, 242
   emulating style, 20
   formal style, 13, 187, 231, 233
   Guardian style manual, 195
   in headings, 161
   Homeric style, 46
   idiosyncratic style, 23
   imitating style, 20
   manual, 192, 193–5
   media release style, 198
   newswriting style, 123, 258
   online style, 133
   personal style sheet, 269, 276, 282
   pompous style, 49
   in proposals, 186
   Publication Manual of the American Psychological Association, 195
   in reports, 182
   simplistic style, 283
   social media writing style, 246, 250, 251, 252, 263
   speaking style, 283; *see also* orality
   speech-writing style, 200–1

style-analysis software, 277–8
style sheet, 169, 192, 193, 195, 269, 276
   in tweets, 259, 262
   typographic style sheet, 169
synopsis, 45
syntax, 71, 78
systematic passthrough, 270

tactility of paper, 33
tautology, 64
telephone apprehension, 260
template(s), 13, 24, 158, 164, 184, 234
tense (historic or universal present), 232
tense (of verbs), 88–9
texting, 259–61
'that' versus 'which' distinction, 109–10
thesaurus syndrome, 56, 64, 65, 69, 188, 233, 261, 281, 283, 292
third person, 89
title tag, 249
tone, 43–4
   appropriate, 91, 180, 244, 271, 281
   in blog posts, 252
   consistent, 122, 124, 125, 203, 233
   definition of, 43
   inappropriate, 44, 69, 177
   less-than-friendly, 43
   positive, 62
   in proposals, 186
   softening of, 90
   in texts, 261
   in tweets, 257, 258
   vocal tone, 131, 241
transitional expressions, 30, 124, 126, 233, 294; *see also* cohesive ties
trolling, 39, 253
tweetstorm, 258
Twitter, 256–9
typography, 167, 173, 177, 178
typo(s), 243, 275, 278, 282, 285, 286

underlining, 167, 294
usability research, 251
usage sites, 287
using computers for writing and editing, 277

verb phrases, 86
verbals
  gerunds (verbal nouns), 85–6, 113
  infinitives, 85–6
  participles (present and past), 48, 85–7
  verbal phrase, 85–7
verbatim, 220–2
verbing, 62
verbosity, 65
verbs, 84–91
  finite, 85
  helping (auxiliary), 84
  imperative, 87
  indicative (declarative), 87
  infinite (non-finite), 85
  interrogative, 87
  intransitive, 85
  linking (copular), 84
  modal (auxiliary), 85
  mood, 87
  phrasal, 87
  prepositional, 87
  separation of, 91
  subjunctive, 87
  transitive, 85
  voice, active, 88–90
  voice, passive, 88–90
visualising your reader, 21, 43
vocabulary, 20, 28, 68, 146, 235, 260, 267, 283
vocation, 3–4
voice in writing, 16, 31, 41, 43, 177

Waynespeak, 67
weasel words, 59, 66, 231, 309

'which' versus 'that' *see* 'that' versus 'which' distinction
white space, in page layout, 167, 168, 169, 182, 186, 190, 236, 282
'who' versus 'whom', 113
widow, 179
Wikipedia, 68, 216, 305
WIRMI, 13
word classes, 77–8
working writer, 4, 177, 203
workplace genres, 177–202
  briefing, 178
  instruction manuals, 195–7
  job applications, 187–92
  letters, 178, 180
  media releases, 197–9
  proposals, 183–6
  reports, 181–3
  speeches, 200–2, 203–5
  style manuals, 190, 193–5
  style sheets, 192–4
  workplace documents list, 179
works cited list, 224
writing
  academic, 231–3; *see also* 206–36
  and allusion, 46
  analysing, 20, 73, 159, 270
  assessment criteria for academic writing, 235
  as avocation, 3–4
  being in command of, 174
  for blogs, 251–6
  for career advancement, 37, 158, 177
  as central to all disciplines and professions, 1
  challenging writing, 20
  changing practices, 75
  as a communicative act, 23
  as a complex skill, 3
  computer-mediated, 240–1, 277
  connections between writing and reading, 19–20

context of writing, 3–4
and cooking, 10
no correct writing process, 15
as a daily experience, 1, 15, 239–40
and design, 150
as a difficult, time-consuming process, 3
digital media changes, 238–9
email messages, 241–6
as epistemic, 5, 21
excellent writing, 14
with figures of speech, 61
formal conventions, 37
free writing, 157
grounding in grammar rules, 71, 100
by hand, 7
how reading helps, 20
importance of error-free writing, 75
importance of high-quality writing, 2
in the information society, 1
with intention to revise, 264–5
for an international audience, 47
job opportunities, 262
keeping a journal, 6–11
as a mainstream activity, 177
mood in workplace writing, 88
myths of writing, 16
oral style, 201
pace and rhythm, 131
paragraphing, 122
pompous style, 49
presentation of academic writing, 233–4

as problem-solving process, 1, 11
proofreading as final check, 273–6
punctuation revealing structure, 130
for readers, 21
as rewriting, 267, 268
rhetorical situation, 165
and running, 9
as selection, 270
sentence structure, 71
social functions of writing, 2
social media, 246–51
Socrates on writing, 22
from sources, 220
speaking versus writing, 131
speechwriting, 200–2
structuring for readers, 29–30, 152
style-analysis software, 277–8
for texting, 259–61
as therapy, 7
tone, 43, 44
for tweeting, 256–9
usage sites, 287
as vocation, 3–4
voice, 43
workplace issues, 158
writing-reliant workplace, 1
writing rituals, 16
writing–thinking–learning connection, 2, 5–6, 7, 13
writing worker, 4, 178

zombie (bogus, phony) rules, 75